BOOK TWO Back in a Year Series

LIFE
STRIKES BACK

Candace MacPhie

Life Strikes Back
Book Two: Back in a Year Series
Candace MacPhie
Published by Candace MacPhie
Copyright © 2023 by Candace Gordon

License Notes

This book is a memoir. It reflects the author's present recollections of experiences over time. For privacy reasons, some names and characteristics have been changed, some events have been compressed, and some dialogue and dates may have been changed.

Cover design by Farrukh Bala

Map and chapter icon designs by Melanie McNicholl

First edition 2024

ISBN: 978-1-7389220-4-8 (paperback)

ISBN: 978-1-7389220-6-2 (hardcover)

ISBN: 978-1-7389220-5-5 (eBook)

CONTENTS

This book is dedicated to my kids, Sloane, Slater, and Anneek.
My nieces, Cristina, Neve, and Harlow.
And my nephews, Christopher, Jack, and Heath.

Do what you love.
Never let anything or anyone stand in the way of what you want.
It's not going to be given to you.
Try, then try again. And again.
Don't give up.
Earn it and have fun doing it.
Love you all to the moon and back.
Mom, Tia, Auntie xoxo

ABOUT THE SERIES

While stuck in a soul-sucking job and grieving my mom's passing, backpacking around the world sounded like a great plan. One year off wouldn't hurt, would it? One year to explore the world and new cultures, meet friends, and maybe even—dare I hope—find love. Thrust into the backpacker's life, my careful-planning nature was ripped from me, replaced by the need to survive because trouble found me at every turn.

If you're looking for a travel guide for city information, this is not it. If you want an adventure, keep reading. These pages are packed with the straight nitty-gritty of the crazy stuff that happened along the way. My actual emails home act as the anchor for most chapters and are my equivalent to a staged social media photo. But my journals, photographs, and memories deliver the juicy substance behind each carefully crafted email that you can dig into and live through.

I share this with the people who took a similar trip but didn't write it down. For the people who didn't have the opportunity to take this journey. For those who are looking for inspiration to take their own adventure. And I hope it gives you a fun escape to cry, cringe, and laugh in the life before smartphones in the late '90s with a crazy Canadian girl.

The five-part Back in a Year series is one continuous story. Each book can be read independently, but I encourage you to take the full trip.

Have fun—because I sure did.

Candace xoxo

CONTENT WARNINGS

Profanity, sexual harassment, sexual assault, consensual sexual content, parental grief, alcohol consumption, smoking, and visits to Holocaust sites.

MAP

CHAPTER 1
NO WAY, MAN

WEDNESDAY, July 8, 1998

RUDE AWAKENING - RUSSIAN BORDER TO ESTONIA

Sharp marching band music blares through our train compartment, waking me from a restless hour of sleep on a hard orange bench. A pulsing ache twitches behind my eyes from the long night celebrating an Estonian guy's birthday in the bar car.

"*Mate*, what's with the music?" Khadejah—my travel partner —asks in her thick Australian accent from the other sleep bunk in our narrow space.

"Ugh" is all I can manage around my swollen tongue that tastes of stale beer and cigarettes.

The two of us set off from London two weeks ago. We're backpacking overland for the next four months to Cairo on a shoestring budget. So far, we've been to Russia and left Moscow last night on this train bound for Estonia.

I grip my nylon sleeping bag and curl into the fetal position as I brace for my ritual of excruciating waking emotions.

A slicing pain in my gut is the harsh reminder that my mom's gone. A part of me died the moment she did and the jagged cavernous void I carry inside has been my cruel companion since that day almost four years ago. It's my first thought every time I open my eyes and my only escape is sleep.

Next, a twinge of sadness nips at my chest for being so far from home.

And the last is the contradictory relief I'm not there.

My mom lit up a room, and everyone loved her. She was the glue that held our family together. Even when sick, she was still our glue as my two brothers, Dad, and I bonded over her lengthy palliative care and held her hand as she died in my childhood home. I miss my family, but those memories of her long years of suffering from cancer are suffocating.

Living on the road is a double win. I've always dreamed of traveling to exotic faraway places *and* being away dulls the painful memories. But my funds are limited. And if I'm not thrifty I'll have to cut my trip short and go home early. And that *can't* happen because even though I miss home, I don't want to be anywhere near there since she's not.

"We must be at the border," Khadejah says as the obnoxious music stops. Her long black hair swishes across the middle of her back before she expertly ties it into her customary slick high ponytail.

I clench my teeth, shoving my sticky morning emotions deep into a box, and slam it shut.

The guys and I had a tactical plan for caring for my mom. Giving medicine, changing sheets, bedside vigils, and doctors' visits. And we were there for each other. But as close as we are, we fell apart managing 'after death' and retreated to different spots in the world. One brother is working in Vancouver, the other is at university in Lennoxville west of Montreal, my dad is still in the death house in Montreal, and I'm out here on the road. We rarely talk about my mom or that time. Since talking to the people closest to me isn't an option, compartmentalization is my day-to-day coping tactic.

My head spins as I crisscross my legs on top of my sleeping

bag in the rumpled clothes I slept in. I reach under the waistband of my green cargo pants, pull out my money belt, warm from being pressed to my skin, and dig inside for my Canadian passport, ready to get stamped out of Russia. I flip through the pages in the small blue book past the many countries' entry visas waiting to be used. I'm excited to experience different foods, cultures, and meet new people. But my personal travel goals are more complex.

I need to get out from under this mountain of grief before I implode.

I want to be fun. I want to be free. And I want to feel like my old self again.

Dejah holds out a blue roll of mints. I take one and swish it around my mouth, hoping it will stave off my bad breath until I can brush my teeth. I press my lips together and crack the icy candy between my molars. Facing grief is a daunting proposition. It's hard, scary, and takes introspective effort. I can do hard. I can do introspective. My obstacle is fear. I feel this pain is all I have left of my mom. And I'm not ready to let it go because I worry it will be like losing her all over again. So here I am, half a world away from the death house, living my dreams on the road and hoping like heck I can figure out how to hang on to my mom in my heart without waking up each day wanting to sob like a baby.

Khadejah taps her burgundy passport, courtesy of her Irish mother, against her palm. My petite friend also has an Australian one from her birthplace tucked in her money belt, but she's using the Irish one because she needs fewer pricey visas with it. The Irish one is real, but it's *super* sketchy. I can't believe it's accepted because it looks fake with a photo booth picture under plastic laminate, and the information page is handwritten. She jokes how she opted out of an Iraqi passport she could have gotten through her dad, who was born there. Her mixed heritage has not only gifted her that awesome hair but smooth dark golden skin and golden eyes with a navy rim.

We met through mutual friends in London. Over a game of cards, she decided to travel with me, and we haven't looked back. We have different accents and grew up on opposite sides of the world, but we get along like I've known her my whole life. She's the best person I could ever ask to do this trip with. We share the common goal of wanting to see everything on the cheap, and she's out here to enjoy herself. And I need her help to remember how to do that again.

I gasp as my bare feet hit the cold floor of the train and cup my boobs over my black T-shirt. The girls are swinging free because I hate how the underwire digs into my armpits while I'm sleeping. Not that I have a lot, and they're decently perky, but support during the day is how I roll. My black bra is dangling over my purple backpack—named Barney after the big purple dinosaur because he weighs a freaking ton—on the other side of the train compartment. I must have tossed it there before I passed out.

"Do you think I should put my bra—"

The door to the compartment bursts open and crashes with a bang as four officers march into our orange oasis. They're carbon copies of each other: white, clean-cut, and young, all dressed in stiff, antique-looking uniforms with huge guns.

One guy shouts harsh, guttural words in Russian. My heart rate triples and my spine straightens while Dejah's serene face looks like she's at a spa day. We both sit still on our benches, clutching our passports between our fingertips. Talker says something, and the other three point their guns at us. My hands tremble. Totally shoot first, ask questions later here. I resist the urge to cross my arms and cover my chest so I don't look like I'm hiding something—other than my boobs.

Talker yanks my passport away and roughly thumbs through the pages. He removes the small beige paper that customs put there when we first landed in Russia. Holding the paper close to his face, he scrapes his thumbnail over the page, holds it up to the overhead light, and flips it over. Then he does the same to

Dejah's—like he's looking for some discrepancy he can get us on. Guilt blooms in my chest, and I haven't done anything wrong. He scowls as he slides the papers into the breast pocket of his stiff coat then tosses our passports at us.

"I hope we don't need that paper again," I say as they leave. "Do you think that's it?" I ask, reaching for my lacy bra.

"Seemed too easy—" Khadejah sharply inhales as three massive German shepherds prowl into our space, each dragging an armed guard on a leash.

The dogs are as serious as their severe-faced uniformed handlers. I clutch my passport and bra between my fingertips and sit statue-still as the dogs sniff their way around the cabin. I hold my breath as their twitchy brown noses work me over and pray they don't take a bite.

I deflate like a balloon as they leave without a word or a bark. I shove my bra deep into my sleeping bag just as a third group enters the compartment. The lead guy is shouting in Russian, waving a customs declaration form, and the other three have their rifles poised for action. We pass the completed rectangular yellow papers we were given when we boarded the train to the lead clone. He points to the cash amount we declared on the form. We dig into our money belts and fan the contents—a couple hundred US dollars and some traveler's checks.

Lead Clone silently paces the small aisle and examines every corner of our space as the three others bar the door. I jump when he says something in clipped Russian.

With big eyes, I shake my head slowly. He could be asking what we were doing in Russia or what we had to eat yesterday —I have no idea.

Lead Clone grinds his jaw, and I clutch my cash in my sweaty fingers as he glares.

He huffs, then robotically spins on his heels, leaving with his clone crew.

My heart races as the door slides shut behind them.

"At least the language barrier worked in our favor this time," I say, zipping my money away as Dejah rolls her eyes.

I've had nothing but problems with communicating since I left Canada. In my first months away living and working in London, I had awkward mix-ups due to accents and different turns of phrase. And it only got worse during our time in Russia. We got lost and bought the wrong items—often. I'm optimistic things will get easier as we travel. But I have nothing to base that on other than hoping our experience brings knowledge and that we'll get better at miming.

I flap the front of my T-shirt to air the nervous sweat on my torso as Dejah flops on her bench, not the least bit ruffled by this police procession or much of anything I find scary. Yet another reason why I love having her as a travel partner. We balance each other out because I'm a nerdy rule follower and she's super chill.

The train slowly rolls across the Russian border into no-man's land.

My stomach swirls with unease as the steel wheels of the train squeak to a stop in Estonia because this is the place where I need a visa I don't have.

But I'm sure it won't be as bad as leaving Russia, right?

210 KROONS - NARVA, ESTONIA

"Border Police," a stern-faced man with white skin and dark hair says as he and three other men file into our cabin.

I balance on the edge of my bench, waiting for orders as they loom over us in drab green uniforms. They're no less intimidating than the Russians, but at least these guys have holstered sidearms—not rifles at the ready.

Stern Man flips through Khadejah's sketchy Irish passport with authority, stamps it, and passes it back to her. He sighs as he thumbs through my Canadian one and says something in pitchy Estonian.

He's looking for my absent visa.

This is one of the many countries where I need a visa and Dejah doesn't. And it stings because they cost anywhere from ten to a hundred dollars each.

Everything from bus and train fares to food, sites, shopping, and hostels is included in my shoestring fifty-dollar-a-day budget. And I diligently track every penny—with currency exchange—in the back of my address book to stay accountable. But I have a separate savings allocation for visas and airline tickets because no way could I stick to my daily budget if I included these expensive variable costs.

I procured as many visas as I could before I left London, but I didn't know I needed one to visit here until I met a Canadian girl at the hostel in Russia two days ago. I freaked out when I saw her visa, then marched to the Estonian Embassy in Moscow the next day. But there was a mob of people outside, and I couldn't get close to the door. I did manage to get through on the phone. Miraculously, they spoke English and said I could easily buy one at the border.

"Me." I point to myself. "Get *visa* … here." I point to my passport, the ground, and then to the outside.

Stern Man frowns and shakes his head. He jabs his finger at me, motions for me to follow, then stalks out, clutching my passport. My eyes go wide. I thought we would be doing the whole visa thing in the comfort of our cabin.

"Candace." Dejah snaps her fingers and gestures to the door.

"Right." I nod.

I've got to follow my passport. Because without it, I'm screwed. I can't go anywhere. It's literally my most important possession.

I tug my hiking boots over my bare feet and cringe as I glide my tongue across my fuzzy, unbrushed teeth. I hope this mint has staying power. I shiver as cold air creeps up the bottom of my T-shirt. Shit. I glance longingly at my rumpled sleeping bag. Why, why, why didn't I put on my bra? I can't do it now because the three other policemen are watching me like I'm a criminal about to make a break for it. I grab Dejah's hoodie, as it's the closest, zip it closed, and reach for my daypack. I slide out past the three officers, leaving my big pack—Barney—for Dejah to watch over.

Stern Man is outside the compartment with his arms crossed. He's no skinny Russian. His muscular shoulders span the width of the hallway, and he's at least a head taller than me. His nose is crooked and dips in the middle like it's been broken, I wager a few times. This man oozes take-no-shit badass.

I wave and smile to lighten the mood, but his scowl remains in place. His left eye twitches as I hurry over. He turns before I reach him and stalks ahead.

I try at a minimum to learn the word for thank you from the back of my travel guide—which has a small list of local words for each country spelled out phonetically—before I visit a place to be polite. But I drank way too much last night and didn't bother. Hopefully, my miming and his few words of English will be enough for us to communicate and get this visa sorted quickly.

The train car attendant lady shouts at Stern Man in Estonian as he lumbers down the hallway. I guess she's yelling—*"Where are you taking her?"*

"Visa," he snips and waves her off.

He pushes open the door and steps off the train.

My mouth gapes. If not in the compartment, then I thought we would at least do this on the train. But I guess they don't have many Canadians traveling in from Russia without visas.

He looks at his watch as he holds the door and tips his head.

I bite my lip as I stare at the dark sky that's not quite night and not quite morning, but that ominous time in between. I glance back down the dim hallway to our compartment. I'm sure I'll be fine, and I know Dejah will raise a fuss if I'm not back in half an hour.

He glares. Okay, here goes nothing. I stumble off the steps

onto the platform. The train door slams, and Stern Man is off. My naked heels rub against my boots as I double-time it to keep up with his speedy long strides. Cool fresh air fills my lungs as we pass too many blue train cars to count. On the plus side, this impromptu hike scrubs the last of the drunken cobwebs from my brain.

Passengers peek out their brightly lit windows then quickly avert their eyes when we make eye contact like they don't want to be misconstrued as an accomplice to whatever nefarious deed I've done to be pulled off the train before dawn.

I look straight ahead to avoid their stares.

Khadejah and I have been allocating Spice Girl names to people we feel a connection with since we left London. I'm Suspicious Spice because of a dubious day in Moscow. Dejah's going to *love* that my name is extremely apropos right now.

Stern Man swings open the ornate wooden door on the long brick building with symmetrical windows and a red roof adjacent to the platform. His heavy boots stomp against the worn tiles as he rushes me through a maze of dark hallways in the station. He flicks on an overhead light, and I squint at the change. He prowls into the small room with wooden panel walls, one filing cabinet, an old desk, a chair, and two wobbly guest stools.

He drops into the spinning chair behind the desk and motions for me to sit opposite.

Spine straight, I wait on the stool while Stern Man aggressively rifles through the narrow top desk drawer. He pulls out a page of green stickers that say *visa* on them and flattens it on the desk. The tension in my back eases because they're the exact ones I saw in the Canadian girl's passport in Moscow.

I grin. I'll be back on the train in no time.

He passes me a two-page paper form and a pen.

I fill it out and return it with two wallet-size photos. I have about thirty for situations like this. Any visa usually requires a photo, and there's never a place to print them when you need to, so I carry them on me.

Stern Man says something as he staples the pictures to my completed form.

I shake my head. He sighs, then rubs his thumb and index fingers together.

Right, time to pay. He keenly watches as I reach down the waistband of my pants and fiddle around to unzip my money belt. I have no idea how much this costs, so to be safe, I pull out a US fifty dollar bill and hold it out to him.

His jaw locks as his face twists into a deeper frown. He doesn't take the money and continues to write something on the paper in front of him.

I bounce in my seat as he places the coveted Estonian entry visa sticker in my passport. Almost done. They were totally right at the embassy; this is easy peasy.

He slides my passport into his stiff green front shirt pocket.

I blink. Why did he do that? My brow furrows as he stands and abruptly stalks out through a side door I missed on my initial scan of the room.

I stay seated and weave the American bill between my fingers.

After a minute, he pokes his head through the side door and gestures for me to follow. I reach for my daypack, and he waves for me to leave it. A chill races over my skin as I shove the bill back into my money belt. I've left Barney and Dejah on the train, and now I'm leaving my daypack and going outside. I rub my chest with my palm as I slink out the side door into the eerie darkness because I have to follow my passport.

The only sound is the rumble of an idling brown van. Like the boxy Mystery Van from *Scooby Doo*, just so much less inviting because this one has no happy graphics along the sides, is littered with dents, and has crumbling rust over the tire arches.

"Get in," he barks as he opens the passenger door.

"What?" I cross my arms over my chest and shake my head as he prowls to the driver's side.

He put the sticker in my passport. Why do we need to get in this van?

My pulse races as I peek into the vehicle. The inside panel of the passenger door is missing. The passenger seat has long, straight slices in the leather, and the foam is poking through. My stomach drops. Are those *knife* cuts?

Stern Man closes the driver's side door and places his hands on the wheel.

My feet are sticky in my boots and my knees wobble as I stand outside the uninviting van and suck in the smell of diesel.

What the hell is going on right now?

He glares at me and pats the shredded passenger seat.

"NO WAY am I getting in this vehicle with you," I shout.

Stern Man's jaw tightens as he adjusts his sidearm in the belt holster. I hug myself tighter as my eyes burn like fire. I have no power here. I can't go back to Russia because my visa was a single entry. And I can't get into Estonia without a visa. He taps his left breast pocket holding my passport. My heart crumbles because I can see it poking out the top. The frustration rolling off him hits me like a punch to the gut, and I step back.

He pats the ripped-up seat again.

Shit, shit, shit. This is so stupid. Everybody knows the general abduction rule 101 is that under any circumstances, *do not get in the car.* I scan the area, but there's no one, absolutely no one, to witness me getting into this van.

There will be no trace of me disappearing.

My teeth chatter, and my body trembles.

He has my passport and a gun. And all the power. I'm at his mercy.

I straighten my shoulders. Now is not the moment to fight. I'll save it for when I need it. My stomach knots as I get in and softly click the door closed.

I twist my fingers in my lap as he drives away from the train station to who knows where.

"Narva?" I ask as I point to the straight road lined with dense pine trees.

Stern Man nods once.

At least I know the name of the city where I'm going to die, go to jail, or worse. My racing heart slows, and an odd sense of calm washes over me. Funny how your mind works in a situation completely out of your control. I stare straight ahead as sadness weaves through my chest for my family. If this goes badly, they'll never know what happened to me. And it will be crushing for them after my mom's death. I feel bad for Khadejah, who I'm sure will be worried sick. And she'll never get her hoodie back, and she likes this one. But mostly I feel exposed not having a bra on.

There are no other vehicles in sight.

The van's headlamps are the only light in the darkness.

I dig my fingernails into the palms of my hands as my calm evaporates and my thoughts turn. I wonder when he'll stop. And what will happen when he does.

I gulp. He's a giant. But I won't make this easy for him.

Every cell in my body is on alert.

Stern Man swerves to avoid a pothole, and I sway with the movement.

I swallow past my dry throat. You know, in the grand scheme of things, maybe facing the daunting job of mourning isn't so bad. I know my mom wouldn't want me to live in a painful haze. She *would* want to be remembered. But not with pain. I promise the twilight sky that if this ends better than the images racing through my mind, I will face my fear and figure out how to manage my grief. And to remember her with love.

Stern Man rolls into a paved piazza lit with hazy light from a single lamp post. He passes shadows of buildings then parks in front of a weathered, white kiosk, reminiscent of a ticket booth at a creepy fair.

He grunts, points at me, then outside, and exits the van.

The rusty passenger door creaks open, and the cold air shocks my spine.

I tense and flex my fingers, bracing for whatever's coming as I take slow steps behind him toward the kiosk.

There's a dim yellow light casting a shadow over the face of a middle-aged woman sitting inside. I still, and the tension in my shoulders dials down a notch at the sight of her.

Who is she? And why are we here?

Stern Man scratches into the chipped paint on the wooden ledge of the kiosk in front of us with his car key then taps the sketch and glances at my beltline.

$15US = 210kr

My eyes flit from Stern Man to the woman then the numbers etched in the wood.

I suck in a breath when it clicks. He's taken me to an all-night currency exchange, and that must be the cost of my entry visa for Estonia.

My knees threaten to give out as my body sags with relief.

He hasn't touched me. He's not selling me to the highest bidder. He's not going to cut me into pieces or keep me prisoner in a rickety shack in the woods. And I don't have to fight, which is good because I'm terrible at it.

I'm here to pay for my visa.

He taps his key on the ledge.

I whip out fifty dollars from my money belt so fast that I think Superman would be impressed. I give him the bill, he passes it to the kiosk woman, she gives him the Estonian kroons, he takes 210 for the entry visa then passes me the balance of the kroons and my passport from his pocket.

I clutch my blue book and cash in a vise grip as I stagger back to the van.

The engine roars as I try to reconcile what the heck just happened.

He's not a killer. He's an honest, law-abiding, Stern Man with a piece-of-crap van.

I sink into the lumpy seat as my adrenaline crashes.

What a cluster. I would have given him pretty much any amount for this visa, but he didn't want to overcharge me and wanted payment in local currency. Meanwhile, I thought I was being kidnapped over fifteen dollars and a severe lack of communication.

My optimism for things getting easier as we travel was grossly inaccurate. My miming was shit. I didn't read his body language at all. And I had no idea what was going on. I better step up my game or it's going to be a terrifying few months. Another reason to be thankful for Dejah because together we can usually puzzle out any situation.

I check my watch as the van labors down the smooth roads. It's been forty-five minutes since the train stopped in Tallinn. It usually takes an hour for the officers to conduct passport business on a train this long. My stomach rolls as the trees blur past. Because now I have a new problem. I'm racing against the clock. When the passport control is done, the train will leave—if I'm on it or not.

And if it's gone, I'm shit out of luck: no Barney and no way to connect with Dejah.

I whimper with relief when we jolt to a stop in front of the station with the long blue train still parked alongside it. We enter the station through the same side door we left from. My daypack is on the floor where I left it. I clutch it to my chest as Stern Man stomps out, leaving me standing in the center of the room like a moron.

I creep to the door and peer out.

Stern Man is talking to another officer in the hallway, probably sharing our tale.

"Can I go?" I wave, point to myself, then point to the door leading outside.

He snips at me in Estonian, flicking his hand to the exit.

I understand that one. He means *Get out of here*.

I'm free. And I need to get on that train pronto. I tear out of the station, leg it to the train and yank on the train compartment door closest to me.

It's locked.

I try another. Locked as well.

Chhhhh, chhhhh, the train engine hisses as it starts.

My heart bounces in my ribcage as I frantically tear down the platform, trying door after door.

Panic flares in my chest. They're all locked.

I yelp when the train car door ahead of me opens.

The eyes of three border police in dreary uniforms' go wide as I sprint toward them.

I need to make it there before they close the door.

One guy yells at me in Estonian. I can only assume he's asking, *"What are you doing off the train?"*

"Visa, Canadian," the second policeman says as he props the door open.

I shoulder past them and lunge inside the train, landing on all fours. The pain from my fall springs me into action. I leap to my feet, hold my boobs in place with my forearm, and run. I sprint down hallway after hallway like Jason from *Friday the 13th* is chasing me.

I'm winded, stinky, disheveled, and on the tipping point of hysterical when I rip open the door to our compartment, expecting to see Khadejah up, waiting, wringing her hands with worry, and ready to search for me.

But no.

Nope.

Soft snores.

"YOU'RE ASLEEP? I could have been killed!" I scream as I slam the door.

She bolts off the orange bench.

I unearth my bra from my sleeping bag and tug it in place as I recount my *not*-easy visa transaction.

She *oohs* and *ahhs* in all the right places.

The train pulls out of the station before I'm finished with my story.

"I'm lucky to have caught the train. Imagine, I would have been stuck in Narva without a bra." I kick off my sticky boots and huddle in my sleeping bag.

That was one of the scariest experiences of my life.

But now I have an even more unnerving task.

A promise to keep.

To finally face the grief that's clawing me from the inside out.

And I have no idea where to start.

CHAPTER 2
PATRICK OR GEORGE?

WEDNESDAY, July 8, 1998

CHANGE OF PACE - TALLINN, ESTONIA

I step onto the train platform in Tallinn, tip my face to the blue sky, and sigh as the morning sunlight heats my skin. *This* was the tranquil Estonia welcome I was hoping for. I shake off the visa mess like a bad dream and declare this moment a fresh start to the day as we enter the airy terminal.

The vast space is bustling with people, young and old, dressed in dark colors. Dejah leads us to the exchange booth near the glass exit doors and pulls out the small brown and black striped change purse that holds our community money, which we named Ken. We've found it easier to have one pot of cash that we each contribute to for shared expenses. We exchange the last of Ken's Russian ruble bills for Estonian kroons, then buy a phone card and a map.

Outside the station, I lean against the plexiglass phone booth as Khadejah calls a recommended hostel from her *Let's Go!* Guidebook. We're taking turns being the tour guide in each location, and she's up with Tallinn.

"We're all set," she says after she hangs up. "They have two beds for us, and I know where we're going." She holds up the map, folded open to our destination.

My chest is light. The quaint, quiet cobblestone streets and colorful buildings are calming after the heavy bustle of Russia. Even with Barney digging into my shoulders with every step, this straightforward four-block walk is a breeze compared to the long, confusing marches we did over the last two weeks.

We stop in our tracks as we reach a paved pathway leading to double doors at the intended address. The sign ahead of us has two intertwined silhouettes of naked ladies with enormous breasts and reads *Erotica*.

"Is this right?" My chest shakes as I giggle—but not my boobs because my bra is taking care of jiggle business.

Dejah flips through her three-inch thick guidebook and sighs.

"Yeah. There are stairs on the side leading to the hostel. It's so dodgy sharing an entryway with a titty bar," she says.

"Oh well, let's give it a go." After Stern Man and the dodgy van trip, this is nothing.

I step on the pathway and veer away from the club to the left toward the wooden switchback steps.

Dejah introduces herself to the blond spiky-haired woman behind the hostel reception desk in the narrow entryway as I wipe my clammy hands on my pants.

"I have two dorm beds available. But you can't access the facilities until noon," Spiky says.

I drop my head. That's in three hours. I need a shower to wash away my pungent stress sweat from last night and am desperate to change out of the clothes I slept in.

"You can leave your backpacks in lockup until then." Spiky points down the hallway.

We pay her for tonight, then abandon Barney and Hulk— Hulk's the name of Dejah's backpack as it's boxy and green—in the hostel storage room. My eyes are gritty and I'm grubby, but I don't have to lug my heavy pack around while we wait.

"Food," I say to Dejah as we lope down the switchback steps to the shared pathway in front of the strip club. "And coffee, or beer, maybe all of the above."

I squint at the sun as Dejah unfolds the map.

"It's two blocks to the main square. They're sure to have cafés there," she says.

Dejah's immaculate ponytail swings as we march through the streets to the open cobblestone area, surrounded by cream-colored buildings with symmetrical windows and peaked orange roofs. This city is not too big to get lost in but not too small to feel claustrophobic.

I cringe at the wide-eyed tourists wearing pink stickers on their jackets as they trail their tour guide, who's holding a matching pink stick. There's also a blue and yellow group milling around. I did a tour in Ireland because I was short on time. I met a few nice people. But mostly it sucked having to be on a rigid schedule, eating in the worst touristy places, and being stuck with people you don't like. Sure, I could have used the help of a guide last night, but I wouldn't give up our freedom for the ease of being on a tour. Not a chance.

Being free to choose is everything. For over a decade, I looked after everyone else, but out here on the road, I don't have to be a caregiver, a parent to my brother, or an employee. I look after myself and Dejah—who's a partner not a dependent. And I relish this coveted gift.

We settle at a table outside a café that edges the square perimeter under a large red umbrella. My stomach growls as I kick back in my seat and unfold the puffy leather menu.

"I can't read Estonian any better than Russian." I slam it closed.

The unfamiliar Russian alphabet was our nemesis, so we ate a lot of homemade sandwiches or pizza while we were there.

"Hang on there, crabby. The letters are the same as ours, we should be able to find something." Dejah traces her finger along the menu and jabs the page. "Omelet. That's weird enough to be universal. And it's kind of hard to stuff up an omelet. And look, they have spaghetti too. We can add them to our food repertoire when we're sick of pizza."

"Now wait a minute." I hold up my hand. "I will never be sick of pizza."

"Fair." She chuckles. "How about an omelet, orange juice, and coffee?"

I nod, and she relays our order to the snooty server as the tourists bumble past.

"Remember when we checked email in Moscow yesterday?" I bite my lip.

"Hard to believe that was only last night." She rubs her eyes.

"I know, right?" Weariness settles in my bones. "It feels like a lifetime ago. Anyway." I fiddle with my paper napkin. "I got an email from Josh."

"You did?" She crosses her forearms on the table and leans forward.

"Yeah." I rub my hand down my face.

A year ago, Josh and I met in Greece when I was on a three-week vacation. He was backpacking and had no plans to return to his life at home in the US anytime soon. His lifestyle intrigued me. *He* intrigued me. He was my catalyst for leaving home after I got back to my black and beige desk job. The only snafu was I thought we would live together in London, then travel. I was wrong on both counts. He chose to live separately before he dumped me and took off to travel on his own.

"What did he say?" she asks as the server places two frothy mugs of coffee and two tall glasses of juice on the table.

My mouth waters. We mostly drink warm water from our reusable plastic Nalgene bottles, so this is a big treat. My hand trembles when my palm connects with the cold glass. I tip it to my lips, and my taste buds twitch from the tart, sweet flavor. I force myself to stop after a few mouthfuls to make it last.

"He *said* he was robbed in Tunisia and that he misses me." I swap the juice for coffee. I balk at the bitter taste after the tangy

20

juice and replace the mug on the table. "I crumbled like a loser and emailed him, gushing about how much I missed him too."

"Nothing wrong with that. Everyone deserves a second chance," she says as she tips a shoulder.

"I'm not sure he does." I press my lips together. "The last time I saw him, he slammed a door in my face." I shudder at the memory of him dismissing me on his doorstep in London after we had sex most of the night. "But I would still be sitting in my lonely apartment if we'd never met. And that thought is worse than all the heartache I've endured at his expense."

"Do you want to see him again?" She taps her thumb on the back of her hand.

"It's not even worth talking about. He told me flat-out he doesn't love me. So it'll never happen." I shouldn't have written him back. He ripped my heart out, then stomped on it just to be sure I got the message. I can't get sucked into his orbit again. I just can't.

I chug the rest of my juice and slam the empty glass on the table. So much for savoring.

Dejah sits back in her chair and steeples her fingers. "Dreams are free, Candace."

She says this often. And it spurs fantastical conversations we use to pass the many hours we spend waiting for buses, trains, or relaxing in the shade. We hypothesize about winning the lottery, life after traveling, or meeting that perfect person. Our far-fetched what-ifs will never come true, but it's a fun escape, like reading a novel or watching a movie.

"I also have an American guy from my past. His name is Dean." She sighs, and I nod. "We met last summer in Prague. We had a fling, but Dean was on a short summer holiday, and now he's back at home. We keep in touch via email. He says he's going to take a break from work and come visit me during my travels. I don't reckon it'll ever happen, but I can always dream. And so can you. There's no harm in it."

The server places two dishes on the table, and Josh is

forgotten as I clap my eyes on the fluffy yellow egg-half-moon that takes up my whole plate. I scramble for my fork and moan in delight as I shove a huge bite in my mouth.

"I'll always love pizza best. But this *is* a nice change," I say as a soft breeze rustles my hair. I catch a whiff of myself and wince. "Man, it's a good thing we're outside. I stink, and my clothes are making me itch." My fork scrapes the plate as I scoop more eggs.

"It's not turning you off your food." Dejah smirks.

"Never." I scoff. "Do you know if they have laundry at the hostel?"

We haven't washed our clothes—other than hand washing underwear and socks in the bathroom sink—since we left London. I have this wild fantasy. If I fold and smooth my clothes when I pack them away, magic happens in Barney. And the next time I open my backpack, my clothes are clean. It sounds ridiculous because it is, but it's how I mentally get around wearing the same dirty clothes over and over.

"Yes, they do," she says.

I sigh at the thought of *actual* clean clothes.

"In an hour we can officially check in." Dejah leans back in her chair and surveys the people promenading the quaint shops on the perimeter of the square. "Since I'm the tour guide for Tallinn, I reckon we boycott sightseeing today to relax and journal."

My mouth drops. Journaling is one of my favorite activities. Recounting my adventures in words is cathartic as it's the only time my mind is quiet. No worries about how to get somewhere, where we'll eat next, or sadness. Just me getting lost in my travel memories.

"I love that idea. But I have twisty guilt at the thought of not visiting sights. It feels like we have to keep busy seeing stuff." I slide my empty plate away.

"We're going to be on the road for a while. We'll need down days," she says.

"Like a holiday from backpacking?" I tilt my head.

"Exactly." She nods with a wide grin. "It's our trip. We can do whatever we want."

I blink. How could I not consider I would need a break along the way? Dejah and I have been away from home for the same amount of time, but her approach is to go with the flow, and I'm about cramming every moment with action. I swallow past the sticky nervous and excited feeling that loops in my gut every time I think about our impending travel to Cairo. Then there's my—solo—four-month adventure through Africa to Cape Town before I go to Australia.

That's a lot of days and kilometers. And factoring in that normal day-to-day tasks like getting around or finding food takes ten times more energy than they do at home, it's exhausting.

Another thing to add to my list—learn to pace myself. I'll add it right next to seeing cool stuff, re-learning how to have fun with the help of my travel partner, not getting diverted by Josh, getting back to myself, and getting over my mom's death.

God, I do need a down day.

***

AFTER SHOWERING and submitting our laundry to the hostel reception, we spent our afternoon relaxing, drinking beer, and journaling in the sunny town square. And Dejah was one hundred percent correct. The downtime was just what I needed after two hectic weeks in Russia and last night's visa fiasco.

After dark, we cross the street to an international pub recommended in the guidebook. There's nothing standout about this place—wooden tables in a row, hard chairs, a long bar, and music pumping behind the chatter. There's a mix of locals speaking Estonian, buff dudes with high and tight haircuts speaking English, and a group of other backpackers. But there's an odd sizzle in the air that makes my skin prickle. Kind of like that peculiar feeling I got walking through the not-quite night, not-quite morning on the train platform in Narva.

We buy two pints of local beer, then score seats with a good view of the room. I sigh as the crisp, rich, hoppy flavor of the golden liquid passes my lips.

"I'm lovin' this beer. Saku is awesome." I snake my finger down the side of the frosty glass.

"As good as fresh laundry?" Dejah asks.

"That's mean. I'm enjoying this." I hold up my glass. "But laundry is better. I almost peed myself when we picked up our clothes." I smile as the waft of fresh laundry soap from my clean T-shirt tickles my nose.

"Day *made*." Dejah's eyes twinkle.

I'm experiencing things I've only ever seen in magazines and movies. But it's the simple stuff I'm learning to appreciate. And clean clothes are at the top of the list. Also up there are cold drinks and crunchy toast because most mornings start with soggy cereal and tepid tea at a free hostel buffet.

"Cigarette?" Dejah holds out her pack.

I slide one out, light it, and take a long drag. I'm instantly hit with the usual mix of delight and disgust as the smoke weaves through my lungs. My delight—the burn of the smoke and the feeling of the lit cigarette between my fingertips. My disgust—it's a revolting habit.

The bar has a dense plume of smoke hanging in the air like it would at home. But unlike at home with its sporadic smokers, everyone smokes here. It's cheap, social, and accepted. Dejah and I enjoy a cigarette now and then. Although … lately it's been more *now* than then. Happy, sad, stressed, waiting for something, we usually find a reason to smoke. But I'm not worried. I can totally quit anytime I want. I just don't *want* to right now.

"Is it just me or is there something dodgy about this place?" Dejah asks.

"I felt it when we entered—" I pause my cigarette before my

lips at the sound of a woman's sharp sob over the Estonian pop song blaring through the pub.

Sobbing Lady is at the table next to us. She's older with scraggly blond hair and blanched skin. The three barely legal, clean-cut, white guys she's sitting with are carrying on with their conversation and ignoring her whimpering.

"What do yah reckon is going on there?" Dejah tips her beer at Sobbing Lady.

"No idea," I whisper and ash my cigarette.

One of the three young guys walks to the bar and returns with a bottle of champagne on ice in a silver bucket. He pours three glasses, not offering Sobbing Lady any. The guys toast and drink while she weeps and blows her nose. No one looks their way—besides us.

A wooden bar stool crashes when it lands on its side as two guys with buzz cuts and US sports team sweatshirts lunge at each other. The one with cauliflower ears lands a gut punch on crooked nose guy. Crooked Nose doubles over. The music blares on as their fight picks up steam. The people a few feet away are chatting casually and much like Sobbing Lady, not one person glances at the commotion. At home, a big shouting crowd would gather. But this is almost like watching TV. I lean back in my seat, oddly not bothered by the fight happening ten feet away because no one else is.

"Those dudes are Eewsahs," I say.

We call Americans Eewsahs, USA said phonetically. Mostly out of spite for my love-hate of Josh, who's from Colorado.

"The hair and clothes give them away." Dejah scrunches her face.

Crooked Nose yanks his arm back. I flinch at the crack when he lands a right hook on Cauliflower Ears, who crumples to the floor in a heap. Crooked Nose steps over Cauliflower Ears, leaving him passed out on the dirty hardwood.

"It's like *Road House*." I shake my head. The movie where

fights would break out constantly and people went about their business. "But here, there's no bouncer to save the day."

"We need Patrick Swayze," she says.

"Oooooh." I rub my hands together. "Patrick Swayze or George Michael?"

"Duh. Like you have to ask." She rolls her eyes, and we both crack up.

Dejah and I both love George. Like, *idolize*. Patrick never stood a chance.

Two men wearing socks and sandals drag chairs across the floor to our table and sit with us. One of the guys has his sunglasses wrapped around his ears backward, so the lenses are on the back of his head. Besides Corey Hart, who does that? The sunglasses at night … and sits with strangers.

Backward Glasses yaps at us in Estonian.

"Pardon?" I ask.

The edges of Backward Glasses's mouth turn down. He huffs and tips his nose, snubbing us but staying at the table.

The sound of shattering glass turns my head. Sobbing Lady has thrown the champagne bottle on the floor. The three guys still don't acknowledge her.

Another fight breaks out on the other side of the bar.

"It's time to call it," I say as I finish my beer.

We abandon our table, much to the delight of Backward Glasses and his buddy.

"You can sit on my lap," a guy with a short military haircut calls out in English as we pass. A few other soldier types join in the lewd catcalls.

My finger itches to flip them the bird.

"Stupid Eewsahs, they're everywhere." Dejah's scowl looks like she's about to dole out the hot slaps.

But we both know it's way too volatile here to respond the way we want.

Instead, she storms out, and I flip my hair over my shoulder as I strut past the last table.

Not as satisfying as a hot slap or the bird but a small dismissal all the same.

On the short trip across the street to the hostel, Dejah says, "That place should be known as Ludicrous Spice."

"Good one." I chuckle then stop and gawk at the long line of rowdy men jostling to enter the Erotica bar, standing between us and our beds.

We drop the shoulder as I learned to do on the Tube in London, swiping wandering hands as we push our way through. One skinny guy with greasy hair grabs my ass. I yelp as he digs his fingers in my fleshy backside.

Dejah sneers at Greasy and shoves him. She's a head shorter than me but way feistier.

"So gross." I elbow another guy on the way to the stairs.

"I'm glad we're only here a few days," Dejah says as we reach the hostel reception.

"Agreed," I say as I rub my sore butt.

I'm still standing from this roller coaster day. The highs of a relaxing afternoon and clean laundry to the lows of train-visa death scares, Greasy groping, and jeers. If today was a test—I totally passed. Besides, how much weirder can things get?

MY SHOULDERS TENSE at the sharp crackling of crinkling plastic bags. I huff. It's my second morning in a row waking to a loud unwelcome noise. Yesterday it was Russian band music, today it's my dorm room all-time pet peeve—early morning bag rustlers. Normally, it wouldn't be this loud, but the smallest noise is amplified at this time of day. This person should know better. I roll over on my bottom bunk, ready to give them a piece of my mind.

But words stall in my throat.

The culprit is a witch.

Like, I'm sure she's a real one. She's dressed head to toe in black and has thick black eyeliner with white makeup covering her face. She's sporting chunky heeled black boots that go up her legs forever. How she backpacks in those I have no idea.

She snarls and shoots me the most lethal death stare. A small squeak eeks past my lips. Maybe I spoke too soon; there are many versions of weird. It's too early for a confrontation I'll probably lose. So I slink further into my sleeping bag and cuff my arms over my ears to block out the grating racket.

THE TWIN CIRCULAR light brick towers with triangular tipped deep orange roofs of the Viru City Gates are the first stop on Khadejah's Tallinn Old Town walking tour—hours after the plastic bag incident.

"They look like paper towel tubes," I say as we stand before the gates. "Like a model a kid would build in elementary school."

"Mate." Dejah chuckles. "They're from the fourteenth century. This was the most fortified city in all of Europe back in the day."

"What can I say, it's not a diss, just what popped in my mind." I shrug.

"Come on then, heaps more to see." She taps her open guidebook.

We pass between the towers to the nearby sweater market. The stalls are laden with Nordic wool apparel, decorated with snowflakes and deer designs. I curl my nose and turn to Dejah, who waves them off. I'm all for buying souvenirs and mailing them home. But this isn't something I would wear, so we keep walking.

We duck into the Pühavaimu Kirik, the Holy Spirit Church, with arched white ceilings and dark brown pews. There's a 17th century wooden clock that doesn't work. We stroll down the cobblestone streets past the white, cream, and butter-yellow buildings to the North Gate of the city that's guarded to limit cars traveling into Tallinn Old Town.

"One more thing to see, then we're done," Dejah says.

"That's it?" I tilt my head as I glance at my watch. "That only took two hours."

"Yup. It's going to take a bit of getting used to after the hours we spent walking around Russia to see one thing," she says, leading us out of town to our last stop—the viewpoint at the beautifully preserved Dominican Monastery Claustrum.

"This is one of the oldest buildings in the city," she says as we pass through the ancient archway to access the monastery.

High mortarless stone walls enclose the quiet courtyard like a miniature Scottish castle. I smile as we poke around in the light rain with a dozen other tourists.

"Done." Dejah snaps her book closed as we exit half an hour later.

"Do you hear that?" I smile at the power ballad floating on the air.

"Michael Bolton." Dejah's eyes twinkle as she wipes the rain from her forehead.

Not only have we bonded over our love of George Michael, but we also love '80s pop music.

"It's coming from that bar." I point to the sandstone building with small windows and music billowing out of the open double wooden doors.

"We need to have a drink," Dejah says as she marches to a table in front of the bar, my boots crunching on the gravel patio as I follow.

We sit alfresco, sheltered from the wet weather under a large blue umbrella, and order two pale frothy Sakus. As the server places the beers on the table, the rain tempo increases, but the air is warm so I'm not cold. I frown at the bar, not keen to move indoors.

"Not sure I can handle full-on blaring Michael Bolton inside. You okay staying out here?" I ask.

"I'm good. The umbrella's keeping me dry." She takes a drink of her beer and sighs. "The best thing about going to Ludicrous Spice last night was discovering Saku."

I nod in agreement.

Rain splashes in the puddles forming on the rocky patio as Michael croons the words to "How Am I Supposed to Live Without You." I pinch my eyes closed and wrap my hands around my frosty pint glass.

Dejah and I were new friends when we took this leap of faith and set off on this adventure from London. She knows my mom's dead but doesn't know the intimate details. It's not like I'm hiding it—it's just not a topic most people are comfortable talking about. Because who likes to talk about death? But this is a sign. I get them sometimes. They come as a song, a smell, a breeze, a person, and even a yellow butterfly, that my mom's still here with me in some way, urging me to be bold or try something new.

In this case, it's to tell my friend what's on my mind.

"In a few weeks it will be the fourth anniversary of my mom's death," I say as my knee bounces.

Her body stills, and she gives me a slight nod.

"I wanted to let you know as I usually get blue around that time." My throat wobbles.

She leans forward, her kind golden eyes encouraging me to continue.

My throat burns as the story pours out of me, and Khadejah listens to every word. How my mom got sick with cancer when I was fourteen and died just before my twenty-third birthday. About the stressful hours waiting for news while she underwent operations. Watching chemotherapy drugs drip into her veins, stealing her hair and vitality. How I took notes at doctors' appointments, dressed her, fed her, stopped feeding her, and held her hand when she died at fifty-two.

I wipe the tears from the corners of my eyes.

"You know how people say nice things about someone after

they died and they were maybe like just okay people? That wasn't my mom. She was everything. She volunteered at school events, timed my swim meets, played softball, and had a way to make the most mundane activities fun." I pull in a slow, steady breath. "She lived life with a passion, and people were drawn to her. You couldn't not be. At home, that passion would be yelling if she was mad about something—she could scream the house down. Then five minutes later, she was happy again. The phone was always ringing off the hook. She was giving advice or catching up on gossip. Her friends were from all walks of life, and she took in strays, making sure everyone had a safe place to land. Our dinner table was always filled with family and friends. And the invitation to join was always there even though she was a terrible cook.

"At her funeral, there were so many people in attendance they couldn't fit inside the church. They had to stand in the vestibule. God, her softball league has an award they made in her honor that goes to the player with the most heart and enthusiasm, and it's the highlight of the annual season-end banquet.

"But most of all, she was over the top with her hugs and loved freely. And she loved me so damn much." I slump in my seat, raw and exhausted. "She would say no one loves you as much as your mom. And I feel that in the big gaping hole she left behind."

Dejah rushes to my side of the table and wraps me in a hug.

I sob in her arms as Michael soulfully sings and the rain drums on the umbrella overhead.

"I heard once that grief is love with no place to go," she murmurs into my hair.

I wipe the tears off my cheeks as she retakes her seat.

"I think that's my problem." I wring my hands. "I have no idea where to start with this undeclared grief. It's layers deep and complex." Pain slices up my spine, stealing my breath. "But

I can't hide from it anymore. Not mourning her is destroying me."

She grabs my hand and holds on tight.

It's not always easy on the road, but it's easier than being at home where I couldn't escape the loss of her. I need *different* to heal. I need wild train trips, going to ludicrous bars, and listening to Michael while drinking Saku in the rain.

I just hope it's enough.

MUD BATH - PÄRNU, ESTONIA

I wave to the woman with thick, black-rimmed glasses behind the desk in the tiny 'i' — Information Office in Pärnu as we enter the following day.

"Hi. We would like a map, directions to a place to stay, and information about a mud bath, please," I say.

My *Eastern Europe Lonely Planet* and Dejah's *Let's Go! Europe* have zero details about this remote town. We didn't let the lack of information deter us. We've made the trip based on a personal recommendation from Damo and Kath, two Aussies we met in St. Petersburg who raved about the mud baths here.

The woman passes me an English brochure called *Pärnu in Your Pocket*. I flip through the novel-sized four-page leaflet that outlines the attractions with a sketched city map the size of my palm on the back. I sigh. Seems not even the town has much to say about itself.

"There are no hostels. Your only option is this hotel." iLady slides me a scrap of paper with the name on it.

I pick up the tatty square and frown.

"The mud bath is here." iLady marks it on my *Pärnu in Your Pocket* map with a sinister smirk then holds out a paper leaflet from the mud bath place.

The back of my neck tingles as we exit the 'i.'

"Why did she have that weird look?" I ask. "She made me

feel dorky about my mud bath enthusiasm. I thought that was kind of *the thing* to do here."

"Who knows?" Dejah flicks her hands in the air.

Using the not-to-scale street sketch, we track down the concrete block hotel that hasn't been renovated since it was built fifty years ago. The concrete continues inside; the walls, floors, and stairs are cold dark gray. Our steps echo as we climb three flights to our room. Khadejah swings the door open, and I shrink back. I cover my nose with my hand, but it doesn't cut the funk of rank mildew leaking into the hallway.

"This is foul." Dejah's nose wrinkles.

Blue striped carpet, two beds, and one window. And eyewatering *layers* of mold. Dejah marches inside and throws open the window. The carpet squishes under the soles of my brown hiking boots. *That* explains the smell. I stand in the middle of the tight space unsure what to do. I don't want to put Barney down, and that's saying something because he spends most of his time under dusty bunks or in storage. I eye the brown polyester blanket covering my single bed, and my stomach flips. I hope it's the carpet and not my bed that smells.

"Let's just get out of here and get a mud bath," Khadejah says as she drops Hulk on the floor.

I place Barney on my bed, convincing myself it's a better option than the carpet, and follow her out.

A bitter, antiseptic hospital odor assaults my senses when we open the door to the mud bath spa. I intake a breath and wrap my arms around my stomach as the smell triggers the reels of agonizing hospital visits with my mom. Needles, vomiting, surgeries, hopeful conversations with doctors that turned into hopeless ones—

"What's with Pärnu and smells?" Dejah scoffs, jarring me back to the present.

I squeeze my eyes shut. Compartmentalizing only goes so far. This sharp scent has cruelly catapulted me back to that time. I clear my throat and shove the raw memories back into the box they escaped from.

"I don't know. The brochure said the mud baths are used for therapeutic purposes," I say as we enter the small reception area.

Khadejah approaches the counter. "We would like to make an appointment for two mud baths and massages, please," she says.

"All our massage appointments are booked, but I can offer you a mud bath without a massage," the woman with her black hair in a top knot behind the reception desk says.

I reach for my wallet, all set to book it up. Khadejah places her hand on mine before I can slide over my cash.

"Can we see the mud bath area?" Dejah asks.

"Good idea." I'm usually a jump-straight-in kind of person, but because of the medical smell, checking it out first is a solid plan.

"Follow me." Top Knot moves down a hallway to the back of the spa.

Top Knot swings open the door, and I step back at the sight of a wrinkly, naked granny in the center of the dark space. There are benches hugging the walls and clothes hanging from hooks around the room. Top Knot points around the corner. I offer Naked Granny an apologetic smile as Khadejah and I tiptoe past to get a better look.

I gape at the young woman lying on an elevated, flat, circular concrete surface. She's swaddled like a mummy in a muddy blanket that smells like hospital. Khadejah spins on her toes and grabs my arm. I barely miss knocking over Naked Granny as Dejah drags me to the door.

"We'll think about it," Dejah shouts as she shoves me outside.

"Not what I was expecting," I scoff as my feet hit the uneven sidewalk. "I was thinking a pool of mud you slide into and frolic around in. That was a mud wrap. Totally not the same." My shoulders fall. "What now? That was the only reason we came here."

"This." Dejah jabs her finger at the picture of children playing on the beach on the front of *Pärnu in Your Pocket.*

"No wonder the woman at the 'i' mocked us," I say as I follow her toward the sound of laughter and waves crashing on the shore.

My eyes light up as we turn the corner. There's a wide stretch of smooth white sand and gentle waves from Pärnu Bay lapping the shore. I yank the Velcro straps on my sandals, scrunch my toes in the warm sand, and sigh. I skip past the kids with colorful buckets making sandcastles toward the deep blue water.

"Yikes," I cry as a frigid wave crashes over my feet.

No wonder only a few people are swimming. It's freezing.

I run up the beach and drop beside Dejah in the sand. I lean back on my elbows and adjust the sunglasses over my eyes to ward off the blinding glare of the sun reflecting off the pristine sand.

At intervals along the beach, there are seven-foot-high hand swings that move like a teeter-totter. I've never seen anything like them. The bright yellow base has a bar across the top with two triangles on each end to hold it up. Two long perpendicular rods are attached to the top bar with handles on each end.

I watch in fascination as two guys use one. One guy's feet are in the sand, knees bent, arms above his head, hands gripping the handles. The dude on the other end is flying ten feet in the air—his only connection to anything is his hands gripping the opposite end of the bar. Flying dude comes down. The guy on the ground pushes off, swinging his body up and sailing through the brilliant blue summer sky. It's insane. It's like a seesaw, but not for butts—for hands.

"We have to try that." I nudge Dejah as they swing like acrobats.

"Pass." She rolls her eyes.

"Oh, come on. Please?" I interlink my fingers at my chest.

"I can't reach the handles." She frowns.

"We'll figure it out." I tip my head to an empty one behind us.

"It'll never work," she says as she stands and walks toward it.

"Oh, it will." I grab my stuff and sprint over.

I push my end up in the air. Her side goes down. She reaches up and grabs the handles. I jump up and wrap my hands around the grips. My side floats down, and my feet land in the sand. Her feet twist as she dangles in the air—until she falls off.

I break out into fits of laughter.

"I don't think that's how it's supposed to work." Dejah huffs as she swipes the sand off her skirt.

"Let's try again," I say as I stifle my giggles.

The same thing happens. Again, and again, and *again*.

"There must be some technique we're missing, or our different sizes are the problem." I scratch the back of my head and study the hand swing.

"Well bad luck, cuz I'm done." Dejah flexes her fingers, then grabs her bag. "The *Pärnu in Your Pocket* recommends a cafeteria place to eat. Are you game?"

"Sure." My jaw works as I contemplate the correct technique for the swing while we walk to the cafeteria.

Open sliding glass doors along the front of the restaurant allow the warm afternoon breeze to fill the space. We weave through the crowd seated at worn wooden tables to the end of the bulging line waiting to be served. My stomach rumbles as I grab a scratched blue tray, dull stainless steel cutlery, and a Diet Coke from the drink area, then glide my tray along the metal runway in front of the glass case.

"Oh, mate, we're a bit stuffed," Dejah says.

The food is hidden under steel covers behind the glass barrier, and there are no pictures. My toe taps as I madly search the room for someone eating something decent. Table after table, people are spooning uninspiring brown beef stew and jabbing at mystery cabbage rolls. My nose curls. No thanks on both options. My shoulders dip with relief as the man wearing a collared brown shirt ahead of me reaches for a plate of chicken and rice from the server wearing a blue hair net behind the counter.

Hair Net turns to me, and I point to Brown Shirt's chicken with a big dorky smile, then hook my thumb to my chest.

"Chicken and rice?" Hair Net asks.

My eyes bulge, and I cough. I wasn't expecting her to speak perfect English.

"Yes, thank you." I nod.

Hair Net piles my meal on a chipped green plate and hands it across the glass barrier.

"Same," Dejah says smugly.

I roll my eyes as I slide my tray to the cash register to pay, then make my way to an empty table.

"Hey, how about I be the Pärnu tour guide since Tallinn was so quick?" Dejah taps the bright yellow brochure as she finishes the last bite of her lunch. "I'll walk us through the six things to visit according to *Pärnu in Your Pocket*."

"Sounds good to me." I drop my cutlery on the tray and carry it to the kitchen window.

The sun's shining as Dejah marches toward the first site, a bunker of some sort.

We can't find it. So we skip it.

The second one is the arched pink and white gate to the road that leads to Tallinn.

The blazing sun heats my bare shoulders as we hike along the moat to the third site, the old circular amphitheater with modern bench seating where they hold concerts.

We continue along the moat to number four, the hundred-year-old stone jetty that stretches two kilometers into Pärnu Bay. I abandon the jetty walk after five steps on the slippery unstable rocks for fear of tumbling into the icy water.

We can't find number five, the cannon.

The heat rolling off the crumbling sidewalk addles our search for the last site, this cliff thing.

"I think we went the wrong way. How can we get lost in this tiny place?" Dejah straightens her ponytail.

"Let's regroup." I stop on a street corner.

Cracks slink through the peeling paint on the pastel-colored buildings surrounding us. My shoulders tense as I wipe my brow with the back of my hand, then dry it on my shorts. It's uncomfortably quiet. No cars, and no other people walking by.

Dejah tuts as she twists the yellow booklet, trying to decode our location.

I scan for a street sign. Nothing.

Across the road, there's a white man hunched over in a shaded doorway wearing a long dark coat. I tilt my head as his wisps of gray hair tangle on the breeze. Why is he wearing a coat on such a hot day? I'm wearing a tank top and shorts and am accumulating under-boob sweat like it's my job.

"We could be here." Dejah points to the map, and I glance over her shoulder. "But it's a guess because I have no idea where we are."

"Uuuunnnnhhhhh." A deep porn star groan makes my stomach drop.

I swing my gaze across the street. Shabby Old Man's eyes are squinted, his mouth a twisted snarl, his coat is open, his pants are pooled at his ankles, and his hand is rigorously moving over his—

"Aww, man." I cringe and twist my head. "He's jerking off."

"Looks like there's a seventh thing to see in Pärnu. Old guy wanking." Dejah's jaw tightens as she flings her arm toward him. "The *Pärnu in Your Pocket* tour is officially over." She spins and stomps away.

"Amen to that." I hustle after her, not caring if we're going the right way or not.

Just outside of town, my heart lifts at the sound of happy voices and '80s music. A grin takes over my face at the sight of an amusement park with five rides, a handful of game stands, and a few food vendors surrounded by tall, leafy trees.

"Check it out." I lift my chin to the banner over the park entryway promoting the annual yacht festival. "Right Said Fred is headlining next week. That would have been cool to see."

Dejah starts, and I join her for the opening lines of "I'm Too Sexy" by Right Said Fred.

"Wait." Dejah stops singing. "What was their second hit? It sounded the same as—'I'm Too Sexy.'"

"Oh, crap. I can hear the song in my head, but I totally can't remember the name of it." I tap my fingertips on my lips as we wander through the rides, stopping at an ice cream cart. "That's going to bug me."

"I'm sure it'll come to us." She pulls Ken from her bag to pay for two lemon Calippos—a new favorite treat, a popsicle in a long triangular tetra pack. I would prefer ice cream, but these are a Dejah-endorsed food as she usually doesn't allow us to eat too much fatty stuff.

We lounge on the lush grass under a shady tree and listen to "True" by Spandau Ballet blaring from the Tilt-a-Whirl.

"What would you do if Dean came around the corner and asked you to marry him?" I tug off my sandals, cross my legs at the ankles, and slurp on my popsicle.

"Well." She takes a bite of her Calippo. "I reckon I would consider it for approximately ten seconds, then you would be on your own because I would be leaving with him." She sighs. "He's really something. I would do anything to see him again. And you, mate, what if Josh was standing here and said he loved you?"

"I would ask him why." I stare at the clouds dancing in the blue sky, breathe in the clean fresh air, and embrace the ridiculous make-believe. "If his answer was good enough, I would jump into his arms and be busy having sex forever." I chuckle, drop my empty popsicle container on the grass to toss later, and prop an arm behind my head.

Song after song we lie on the grass, smoke, and talk about nothing as kids scream from the top of the Ferris wheel until the blazing afternoon cools.

We make our way to the beach to watch the sunset. The sky is a peaceful wash of pink, blue, and purple as the sun dips into the bay. The smooth sand is cool under my bare feet as we crash through the kiddy sandcastles and carve our names in the hard-packed shoreline with our toes.

My mouth parts as a naked gray-haired couple dash hand in hand across the sand. Their voluptuous bodies jiggle, and they let out a loud whoop when their bare skin hits the cool water. They embrace in the waves to the backdrop of the pastel sky. My heart lurches as envy swirls in my chest. I long to share happy moments like that with someone. Such a simple wish yet seemingly impossible to fill. I rip my eyes away from their private moment to the other end of the beach.

"Hold up." I tap Dejah's arm. Two different-sized guys are crushing the beach swinging game. "Check it out."

They stop. One guy climbs onto a garbage can, jumps for the handles, and they're flying. Up and down in perfect swinging synchronicity.

"That's the technique we're missing." I snap my fingers. "The jump gives the momentum to get it going. We have to try it again."

"Uh …" Her forehead wrinkles.

"Don't even try to say no." I drag her up the beach to an empty swing. "You get ready at your end, and I'm going to get that garbage can." I race to the nearby waist-level metal barrel, tip it to the side, and grunt as I wheel it on its edge over to my side of the swing.

Dejah stands on the ground, her arms up as she grips the swing handles. I lift one foot to the lip of the thankfully-not-full garbage barrel. Then I lean over, grip the opposite side of the round top with my hands, and hoist my other foot up. My ass is in the air, doing a downward dog on the rim of the garbage can.

I squat, then leap to the swing handles, catching them on the first go.

I smile. Fucking A. This is it.

Gravity pulls me down. Dejah goes up and sways until she falls off.

"Okay. I admit defeat," I say as I fall to the sand opposite her.

Our laughter fills the dusky sky.

We never had a mud bath *and* were old man jerk-off material, but we still had a great day—making my heart that bit lighter. I lie back in the sand and close my eyes. Now we just need to get through the night in our moldy room.

WELCOME NEW ADDITION - BUS STATION, PÄRNU, ESTONIA

After a sleepless night in a damp bed, we circle the streets in the pouring rain searching for the bus station. Frustration leaks from my pores; I hate being lost. Sweat soaks my T-shirt under my yellow jacket from the strain of carrying Barney on this marathon hike, and the useless map on the back of *Pärnu in Your Pocket* is a soggy mess in my hands.

I bought my bright rain jacket on a rare British sunny day, and it draws a lot of attention. I'm the only person in Eastern Europe who wears yellow or any color besides black, gray, or blue. I wear the vibrant color with pride. I just wish it was a little better at keeping out the wet.

After an exceptionally long detour and lots of swearing, we find the bus station. I huff as we enter the parking lot. My wet hair is a tangled mess, and my feet are wrinkling in my damp boots. Days like this suck so bad. I'm going to be wet all day, and we still have no idea when or even if the bus is coming.

"Hey, you two looking for the ticket booth?" a skinny hippie backpacker with light brown skin who's standing under the overhang outside the bus station asks. "Took me a while to find it. It's over there." He gestures to the small window on the far side of the building.

"Thanks," I say as we duck under the overhang and introduce ourselves.

"I'm Keith from Vancouver." His big brown eyes twinkle as he adjusts his long brown ponytail that falls to the middle of his back.

"Nice to meet yah." Dejah nods to Keith and drops Hulk at my feet. "I'll get the tickets, then I'm going to see what Ken can buy us to eat."

Dejah leaps over a puddle as she dashes out in the rain.

"Hey, you wouldn't happen to know the other hit song by Right Said Fred, would you? The one they released after 'I'm Too Sexy'?" I ask.

Keith's brow creases as he shakes his head.

"Not knowing this song is driving me crazy." I explain the amusement park banner as I drop Barney next to Hulk then toss the sodden *Pärnu in Your Pocket* in the trash can.

"Now I get you." He chuckles. "I wasn't sure what you were talking about."

"Hey, do you like peanut butter?" I ask.

"Yeah." Keith shrugs.

"Excellent." I grin. "I have a one-kilogram container my dad brought me from home that I would love to share." After carting it around since we left London, my clothes have a tang of peanut smell, but I don't have the heart to throw it out.

Khadejah returns, flapping the water beads off her navy coat.

"I looked everywhere, and all I found was two Snickers bars and some orange juice." She frowns because artificial fatty food for breakfast is a Dejah no-no.

"Chocolate is good for me." I smack my lips, happy for the treat. "Guess who likes peanut butter?" I tip my head in Keith's direction.

"Thank God. Can't stand the stuff." Dejah wrinkles her nose.

We all crack up.

And just like that, in a downpour outside the bus station in Pärnu, we make a new friend.

"It's time." I nod to Dejah as the bus pulls into the station.

We hoist on our packs and race through the bus boarding mob to the open under-bus luggage compartment. Keith's arms are crossed as he leans against the bus station wall, safe from the rain under the overhang. He'll be sorry he didn't join us when he gets a crappy seat. The locals are ruthless, and Dejah and my get-on-the-bus routine ensures we don't get boxed out by the feisty crowd and get a decent seat.

Water drips down my face as I leave Barney with Dejah to ensure both bags are stowed under the bus. I angle my shoulder and shove my way to the front of the chaotic mob for the door.

"Where is my girl?" I shout, as I stand on the first step into the bus.

"Over here." Dejah waves her arms in the air as she bumps her way through the grumbly crowd.

I wait on the step until our cold hands connect, and I haul her inside. We high-five our success and score a seat together away from the toilet.

Keith is the last to board. He waltzes down the aisle and takes a seat beside us. I roll my eyes. He's even more chill than Dejah. Okay, so we didn't need to use our get-on-the-bus routine today. But it's always good to practice because you never know what lies ahead.

THE BIG FINALE - RIGA, LATVIA

It's pouring when the bus rolls into Riga. At the exchange window outside the small, dank bus station, I swap my remaining Estonian kroons for nineteen Latvian lats. Converting back to Canadian currency is the easiest way to grasp the value of things, and nineteen lats is about fifty dollars.

Now we need a map and a place to stay. I approach the information center next to where I got my lats.

"Hi, I was hoping—" The woman slams the small window shut.

I sigh, and my shoulders droop as she turns her back.

"I have a map." Keith taps his front pocket. "And my book suggests two places to stay. The university dorms and the Arena, that's where the circus performers live in the winter. I suggest we try the dorms first. They're closer."

"Keith, you're a welcome addition to the team." I slap him on the back, relieved he's taking charge.

He gives me a toothy side grin.

My breath coils on the cold air as the three of us traipse over to the university dorms. They're full, and we're waved off with a scowl by the reception lady. I think if she had a window, she would have slammed it shut too.

The sideways rain soaks my pants as we trudge the wet cobblestone streets to the Arena. They have vacancies. Even better, they have a fluffy tabby curled up under a black lamp on the check-in desk. I stroke the soft fur under his chin, and his loud purr soothes my pouty mood while Dejah arranges our beds. They have single rooms for three lats each. And no elevators. I swear the whole way as I lug Barney up five flights of steep concrete steps to my small room with a single bed, a nightstand, and not much else.

We drop our gear and change clothes, then attempt sightseeing in the lashing rain. But the dark skies are miserable and the cold air chills me to the bones, making this walk as welcoming as the first two Latvian ladies I met.

"Hey guys, I'm going to have a nap. Wake me when you get back?" I leave Khadejah and Keith to touring because I'm way past ready to climb into my warm sleeping bag.

Khadejah jumps on my single cot, and I startle awake.

"Wake up, sleepyhead." I swipe my drool as she flops on the bottom of my bed. "We heard the local Irish pub is the best place to watch the game tonight."

World Cup soccer has been playing on every TV in every country for the last month, and they're down to the final two games.

"Irish pub, shocker." I rub my eyes.

Every city has an Irish pub—which totally makes sense after visiting there. They even have a pub at the shoe cobbler. Heaven forbid the Irish leave Ireland and have nowhere familiar to drink.

"Come on, Candace, we need to get going." Keith pokes his head through the doorway. "For sure Croatia is going to kick the Netherlands' ass in the game."

He was in Croatia a few weeks ago and has been raving about the brilliant sunshine, clear blue sea, and endless coastline all day.

"I'll be ready in five minutes." I shiver as I crawl out of my warm bed and throw on some clothes.

The packed, smoky pub has dark brown walls, floors, and tables, and a huge white projector screen airing the pre-game show.

"There's a semi-open table," Khadejah shouts over the English announcer chatting about the game blasting through the bar. "There's not much else. Bad luck it's in front of the big screen, but it'll have to do."

I hand signal with the table occupants, pointing to us and the chairs, trying not to be like Backward Glasses from Ludicrous Spice bar in Tallinn. The couple nods, not that they have much choice as Dejah is already parked in a seat opposite them and Keith is at the bar buying beer.

The second the game starts, Keith is on his feet screaming for Croatia. My mouth gapes. Our quiet Keith is gone, but *other* Keith's enthusiasm is infectious. By the end of the game, Dejah and I are cheering along with him when Croatia wins the bronze medal.

"You two have to go to Croatia," Keith shouts over the screaming crowd. "The country and the people there are amazing. You know I wouldn't lie."

Disregarding the last two hours of *other* Keith, he's a reserved guy, so for him to go on and on about Croatia, it must be something special. It's not a place we planned to visit but is now a consideration based on his sunny descriptions and enthusiasm.

"I have the perfect Spice name for him." Khadejah explains to Keith how the Spice names work. He's smiling and keen to be given a name. "In honor of your passion for Croatia, your Spice name will be Hrvatska Spice."

"Yes." He throws his fist in the air, ecstatic to be named Croatia Spice—said in Croatian.

It never fails to amaze me how delighted people are to be given a Spice Girl name.

WE SPLASH through rivers of rainwater on the cobblestones as we search for a healthy breakfast place for Dejah that also serves vegetarian food for Keith. Nothing fits the brief, and because of the downpour, Dejah concedes to eating at a bakery.

My mouth waters at the smell of freshly baked bread filling the shop. I blow into my clasped hands as I scan the fluffy baked goods behind the glass counter. I intend to take full advantage as Khadejah would normally only allow a place like this on a special occasion—like a birthday or a *really* bad day.

I skip to the table, carrying a chocolate croissant that covers the entire medium-sized plate. Her lips flatten, and I ignore her disappointed glower over her fruit cup as my teeth sink into the buttery, chocolate goodness. I devour every crispy morsel.

After we eat, we attempt to tour around Riga, but it's Sunday, and most sights are closed. The totality of my rainy Riga sightseeing is my somber photo alongside two military guards at the forty-two-meter-high granite Freedom Monument.

"Anybody want a coffee?" I ask.

"I'm going back to nap." Keith rubs his mouth.

"I'm gonna walk around. Meet back at the Arena later?" Khadejah tugs the hood up on her jacket, then we depart in different directions.

My foot splashes in a deep puddle. Icy water seeps over the top of my boot, drenching my sock. I groan. Despite my epic breakfast croissant, today isn't roses and rainbows and seeing beautiful new things in the sunshine like I envisioned every day would be when we started this trip.

I shake the water off my boot and intake a breath at the blinking red neon sign boasting *Internet* across the street. Connecting with home is a pot of gold at the end of today's absent rainbow and just what I need to lift my spirits. I leap over the lake-puddle and race to the door.

The warmth of the café heats my frosty fingers, and I smile at the boxy '80s computers. I order a hot milky coffee and buy an hour on the Internet. I light a cigarette and toe off my sodden boots under the desk. The dial-up slowly beeps and wails as my toes tingle and defrost. The screen flickers then loads my inbox with ten new Hotmail messages.

My heart wobbles at the new unread message from Josh in the middle of the rest.

I pinch the bridge of my nose. This is a disaster. And totally my fault. I've been copying Josh on my group emails since I left London—*only* to shove in his face how much fun I'm having without him. And now after responding to him directly while I was in Moscow sharing my stupid gushing—*I miss you, too*—he thinks we can communicate on the regular. Well, didn't my spiteful idea just gloriously backfire? Seeing his name in my inbox is like re-opening a thinly healed wound, and for him, it's probably no big deal.

I stub out my cigarette and scan my other messages. An unforced smile tips my lips at Vasilii's name. He's the Russian friend of a friend with the perfect smile we met in Moscow. Dejah and I both crushed on him for days—he even introduced us to his mom and sister. Before we left Moscow, his sister alluded to the fact that he likes me and wants to meet me again.

I double-click on Vasilii's note and shimmy in my seat as I read his words saying he's planning on meeting me in South

Africa after Christmas. I hit reply. My fingers dance across the keyboard letting him know I can't wait to see him. Because Josh lives in fantasyland, but Vasilii? He's 100 percent real.

I delight in reading every word of my other notes until only *his* remains.

I hope you're safe. Do you know where you'll be over the next month? I would love to meet up. I miss you.

Josh xo

My jaw drops.

For months—*months*—I longed to make travel plans with him, and he dodged me at every turn. But now? *Now* he wants to bust out of fantasyland and meet me somewhere?

I light a new cigarette and take five deep lungfuls as I re-read every word twenty times. My brain spins with confusion. I have this charming Russian—who likes me and can't wait to join me in South Africa. And then there's Josh—who doesn't love me, said he never could, but wants to meet up.

I tap my cigarette over the ashtray and stare at the crack in the plaster wall above my monitor. Never in my twenty-six years have I lived this freely. I have no obligations to anyone other than my plan to travel with Khadejah to Cairo, then safari over Christmas, and as of four minutes ago committing to meeting Vasilii in five months.

I get to choose who I spend time with and do what I want, when I want.

But choosing to meet Josh would be a colossally terrible idea.

I bite the edge of my thumb.

Infinitely bad.

I push away from the desk.

He was supposed to only live in my dreams. *Dreams.* I huff. They're free, but they're also dangerous. There's like a 90 percent

48

chance he won't follow through, but his note ignites a treacherous flicker of hope for the 10 percent chance he might.

But … if I've learned anything on this trip, it's to leave my options open. I ignore my brain shouting at me to leave Josh in the past as my heart responds by sharing our travel plans to Poland and the Czech Republic and that I *might* be open to meeting up. But I'm not going out of my way to do it—I have to maintain *some* dignity.

As soon as I hit send on Josh's note, I fling his preposterous proposal out of my mind because there's no way it will amount to anything. I compose an airy group note home, avoiding the difficult specifics, like the train incident in Narva and the old wanker because no one wants to hear *those* details.

From: Candace

To: My Friends

Date: July 12, 1998

Subject: Hello from Latvia

Tallinn, Estonia was our first stop after Russia. It's lighter there, in spirit I mean; it's a sharp contrast to the hard, tough, busy feeling of Moscow. Tallinn is a small town with cobblestone streets and old-world buildings, with loads of tourists, and the locals are friendly if not slightly strange. It also made us appreciate how expensive Russia was as food and accommodation there are cheap in comparison.

After Tallinn we headed to a place on the coast of Estonia called Pärnu. It's a town known for its healing mud baths, lovely white sandy beaches, and lots of interesting sights. In the end, we opted not to have the mud bath as it was a mud wrap, not a *bath*.

We're now in Riga, Latvia. It's a lovely town with so much to see and do.

Candace xoxo

DEJAH, Keith, and I return to the Irish pub to watch the Brazil vs. France World Cup final game. The fine hairs on my neck tingle as we enter the packed bar. The mood is electric, and Ronaldo is in the house. Loads of Brazilian fans are wearing the #9 Ronaldo yellow jersey. There are also tons of France fans wearing blue.

"Go France." Keith throws his arms over his head as the game starts.

We decided on the walk over that we're cheering for France as they're hosting the World Cup. The sea of people wearing yellow and blue are good-naturedly side by side singing the team(s) 'theme song' as the players race across the screen. I played soccer for ages but freely admit I have no idea about the ins and outs of professional soccer fans' habits.

The referee on the large projector screen blows his whistle three times, signifying the end of the game—France wins the World Cup 3-0.

My ears ring as people in blue shirts stand on their chairs and belt out the French national anthem. A massive French flag is passed around. Fans in yellow and blue are toasting and dancing. Keith, Dejah, and I dance along with them with massive silly smiles on our faces. Dejah throws her arms around my waist, and Keith wraps his arms around the two of us. The three of us bounce in a hug as the crowd in the bar chant and sing.

Man, this place is fun. I can only imagine how wild it is in France.

COINS - BUS STATION, RIGA, LATVIA

I groan as I drop my backpack next to a bench under the narrow overhang outside the bus station in Riga. The small semi-dry entryway offers a slight break from the persistent rain we've experienced since arriving here two days ago.

Our bus departs for Lithuania in ten minutes. I reach into my pocket and pull out a pile of Latvian coins that weigh heavy in my hand because we can't exchange them. Bills yes, but coins no. I can't afford waste on my tight budget.

"Give me all your coins." I cup my palms to Dejah and Keith as they shake the rain off their coats.

I'm going to spend every bit of our Latvian change on something useful at the bulging market stalls selling fruit, snacks, and household wares in front of the bus departure area.

Coins clang in my palms as they empty their pockets. My jaw clenches as the bright silver circles twinkle under the dull light. I must have like sixty dollars' worth.

But there will be no waste today.

Khadejah and Keith kick back on the bench under the covered area surrounded by our three large backpacks as I frantically race between stalls in the heavy rain. With two minutes to spare before the bus departs, the coins are gone, and my spending mission is a success.

My chest expands with pride when I return to them dripping wet carrying four heavy plastic bags filled with Diet Coke, fruit, chips, mystery cookies—I think they're cookies, but I'm unable to read the label—bread, cheese, and pickles for us to eat on the eight-hour bus trip to Vilnius.

"Mate." Khadejah coughs as she chuckles. "You're too much."

"We need to manage our money better." I pinch my lips and tap my toe as the plastic bags cut into my fingers.

Dejah's warm golden eyes soften.

"We just started, it's all good. We'll get better," she promises as she slides off the bench and squeezes my arm.

"Okay." I nod sharply, and my fervent grip on the food bags loosens.

My erratic mood is not *all* about wasting money. Each day that passes is another day closer to death day. And each day leading up to her death also has an anniversary.

The day she stopped getting dressed.

The day she stopped eating.

The day she stopped being able to talk—

"All part of the deal. We look after each other," Dejah says as Keith loads our big packs under the bus. And we don't need to do our get-on-the-bus routine today since there's no mob waiting to board. "I'm knackered. Let's get out of here."

The snack bags twist and bang against my knees as I climb on the bus behind her. The familiar odor of mildew soaks the air. The seats are covered in dubious-looking stains, and the murky windows are covered in years of grime and breath. I pretend it's not that bad because this is our only option for travel. I throw myself in an empty seat with Keith taking the adjacent one. Khadejah lies down on the bench in front of me and is asleep before we roll out of the station.

Found friends like Keith are like a shooting star. They shine bright and bring joy as they pass through, but they don't stay long because they have other places to be. Which is why I'm so thankful Dejah and I are in this together for the long haul to Cairo. This trip would be unbearable on my own. I already carry a deep hollow ache in my chest from missing my mom, and the sheer loneliness of trying to figure things out with no one to commiserate with would be agonizing. But I have to be more diligent. Money management is vital and is the one tangible thing that can derail my master plan to travel and stay away from home as long as possible.

I unravel the red metallic wrapper around the mystery cookies. I shove one in my mouth and pass the package across the aisle to Keith. My lips pucker as the cookie turns to cement on my tongue. I scramble for a Diet Coke out of the station snack supplies and take three big gulps to wash it away. Keith is munching on his third cookie with a smile—at least one of us likes them.

"Got any chips over there?" Keith asks.

"Yeah." I toss him a bag and pinch open a small package for myself.

The mystery flavor I selected is a cross between stinky cheese and tart vinegar. I shiver as the odd chip flavor spirals around my taste buds. The bag crinkles as I dive in for another to double-check if they're really that bad. I frown as I chew. Yup, terrible.

"These are the best," Keith says as he shovels another handful into his full mouth.

I soften into my threadbare seat. The prospect of going home before I untangle my heart terrifies me more than bad weather, mold, rude people, strict money management, these chips, and anything else I might face on the road.

My *only* way is forward. And nothing is going to stop me.

CHAPTER 3
SOME DAYS ARE HEL

MONDAY, July 13, 1998

ROBOT - VILNIUS, LITHUANIA

Wet icy wind blasts my face as I step off the bus in Vilnius. I shiver as I pop the hood on my yellow jacket. Keith's bony ass is in the air, the top half of his body lost in the under-bus storage compartment digging around for our backpacks. Khadejah stumbles off the bus steps, and I catch her before she crashes to the sidewalk. Her eyes are glassy, and her normally bright dark golden skin is ashen. I swipe her dark hair out of her eyes and press my hand to her forehead.

"You're burning up." I frown.

I tuck my hand under her elbow and lead her over to Keith, who's successfully rescued our bags from storage. Keith and I throw our big packs on our backs, then I strap my smaller daypack to my front. I hook my forearm through one of Hulk's shoulder straps, Keith takes the other, and with my last free limb, I crook arms with Khadejah.

Linked in a row, the three of us hobble inside the gray brick station. The inside of the cavernous space is no warmer than outside, but it's dry. We drag ourselves to a wooden bench away from the drafty door.

"Okay, here's the deal. Dejah, you sit here with the big bags," I say as she collapses on the bench and we drop our packs at her feet. "Keith and I'll change money, buy a map, and figure out how to get to the hostel."

She nods and passes me Ken.

Keith and I weave through the crowds to the currency exchange booth on the opposite side of the bus station. I exchange our leftover colorful crisp Latvian lats bills for Lithuanian litas. These new bills feature dour-faced old people and are slippy between my fingertips—almost slimy like lots of people have touched them. I chuckle as I tuck the notes into Ken. Seems fitting. No one smiles in the Baltics, not even on their money.

We score a map from the information kiosk beside the exchange booth. They have *Vilnius in Your Pocket*, like the one in Pärnu, but this one has pictures of churches on the front and a map on the back highlighting the top sites around town.

I grab a handful.

"Why did you take so many?" Keith asks as he saunters across the bus station to the bench where we left Khadejah.

"What?" I'm clutching ten brochures. "Oh. It's a bit like napkins. I always take extra since I usually lose or spill something on them. Plus, Dejah will want one. *And* I'm collecting all my entry tickets, bus tickets, and anything I come across to mail home."

"Dude, no wonder Barney's so heavy." He shakes his head.

"I know." I sigh. "It's hard to be a packrat and live out of a backpack. But I'm managing it."

Barely. Barney weighed a whopping twenty-two kilograms when I left London, and he hasn't gotten any lighter. The extra papers, maps, postcards, and small souvenirs are adding to his considerable girth. But one day when this trip is all said and done, I'll arrange everything in an album, adding my ticket stubs alongside my photographs for a little extra pizzazz.

Khadejah's slumped on the bench looking even smaller than her five-foot frame. I pull my *Lonely Planet* out of my daypack and thumb through the pages to the section on Vilnius. Keith flips open the large map as I read out the location of the only hostel in town.

"It's too long to walk. We'll need to take the bus," he says, tracing the distance.

"The guidebook says to take bus number thirty-four. The stop is across the street outside McDonald's. Will it harm your delicate sensibilities to stand outside one?" I tease.

"Funny." Keith's dark eyes twinkle.

He's not into anything mainstream, anything to do with big business, or 'the man.' It's too much for his vegetarian-hippiness to handle.

"I think we get bus tickets there." Keith points to the thin yellow box near the entrance to the bus station that appears to be spitting out tickets.

"Back in a jiffy." I pat Dejah's knee and jog after Keith.

He and I get in the short line, but I can't see around the giant bald man ahead of me to get a clue how the machine works. I randomly press buttons when it's our turn with no luck, then Keith has a go with the same result.

"How are we going to figure this out—" I jump at a light tap on my shoulder.

A lady with tight gray curls and a cane points to us then to the machine.

I nod and smile, relieved for the help. I hold up my thumb and two fingers, indicating I want three tickets. We learned the hard way in Russia that the thumb counts as one unit if you're holding it up or not.

Keith points to our destination on the map, and I hold out my palm filled with change. Tight Curls plucks five coins, inserts the money, presses some buttons, and three label-sized white tickets pop out of the bottom slot.

"Ačiū," I say—exactly like a sneeze—which is thank you in Lithuanian.

Before we got here, I made sure to check the back of my travel book so I knew how to say it. Unlike when I arrived in Estonia. Not that knowing how to say thank you in Estonian would have salvaged my visa communication disaster with Stern Man. But at least I would have been polite.

Tight Curls dips her chin—no smile, of course—then takes her turn at the machine.

I press my lips together as I stand over Khadejah, who's splayed out on the bench with her arms draped over our bags. She's deathly pale. I'm not sure if she has the flu or a bad cold, but I know for sure she needs rest.

I touch her shoulder to rouse her. "Hang in there, Dejah. We'll be at the hostel soon. I'm sorry I can't carry Hulk for you. I can't manage him and Barney."

"It's okay, mate." She groans as she drags herself upright and grimaces as I hoist Hulk on her back.

Mercifully, we don't have to wait long for a city bus, and it's a straightforward trip following the directions in the guidebook. The hostel looks like a Swiss chalet. It has a rich brown roof with scalloping around the edges where it meets the white walls. The reception area is cold and sparse; they must have spent all their cash sprucing up the outside.

The three of us are assigned to the same large, damp, eight-bunk-bed dorm room. On the plus side, the basic wooden bunks are high enough to sit on the bottom bed without hitting your head. This is a win because normally the bunks are so low you have to roll out of bed so you don't injure yourself. It does mean the top bunk is like sleeping in the clouds, but we get lucky and each score a low bunk.

"Come on, Dejah, let's get you into bed." I pull back the stiff white sheets and guide her under the covers. There's no blanket, so I put my sleeping bag around her, and she's out like a light.

"What do you want to do?" Keith asks as he lazes on the bottom bunk adjacent to hers.

"I need a shower before I can decide anything," I say, unzipping Barney to grab my toiletries.

"Cool. Take your time. I'm reading up on churches." He sticks his nose in his guidebook while munching on the leftover cement cookies from the bus. He loves the big pipes that fan out like a silver peacock behind church organs and has made it his mission to see every one in every city he visits.

Hot water pounding on my skin washes away the dirt from the bus and the cold weather. I flinch as it hits my belly button. I was excited when I got it pierced in London three months ago.

Today—not so much.

There's a bumpy, dark, itchy, red rash an inch in diameter around the small golden ring looped through the hood of my belly button. I gag as clear pus drips around the piercing. As I get dressed, I stick a tissue through the ring to catch the seepage.

I know I should, but I refuse to take out this belly button ring. This piercing was a departure from my usual nerdy straitlaced ways. It's my visual reminder that this trip is about branching out and trying new things. So it's staying. I just hope it gets better soon.

Dejah's chest rises and falls as I hover over her sleeping form with my fists clenched. I stand up straighter, grab her water bottle, fill it up, then place it beside her bed.

My fingers tremble as I take a step back.

Khadejah, my fun, vibrant friend who is quick to laugh and joke, is sick.

Sick.

Tears sting my eyes. After eight years of looking after my mom—I'm drained. I no longer have it in me to offer care and compassion. That part of me is empty. It guts me, but I just have nothing like that left to give.

My chest ripples with guilt as I take another step back and stare at her gaunt face.

I *can* do tangible.

I place two Tylenol next to her fresh water with a note letting her know we're popping into town and will pick up food on our way back.

My stomach burns as I back out of the room and softly close the door, feeling like I've let her down. But I can't sit by her bedside. I just can't.

Keith and I catch the bus into Vilnius city center.

I can confirm from our rainy tour that there are a lot of churches in Vilnius.

Our third church has an imposing circular stained-glass window over the twelve stone steps leading to an enormous entryway. A woman about my age is cowering on the bottom step, begging for money. I stop in my tracks, and my heart squeezes when I see her face. It's swollen, smeared in blood, and she can't open her left eye. I have so many places I could go if something like that happened to me, even out here on the road. I could call my dad and he would help me. But here she is, begging and alone.

As we enter the church, a dark thought crosses my mind, and a wave of nausea rips through me. "Keith," I whisper, stealing his attention from the ornate organ on the church balcony. "What if someone did that to her on purpose? So we would give her money, *which we did*. Have we contributed to the cause rather than helping her with a solution?"

The color drains from his face, and my heart sinks. I didn't want to be right about her.

We trudge through the streets of Vilnius in the torrid rain that's been following us like a Charlie Brown cloud. It seems like a nice town, but I'm not inspired.

"We should head back." The rain is miserable, that poor woman has soured my spirits, and my guilt runs deep for leaving Khadejah alone at the hostel.

"Sure. There's a grocery store not too far away. I can make us dinner tonight," Keith says.

"I saw that one. It looked like you can touch the food," I say.

A crease forms between his eyebrows.

"Oh man, in Russia, we couldn't touch the food. It was behind glass, so we had to point and mime our way to buy a loaf of bread. It was bad." I wrinkle my nose.

We touch and buy food for dinner and breakfast. We also buy tissues and cold medicine for Dejah—a label I recognize from London after my many colds there.

At the hostel, Keith heads to the communal kitchen with the groceries to whip up veggies and rice while I check on Khadejah.

"You left me," she says as I enter the cold dorm room.

"We got supplies." I hold out the bag of stuff we bought for her.

She crosses her arms.

I clear my throat, place the box of tissues on the bed, pop a pill out of the blister pack, and pass it to her with a small bottle of orange juice.

"What's wrong with you? It's like you don't care … and you're acting like a robot," she says as she takes the pill and juice.

I go still.

"I'm sorry." My spine straightens as I stand beside her bunk. "You know I care."

It's because I care that it's hard when someone's sick.

But she's right. I'm nothing more than a robot.

"How about a hug then?" She sighs.

"I can do that." I sit on the edge of her bunk and wrap my arms around her slight frame.

My heart breaks in a new place as I tighten my embrace. Usually, I anticipate needs, I sense moods, I commiserate, I listen, I help, I love—my empathy is the foundation of who I am. But it's broken. I feel like I've been replaced with a stranger. And I hate it. I have to figure out how to put my pieces back together because I don't want to be this person I've become.

THE SANDWICH - VILNIUS, LITHUANIA

Khadejah rallies the next morning. It's my turn to be the tour guide, so we start at the Gate of Dawn, the last remaining city gate from the 16th century. Rain drips down my cheeks as we admire the baby blue two-story archway over the street with a church cross on the top. It's *the* iconic religious, historical, and cultural monument in Vilnius. It's lovely, but my hands are numb from the cold, and my mood darkens with each new raindrop that pelts my face.

Also, yesterday's conversation with Khadejah is rubbing against my insides like sandpaper. I spent ages lying awake in my damp bunk analyzing if my broken empathy is tied to my grief emptiness. I didn't come up with an answer, but I did manage to wind myself up because tackling grief is heavy enough on its own … and now I've identified a whole new challenge to deal with.

My cheeks puff as I blow out a long breath. I'm ready for another down day.

"Hot drink?" Keith points to the small tea shop across the narrow cobblestone street.

"Yes," I say, ecstatic for the distraction.

We race over and slide into dainty spindle chairs around a tiny table covered in a macramé tablecloth.

"Tea? Ačiū," Keith asks the server, pointing to the three of us.

"Pieno?" the server inquires, holding up a pitcher of milk.

Keith blushes as Dejah and I crack up like teenage boys because it sounds like she asked us if we wanted a *penis*.

"Pieno, ačiū," Dejah replies with the first smile I've seen from her all day. "This is fun. We know two words in Lithuanian: penis and sneeze."

Keith goes even redder as the rain batters the glass storefront.

"It's pretty lame to be drinking tea to warm up in *July*," I say as the server places a white porcelain teapot with an elegant spout and three mismatched flowered cups and saucers on the table.

Keith pours the tea, and steam swirls from my delicate pink peony cup. I add a dollop of pieno and take a sip. I slouch. It's hot but tasteless.

"The *Vilnius in Your Pocket* recommends a nice place for sandwiches," Keith says.

Usually, our sandwiches are made with a Swiss Army knife while we sit on a park bench. A popular specialty sandwich would be a treat.

"I'm down." I place the bland drink on the table.

It's been a tough couple of days, and this is the perfect suggestion to turn spirits around.

"How about an early lunch?" Dejah frowns at her full cup.

"Oh, yeah." Keith glugs his tea as Khadejah shrugs on her coat.

We leg it three blocks and up some stairs to the *Vilnius in Your Pocket*-recommended sandwich place. There are twenty tables with most of the seats occupied by grinning tourists.

I rub my hands together. This is a good sign.

I caress the menu as I evaluate the extensive sandwich options. I can only read the titles. The rest of the words are in Estonian. But based on the content buzz of happy mingled conversations in the room, I can already tell it's going to be fantastic.

"I'm going for the 'American Sandwich,'" I say as I close the menu.

I giddily place my order, Khadejah opts for the same choice, and Keith orders a veggie version.

"I wonder if it's like a club sandwich with chicken, bacon, maybe some tomatoes, lettuce, and a bit of mayo." I sigh.

Lunch can't come soon enough.

My lips part as the server places the sandwiches on the table.

I crinkle my nose. It has three slices of bread, but that's where the similarities to a club sandwich end. It smells funny like overused fryer oil. The dark brown bread has a shiny sheen, like a French fry. I stick my fork between the layers and pop the top piece of bread. My gut rolls as the sharp scent of horseradish waters my eyes. Scraggy chicken is wedged between the thick layer of white sauce.

I stab my fork into the stack of bread and saw my knife along the corner.

Brown grease oozes from the deep-fried bread, puddling onto my white plate.

It smells rancid and turns my stomach.

I glance around the restaurant. Empty plates. Smiling patrons.

I *must* be overreacting.

I bring my sandwich-stacked fork to my mouth. My throat constricts as the combination of brown grease, stringy chicken, and horseradish hits my tongue. My fork clangs on the plate as I clamor for my napkin. I spit out the unchewed grossness and reach for my water. I madly swish the liquid around to dispel the taste.

Khadejah shoves her plate away. I don't know if Keith even took a bite of his. And I know it's bad when Keith refuses to eat because he eats everything.

Bitter disappointment hangs over our table.

"I need a purge and a shower," I say quietly.

"Lunch is over," Dejah sighs, crossing her arms.

"I'll ask for the bill." Keith grimaces, signaling the server.

We resume our sightseeing to forget about our failed lunch. We plod along in the light rain to the round, three-story, red-brick Gediminas Castle Tower. Heights and I are not friends, but this tower is short and the stairs aren't claustrophobic, so I make it to the top. The tower is on a hilltop and has sweeping views of Vilnius. Brilliant orange rooftops and majestic church steeples brighten up the murky sky. I breathe in the cool air and let this good moment of being in a pretty place soak under my skin.

"I count sixteen churches," Dejah says.

"We've only been to six. I have more to see." Keith grins.

"The fresh air is helping me recover from *the sandwich*," I say.

Dejah's face twists, and Keith shakes his head.

"Right." I shudder. "Nothing can fix that memory."

The sandwich is definitely a bad moment.

"Let's stop at the good grocery store to get stuff for veggie pasta tonight. I don't think any of us can tolerate another bad meal," I say as we exit the tower.

"And lots of beer," Keith adds.

Khadejah has a rest while Keith and I prepare dinner in the hostel kitchen. We chop, drink, and chat with a baby-faced white guy also preparing food.

"Where are you from?" I ask Baby Face.

"Polska. My friend and I cycled three hundred kilometers in the last two days to get here," he says.

"I would love to cycle, but not in the rain," I say as I place our dented pot of sauce on the ancient six-burner gas stove to simmer.

The metal chair scrapes across the linoleum floor as I take a seat at the long wooden kitchen table. I rifle through my bag, pulling out my travel guide and cigarettes. I slide one out and offer my open pack to Baby Face. He takes one, snatches my lighter, and lights mine then his.

Keith—the non-smoker—stirs our sauce and frowns at the cigarette hanging between Baby Face's lips as he scrambles a big pan of eggs at the adjacent burner.

"We're going to Poland next; do you mind if I practice on you?" I ask Baby Face.

He smirks as his eyes land on my chest.

Ew. He thinks I'm coming on to him. Just no.

"My *words*." I roll my eyes. "I just want to practice Polish words."

"Shame." He glides his thumb across his bottom lip as he talks to my boobs. "What have you got?"

I open my *Lonely Planet* to the phonetic Polish words section.

"Okay, poprosie beelet. What am I trying to say?"

"Again," Baby Face orders.

I say it again. And again. Changing the inflection each time.

He purses his lips and sharply shakes his head.

"I was saying, ticket please." God, I'm terrible at this. Even with the words written out phonetically, I can't say them properly.

My hopes of getting better at communicating are not looking great.

"Let me introduce you to a word that will not be in your little book." He smiles then whispers conspiratorially, "Kurwa."

"Kurwa," I repeat. "That's a pretty word. What does it mean?"

Baby Face chuckles. "It's like slut, bitch, whore, all rolled into one."

"Ugh. I'll never use it." I crinkle my nose.

What a loser. He's trying to shock or upset me, but after all I've seen on this trip, it's going to take more than a bad word to get under my skin.

IN BROAD DAYLIGHT - BUS STATION, VILNIUS, LITHUANIA

My heart warms as sunlight streams through our dorm room window. Finally, the rain's stopped. No more wet feet and freezing fingers; we get to enjoy a sunny summer day. And it's going to be awesome because we're day-tripping to the fairytale Trakai Island Castle which stands on an island in the middle of a lake.

My T-shirt rides up as I stretch my arms above my head, dragging a trail of foul-smelling pus in its wake. My stomach pitches as my fingers slip through the slime around my belly button. The rash circle looks bigger than yesterday. But I'm still not taking it out. I tug my shirt down and roll over to check on Khadejah. She's not *better,* but her eyes are clear, and she promises she's well enough to visit the castle.

We exit the city bus beside the food market stalls in front of the central bus station.

"I'll go buy the tickets. Can you guys scout for snacks out here?" I ask Keith and Dejah.

"On it," Keith says, leading a still-pale Khadejah in the direction of the booths.

The sun heats my face as I zigzag through the stalls to the front door of the gray brick bus depot. I waltz into the station filled with frowning people rushing to their next destination and scan for a place to buy tickets. There's a stand-alone kiosk, not far from the exchange booth Keith and I visited yesterday. It's odd, reminiscent of an ice cream cart, but there's no lineup so I take it as a good sign and mosey over.

I smile brightly at the ticket guy with a heavy brow and olive skin sitting on a wooden stool behind the kiosk. Black stubble surrounds his scowling thin lips. What a surprise, another frowner. I maintain my happy face as I hold up my thumb and two fingers. "Three tickets for Trakai, ačiū," I say slowly as I slide money across the kiosk desk.

Ticket Guy's nostrils flare as he takes the slippy bills. He stands, pushing his stool away as he rips off three small squares from a booklet then steps around to the same side of the kiosk as me. He leans forward so his body is a foot from mine and holds out the tickets and change in his right hand.

My shoulders tense as I flick my gaze up at him.

His dark eyes are narrowed on the modest V of my T-shirt.

My smile slips as he licks his lips.

The back of my neck itches as I reach out with my right hand to take them.

As my fingers clasp the papers and change, his left hand seizes the elbow on my outstretched arm. I yelp as he yanks me off my feet, spins, and maneuvers me so I'm pressed between the kiosk desk and his tall, bulky frame. I jolt from the sharp pain as his hips snap into my infected belly button piercing, locking me in place between him and the ledge of the kiosk.

No sound passes my lips because my brain is unable to reconcile what the hell's going on right now. I can't see anything but him; he's blocking my view of everything around us.

My throat pulses and my body freezes as his hands roughly grab my hips.

My stomach bottoms out at his deep, excited pants.

What is happening?

Hard stubble scrapes across my skin as he cruelly pinches my breasts then bites my neck. I retch as his hot tongue leaves a sticky trail of saliva as it slides up the side of my face.

Oh my God, please stop, I scream in my head.

Panic flares inside me. My tickets and change clatter to the floor as I fight and scratch to get away. But he has me pinned. He jams his thighs between my legs, pressing his heavy erection into me as he continues his brutal attack.

Stale breath hits my cheek as he gropes under my shirt.

I scream, writhe, and yank at his arms.

It makes no difference.

My eyes burn as he widens his legs, forcing me to spread mine. He yanks my skirt up, and his callused fingers press into the flesh on my thighs. I stomp my feet but can't move out of this hold. The kiosk ledge cuts into my lower back as he presses his body harder into mine.

His hand thrusts inside my underwear.

Time stops. I don't move. I don't breathe. I don't make a sound. I've disconnected. It's like I'm seeing this from outside my body. I know I should continue to fight, but I'm frozen.

He's relentless, ruthless, and intimately invasive.

Minutes pass like hours before the pain he's inflicting overrides my fear.

My chest heaves as I rotate my shoulders from side to side. His grip around my waist and arms loosens. I take advantage and twist out of his hold. I jump away as he nonchalantly retakes his seat behind the ticket kiosk like nothing happened.

I sway as I cross my arms over my chest.

What.

The.

Fuck?

Blood races through my veins. I snarl as I scour the area, glaring at everyone in here who looked the other way while he attacked me. Maybe they couldn't see it, but I *was* screaming, just not during the worst parts.

I jut my chin upward and throw my shoulders back. I look him in the eye as I pull my skirt down, then adjust my T-shirt and underwear.

Anger is bursting out of my every pore at *him* and *them*. No one said or did anything to stop him or help me.

I glance down at the tickets strewn at my feet.

My heart withers. God. I have to kneel in front of him to pick them up. My breath stutters. Fuck, *this* is what's going to make me cry? I grit my teeth. He's not getting the satisfaction of my tears. I choke them back. I bend at my knees, keeping him in view, then scrape the tickets and money off the floor.

He snarls and laughs. It's harsh and demeaning.

The sour taste of bile rises to my throat as I stumble away.

Why is it that I was the one who was violated yet *I* feel like a dirty whore?

A *kurwa*.

I was never planning on using that word.

I bite back a sob. Turns out the word I learned last night *does* upset me.

I stagger outside and lean against the gray brick wall a few feet from the exit. It happened so fast. It's hard to believe it happened at all. I'm tall and strong. I never thought it could happen to me. I always believed I could defend myself.

I suck in a breath. I fought hard, but undoubtedly, *he* let me go.

How can one moment change my perception of … my ability, my trust in others, and my sense of safety? I walked into the station to buy tickets on a sunny day to see a castle and I left humiliated, feeling like a *kurwa*.

Nausea rolls over me as my vulnerability smacks me in the face. If he could get under my clothes in broad daylight, in a public place, in full view of other people, what would have happened if it had been dark? Or if I'd been in a remote place, where he wouldn't have stopped?

I lean over and dry heave.

I cover my mouth with my hand and crumple against the wall.

People rush past and throw me glares. Sure, *now* they notice me.

I unzip the front pocket of my daypack and pull out my cigarettes. My hands shake as I bring one to my lips. My thumb slips across the flint wheel a few times before I get a light. I take a deep drag then press the heels of my hands into my eyes.

The smell of the cigarette is calming as it swirls around my face.

I hunch in a ball and rock back and forth.

This will not break me.

This will not alter my path.

This changes nothing.

"There you are." Dejah's voice.

But I don't look up. I stall in my protective position and swallow the emotions clogging my throat.

"The bus stop is in the third stall. We got some snacks but nothing for lunch. We'll need to track something down in Trakai." Keith's voice.

I rub away my tears before I stand.

"Is everything okay, Candace?" Khadejah asks.

My lips part and my words freeze on my tongue. My mouth opens and closes. What exactly should I say? *Oh hey, no biggie, the ticket agent just held me down and brutally shoved his dirty fingers inside me.*

I shiver as shame weighs on me like a heavy cloak. I *can't* share this. I refuse to share this. I won't. Instead, I plaster on a fake smile and lie.

"Yeah, I'm good." I stomp my cigarette out on the pavement. "I got the tickets."

I speed past them in the direction of the bus stop. I could tell them, and they wouldn't judge me, but I'm mortified by what he did. No one helped me when it was happening. And especially with the language barrier, what could Keith and Dejah do about it? A big fat nothing is what. So it's not worth reliving in words.

I square my shoulders and shove the last twenty minutes deep inside *a deal with never* compartment. At a loss for what else to do, I focus on the cloudless blue sky, that I have two wonderful friends, and we're setting off on a day trip to see something amazing.

GOOD FROM FAR - TRAKAI, LITHUANIA

Tall evergreen, spruce, and birch trees line the rocky lane on our stroll from the bus stop to the castle in Trakai. The trees help soothe my battered nerves as they remind me of happy times at the family cottage in the summer. My chest pinches with homesickness quickly followed by my usual calming relief I'm not there. Five steps later, I stop in my tracks as a yellow butterfly swirls and glides through the air in front of my face. My lips quiver as I track its dance.

Mom.

After she died, I walked every day for hours to clear my head. I would walk until my body could go no further. During those walks, a little yellow butterfly would come out of the fields, trees, or wherever I was and circle me, just like this one, and I felt less alone with it nearby. It also appeared during random times, like when I was sitting alone on my apartment patio at night in the city. So I started talking to it, figuring it was my mom's way to cheer me up or bring me comfort.

And here she is today. When I need her so very much.

"What's with the butterfly?" Dejah asks as she stops to watch the yellow wings flutter around my head.

"Ever since my mom died. On good days and … bad ones." I wrap my arm around my middle as I recall *his* cruel fingers sinking into my skin. "I see a yellow butterfly. I just kind of refer to it as my mom."

I tense, ready for a negative reaction because it's crazy to believe my mom's spirit lives in a yellow butterfly.

"That's cool." She smiles kindly as it pirouettes between us. "And it's yellow, like your jacket."

"I never thought about that." Goosebumps sweep up my arms.

Maybe it's not so crazy to believe. Especially on days like this when I need it most.

"Check this out," Keith shouts from twenty meters down the road.

The butterfly darts to the bushes as we rush down the rocky path to Keith. There are swings and a massive metal slide beside a long wooden dock leading out to a placid round pond. Keith kicks off his shoes, rips his shirt off, and sprints down the dock. He leaps off the end, curls into a cannonball, and splashes into the water.

"Ahhhhhhhggghhh." An uncharacteristic high-pitched scream from Keith. "This is way colder than I expected."

Dejah and I dangle our feet over the end of the dock as Keith floats on the surface of the pond.

"I wish I brought my swimsuit." I sigh.

The cold water would numb my skin, and I could do with a full body cleanse.

Keith swims over and hoists himself out, his bare feet landing next to us with a light thud. I twist my lips at the protruding ribs on his gaunt body as he reaches back to squeeze the water out of his long dark ponytail. He's a fun and sweet guy, but *totally* not my type. Zero attraction. Besides, I think I would break him if we had sex.

My stomach turns as I rub the side of my face where *he* licked me. I scoop icy water from the pond, then scrub my face and neck. But it does nothing to alleviate the memory of what *he* did.

So much for shoving the encounter in a box.

Trakai Castle is an immaculate structure with sand-colored stone walls and orange triangular turret rooftops perched benevolently on an island surrounded by Lake Galvė. The deep blue lake glistens from the rays of the sun as we stroll across the dark wooden pedestrian bridge to the castle. Along the beachfront where the bridge starts, there are vendors selling trinkets and renting pedalos giving off a relaxed vacation vibe.

The peaceful feeling from strolling across the bridge evaporates when I step inside the castle courtyard. Every corner has a market stall selling the same cheap plastic castle replicas and metal key chains. But it's the vendors' competing voices echoing off the high stone walls shouting for business that grate my skin. I creep closer to Khadejah so my arm grazes hers for comfort.

"This is nuts. The castle is better from far." Dejah sets her hands on her hips.

"I'm so glad it's not just me who thinks so," I say.

Once again, we feel the same way just with different reactions. I'm overwhelmed and want to shrink into a ball, while her jaw is tight and her fingers are clenched, poised for action.

"Yeah." Keith frowns, and his brow wrinkles. "We should rent a pedalo."

Dejah marches us back across the bridge to the beach boat rentals.

Water churns beneath us as Keith and I work the pedals on

our small green boat while Dejah rests in the back. Keith chatters away about his favorite church organs as a light breeze kisses my face and I savor the crisp smell of pine and citrus from the trees lining the shore. I swish my fingertips in the cool, clear water, soak in Keith's carefree vibes, and scrub the bus station encounter from my mind. Because it doesn't deserve space in this sunny day I've been longing for and finally got.

FOURTH CLASS - BUS STATION, VILNIUS, LITHUANIA

Even after a long shower, my belly button is still red and seeping. Add that to the bruises on my thighs, breasts, arms, hips, and ass from yesterday's encounter and it's all I can do not to rock in the fetal position on the moldy tile floor. But I don't because for one, the floor is gross, and for two, I'm not going to let it get to me. Instead, I focus on hiding the bruises and packing Barney because we're leaving Vilnius today.

A sick feeling pools in my gut as we enter *the* bus station. My body relaxes and my nausea slips away when there's no sign of my assailant or any ticket agents at the open kiosks. We ask at the information booth where to purchase tickets and are told to ask the bus driver.

We find the stop, and I step onto the blue double-decker bus.

"Hi, can I get three tickets to Klaipėda?" I ask the bus driver while Dejah and Keith watch the big bags outside.

"You have to wait." He jams his finger in the direction of the door.

My shoulders droop as I slink off the bus.

We wait like fourth-class citizens at the curb as locals who arrived after we did are welcomed on board.

"Will there be any room left for us?" Keith frowns and taps his toe.

"This is complete bullshit!" I throw my arms in the air and pace the sidewalk. "Vilnius is the capital city of Lithuania, but don't be a tourist here and expect to get treated like a normal person. Fucking assholes."

Keith and Dejah gape with slack jaws.

I absently rub one of the larger bruises on my side and glare as another four people climb on the bus.

"Candace, if we don't catch this one, we'll just get the next one." Dejah pats my arm.

"That's not the point," I huff.

"Are you okay?" She narrows her eyes. "You seem off."

"I'm good." I shake out my hands. I need to chill and compartmentalize better. I shove this stupid moment and *the encounter* deeper inside. "I just want to get out of here."

"If you're sure," she says as the bus driver stomps down the steps.

He scowls and reluctantly nods, permitting us to store our packs under the bus and board. Only single seats are available. I'm disappointed to be separated from my friends but desperate to leave Vilnius, so I'll deal. I collapse in a seat beside a ten-year-old boy whose mom and older sister are sitting ahead of us. The kid is by the window, and he's up, down, up, down, moan, moan.

I clench my teeth. This is going to be a long five-hour trip.

I pinch my eyes shut and smack my head against the back of my seat. It's days like this—and yesterday—that make me question why I'm out here. I walked away from a good-paying job and an impending promotion in a pharmaceutical market research company in Canada. And I'm old to be out here. People my age are usually at the bank securing a mortgage and gearing up to start a family, not living out of a purple backpack. Dejah and Josh are a year younger than me, and we occasionally meet travelers our age, but they're on vacation, not living this as a life. Most backpackers are wide-eyed and fresh-faced, barely into their twenties, like Keith.

I rub my hand over my chest. I worked hard to earn my

undergrad, and I fear this time away from work is creating a gap on my resume that I won't be able to recover from. Maybe I would be better off sucking it up at home, working, and progressing my career.

I drum my fingertips on the plastic armrest. I hate having travel doubts. Or any doubts at all. I'm going to blame this waffling on *the encounter*. Oh, and these freezing rainy days in *July,* the fact we get lost all the time, our bad luck with food—*the sandwich*—PMS, my disgusting belly button, the asshole bus driver, and the approaching death date.

I sink deeper into my seat. The backpacking honeymoon period is over. I'm in the thick of it now. And it's hard. Really hard. But I'm no quitter. I exhale and roll my shoulders. I've got this. We're headed to Klaipėda for sun, sand, and relaxing. And everyone always has fun at the beach, right?

BE SMART LIKE THE PUPPY - KLAIPÉDA, LITHUANIA

I smile as I admire my freshly painted burgundy toenails and place the bottle next to a twisty candle on the '70s console in our new room. Every surface in this private rental is packed with bulbous knick-knacks, vases, figurines, and bowls that match the retro orange and brown geometric wallpaper. It's trippy, but it's not a dorm room, is clean and dry, and has loads of space for the three of us to spread out, so it works. Keith and Dejah—who's thankfully feeling better—are roaming around town with the help of the *Klaipėda in Your Pocket* we scored at the bus station. I stayed behind at groovy central to pamper and purge my rotten mood.

Clean, plucked, and polished, I saunter alongside Keith and Khadejah to a bar they scouted earlier. My black going-out shoes —that show off my shiny toenails—click across the thick wooden floor slats as we walk to a booth on the side of the room. My skin tickles with delight as "Pour Some Sugar on Me" by Def

Leppard booms out of the speakers. I love this song. I open the plastic menu and scan the options. Burgers. Oh yeah, this day is shaping up nicely.

Halfway through my tasty burger, three jacked Eewsahs with crew cuts enter. I'm captivated by the one who prowls rather than walks. His broad shoulders roll with every step, and the confidence oozing off him makes me sit up straighter.

"Dibs on the Eewsah in the blue shirt." I angle my chin to the three guys who take up residence at the long bar in the center of the room.

"Knock yourself out, mate." Dejah chuckles, and Keith shrugs.

The last part of my formula to replenish my spirit and snap out of my funk is some attention from a guy of *my* choosing. I crave and need physical contact for comfort. It's why I hug everyone. And whether I meet Josh or Vasilii sometime down the line on this adventure doesn't change the fact that at this very moment, I'm single. So why not flirt with the Adonis with light brown skin and thick dark hair?

I dab my mouth with a napkin, apply a coat of lip gloss, and fluff my hair.

"I'll be back," I say to Dejah and Keith as I zero in on my target.

"Hi, I'm Candace." I flip my hair over my right shoulder. "I heard you speaking English. Where're you guys from?"

My opening chat-up line could use work, but they don't *know* I can tell they're from the US.

"I'm Juan Manuel." A racy crooked smile from hotty-hotness in the tight blue shirt sends shivers up my spine. "Noah." He points to the blond guy with dimples on the stool to his left. "That's Austin." He gestures to the off-putting guy on the right with beady eyes and a scrunched-up face.

"We're doctors from the USNS *Comfort*. It's a hospital ship here on a peace exercise," Beady-Eyed Austin says.

Doctors. Hospital. Talk about a stroke of luck. These guys might be able to tell me what's going on with my leaky belly button.

"What's this?" I slide up my T-shirt and point to my stomach, which now looks like a puffy red bullseye.

Without hesitation, and in unison, the three of them diagnose me. "Cellulitis."

"Ew." I wrinkle my nose, having no idea what that means. I scrutinize the itchy red ring. Well damn, it's even bigger than it was this morning. "Is it serious?"

"If untreated, it can spread." I shiver as Juan Manuel's rich Spanish accent whispers over my skin.

"How does it go away?" I stare into Juan Manuel's deep brown eyes.

"Antibiotics," Dimples Noah says before the others can.

"Huh. Thanks." I have antibiotics in my medical kit. I left home with three doses in case I got into trouble and was unable to get to a doctor. Another win with this day. These guys just saved me an awkward doctor's visit, *and* my belly button should feel better in a few days.

"Do you want to join us for a drink?" I tip my head to Keith and Dejah.

"Hell, yeah." Beady-Eyed Austin rushes over to our table.

But I don't care about him.

I focus on the tall drink of water dressed in blue.

"You can call me Juanma." His warm paw engulfs mine as he smoothly flexes his massive bicep while he shakes my hand. "Nice to meet you, neña."

The sexy guy vibes rolling off him hit me in the center of my chest. Oh boy, he's potent, and I was spot on with my initial assessment. The energy from our palms connecting rings through me like smashing the bell in the strongman game at the fair.

I introduce the guys to Dejah and Keith, then the six of us

head to a techno club around the corner. Dimples Noah rubs his hands together at the blinding colorful lights twisting around the room. He rushes to the center of the busy dance floor directly under the disco ball, adjusts his T-shirt, and starts cross-stepping. He executes a perfect knee drop, spinning into a shoulder freeze.

I blink. He's … *breakdancing*. The dancing crowd makes room as he does a series of kicks and arm pops. It's high school all over again. We're just missing the large piece of cardboard, but to his credit, Noah backspins just fine without it. I revert to my teens as I stand in a semi-circle and clap as he does the worm.

"Let's dance." Beady-Eyed Austin grabs my hand in his clammy one and drags me away from Dimples Noah's show.

Austin's pushy and giving off a miserable, just shy of creepy vibe. I suffer through one song, then make pleading eyes to Khadejah to step in and dance with him so I can find Juanma. She rolls her eyes and cuts in, and I make a hasty exit.

Juanma's leaning against the bar. I lead him to the dance floor and swing my hips to the electric techno. His large hands gently engulf my waist, and I list into him.

"Where's Austin, corazón?" Juanma asks over the music.

"No idea." And I don't care.

"The thing is, Austin likes you," he says.

"But what if I don't like Austin?"

I huff as Juanma is yanked away by an Eewsah girl with a boxy short haircut wearing neon painter pants. I watch him point her in the direction of another guy and preen as he returns to me.

"You're beautiful, preciosa," he whispers in my ear as he pulls me closer.

I dance to the melody, but Juanma dances to the beat. He expertly dips, grinds, and spins while I soak in every bit of our physical connection. Ding, ding. My cup is filling. This attention is exactly what I need. After three songs of me unashamedly rubbing myself against his jacked-up chest, he pulls away.

"Carajo, I have to catch the last shuttle boat back to the ship. Meet me here tomorrow night?" He grazes two fingers down the side of my cheek.

"Yes." I could swoon right now like the ladies did in the olden days.

Juanma flashes me his cheeky grin before he's dragged out by Boxy Haircut Girl with Dimples Noah and grumbling Beady-Eyed Austin in tow.

I kick back on a stool at the bar as Keith spins Khadejah on the dance floor. I'm relaxed and warm all over from Juanma's attention. Turns out this beach town is just what the doctor ordered.

I TAKE a drink of warm water from my reusable bottle and sink my toes into the white sand of Smiltynės Beach on the tip of the Curonian Spit, a two-minute ferry ride from Klaipėda. The massive USNS *Comfort* with three medical red crosses along the side is floating in the Baltic Sea just ahead of us. Funny to think the guys we met last night, specifically Juanma, are on that boat right now.

Khadejah and Keith are passed out on their towels fast asleep. I whip off the T-shirt and shorts I've been wearing to hide the bluish-purple bruises that litter my body, splay on my towel in my bikini, and sigh as the sun heats my skin.

Finally, no rain, and no personal pity party.

I giggle as I rummage through my daypack for my camera. I get up and stealthily reach around to extract my creeping bikini wedgie out of my ass crack. Then I snap a shot of the snoring duo with the ship in the background.

A loud moan steels my spine. I reluctantly glance over my shoulder. An old dude with a beer gut is leering at my ass. His boner's straining his tiny bathing suit. He gives me one last look before he rushes to the beach changing hut.

Ew. Seriously? I sigh and pull my clothes back on. At least he didn't approach or jerk off in front of me. I hang my head. Wow, you know you've truly lowered the bar when 'not masturbating at you' is a benchmark for acceptable human behavior.

After we shower and change in our groovy room, I convince Dejah and Keith to go back to the same bar in hopes Juanma might be there. My shoulders sink when I don't see him. We order a pitcher of beer and a Diet Coke for me—since I started the antibiotics this morning—then slide into an empty table at the side of the bar. I sit with a view to the door and tap my toe to the techno as I wait.

My cheeks flush as Juan Manuel enters the bar with Beady-Eyed Austin trailing behind him like a miserable toddler.

"Good to see you, gata," Juanma says, flashing us a warm smile as he stands beside our table. "I thought we might miss you. Admirals were visiting our ship today and us regulars couldn't use the jetty to come ashore so it was available for them. Mierda, they were supposed to leave at two but only left at eight."

I nod and smile as I count his abs through his ridiculously tight white T-shirt. Dejah kicks me under the table. I reach down to rub my ankle and curl my lip at her.

She tilts her head, shakes it, and widens her eyes at me.

Oh. *Ohhh.* I need to talk, not just ogle him.

"Hi." I wave.

God, I have zero game.

"Grab a couple of glasses and pull up a seat, man." Keith saves the day as he points to the empty spots at our table.

"We saw your ship today when we were at the beach," I say as Juanma takes the seat beside me.

Dejah rolls her eyes.

My mind blanks. He's so hot that any interesting chat evaporates on my tongue.

"So, Juanma, tell us why you decided on the military," Dejah asks, salvaging my lame conversation skills.

"My dad was a pilot in Vietnam. That's what got me interested in the military," he says.

"My father was also in the military. Like you care," Austin interrupts. He chugs his beer, slams the glass on the table, and reaches for the pitcher for a refill.

My eyes crinkle. What's wrong with him? Did he leave his manners at sea?

"I was a Marine for six years. But I always wanted to be a doctor, so I enlisted in the medical core." Juanma smiles, his dreamy eyes focused on me.

My skin crackles.

"I've been in for twelve years." Austin scoffs. "And have been to *way* more interesting places than *Juanma*. You should ask me about those."

"What's it like living on a ship?" Keith directs his question to Juanma, ignoring Austin.

I bite my cheek, relieved it's not only me who's annoyed with him.

"The pendejo who sleeps next to me has terrible hygiene and an annoying alarm clock." Juanma chuckles.

"What about fat Jenkins whose farts are lethal and who struts around in his tighty whities?" Austin ends his sentence with a rumbling burp.

I cover my nose with the back of my hand when the foul waft hits me.

"Or Jonesie who never changes his socks. You can smell them all over the ship." Austin dangles white chewing gum out of his mouth like a cigarette, and it bounces up and down on his lips with each stupid word he utters. And he utters a lot of them.

Is Austin drunk? I mouth to Dejah across the table.

No idea, she mouths back.

My gut was spot on. Austin's a weirdo.

"We have to leave. There's a party down at the landing dock. We'll be there a while before we catch the ferry to the ship. Do you want to join us there, mi cielo?" Juanma asks as he stands and scowls at Austin.

Austin smirks and slides out of his seat.

"We might meet you down there." I nod, trying to look casual.

"I hope so, preciosa," Juanma says as he leans forward and presses his soft lips to my cheek.

"Come on, mamabicho." He grabs Austin's arm and drags him out of the bar. I don't know what a mamabicho is, but I hope it's a bad word because Austin's being an ass.

I rush Khadejah and Keith through their drinks and they *reluctantly* go with me to the dock. A soft beige puppy with a dark brown patch over his right eye trots alongside us through the dark streets of Klaipėda to our destination.

The puppy whimpers and takes off when we arrive.

Eyes wide, the three of us crouch behind waist-high bushes and take in the creepy scene at the boat landing. It's pitch black except for a raging bonfire that eerily flickers large embers into the wind as "Sabotage" by Beastie Boys booms from some random source.

"I can't see Juanma," I say as I part the craggy branches for a better view.

A group of ripped guys are dancing and stumbling around the fire with their shirts off. Four of them smash their beer bottles on the pavement in unison, then toss their arms up in the air in triumph.

What a mess.

"It's like *Top Gun* gone wrong," Dejah says.

"Duuuu—de," Keith says.

"Juanma's cute, but just no, totally not worth *this*." He filled my cup. I got attention and the desired physical contact I was craving. I'm good for a while now.

"No Spice Girl name for him." Keith snickers.

"Nope," I say as we walk back to our room. "Ugh, I'm sorry for dragging you guys there."

Klaipėda totally got me out of my funk, but we should've been smart like the puppy who left as soon as we arrived or better yet not come at all. I won't be insisting on that again—not that we'll meet more doctors from a medical ship ... but you never know.

GRYBAS - NIDA, LITHUANIA

"I'm going to miss you," I say to Keith as I give him a heartfelt hug on the sidewalk outside our groovy room.

Mark this day. Keith and I finished the dregs in the peanut butter jar this morning. And just in time as he's leaving us and heading to Germany to catch his flight home from Munich next week.

"Aw, mate, it's been a blast," Dejah says as she hugs him goodbye.

"It's been fun, girls. Go to Croatia. I promise you'll love it." Keith waves, and I frown as our shooting star strolls out of sight.

"Ready?" Dejah adjusts Hulk on her back.

"Yes." I smile softly, so glad to have her as a partner on this trip.

We trek to the ferry dock and catch the boat to Smiltynė for our trip down the Curonian Spit to Nida. The first few lines in Dejah's guidebook say it's one of the nicest towns in Lithuania, boasting quaint streets, sand dunes, and wide beaches. That was all it took for us to decide to see Nida for ourselves. Plus, you can't really say you've seen a country if you only visit the capital city. We figure it's best to see a few places to really get the feel of things.

My heart warms when the bus driver *smiles* at us. My first real smile from a Lithuanian, or any local in the Baltics. And as another first, he insists on putting Barney and Hulk in the luggage hold under the bus. It's a nice change not to be treated as a fourth-class citizen in Lithuania.

I duck my head as I board the short bus. Khadejah takes a

seat at the window, and I slide onto the wooden bench beside her.

"The Curonian Spit's ninety-eight kilometers long. The northern fifty-two belong to Lithuania, while the rest of the spit is a part of Kaliningrad Oblast, Russia. Nida is the town at the most southern point of the Lithuanian side," Khadejah reads from her guidebook. "This spit separates the Curonian Lagoon from the Baltic Sea coast. Its width varies from four hundred meters in Russia to almost four thousand meters in Lithuania. How cool is that?"

"Very cool. We'll be right beside Russia?"

"Looks that way. Just so you know, that's all the information I've got about Nida. I've no idea where to stay." She shrugs, and I chuckle.

"It's better than what I have in my book, which is zilch. I'm sure there'll be an information office or something." We'll figure something out.

A few hours later, we're lugging Barney and Hulk through the quiet streets of Nida, looking for a place to stay. The guidebook's right. It's beautiful. Tall, leafy trees rustle on the salty breeze. Red, blue, and brown cottages with tipped red roofs all have a small patch of lovingly maintained vivid green grass and wildflowers weaving between the waist-high fence posts. It's like a picture-perfect postcard. But there are absolutely no signs directing visitors.

We stumble across a small white cottage with an 'i' over the door.

"Hi, we're looking for a place to stay," I ask the lady behind the desk as we enter the tiny office.

She nods, picks up the bulky black receiver, and uses the blunt end of her yellow pencil to dial the rotary phone.

"Someone will be here soon," she says as she hangs up.

Minutes later, a woman with transparent white skin bursts into the tourist office wearing an apron and carrying a wooden spoon dripping with red sauce.

"You can both stay with me for sixty lats a night," Apron Woman says.

I glance at Khadejah, who lifts a shoulder.

"That would be wonderful. Thanks," I say.

She lives on the top floor of a four-story walk-up. Each step is work. Sadly, even without the peanut butter, Barney doesn't feel lighter. Those souvenir papers bulging in Barney's front zipper pocket better look amazing in my future photo albums.

Apron Woman opens the door to a bright and spacious room. It has two single beds on either side and *total luxury*, there's a small radio with a cassette player on the table between the beds. I have my Walkman, with five mixed tapes which I listen to often, but being able to play music out loud is a real treat.

Ken pays Apron Woman for two nights, and she hands us the keys.

We leave our room in search of food. The sun is shining, and the air's so fresh it makes my lungs feel clean, but street after street, there's nothing but small houses and closed cafés.

"I'm starting to think that we should just stick with homemade sandwiches." My stomach grumbles.

"There's a place. It looks promising." Dejah races to the door.

"You said that about the last five places." They were all closed, and my heart sank a little more with each locked door we tugged on.

"Looks like we're in luck." She yanks the door open.

"Sadly, no one else is here so we can't meal copy," I say as my eyes sweep the sparse room with dirty worn floorboards.

"We'll figure it out." Dejah grins as we park ourselves at a wobbly table by the window.

I scan the white paper placemat with two columns of food choices written in Lithuanian. "You know, I hoped my knowledge of French would help a bit with other languages, but French isn't related to Lithuanian, Latvian, or Russian, which sucks."

"They have spaghetti. What do you reckon grybas spaghetti is?" she asks.

"No idea, but it's in almost everything on the menu. I hope grybas is some type of vegetable and not some unidentifiable meat product." I drop the placemat on the table. "I'm going to chance it."

"Same." Dejah relays our order to the server.

The server probably thinks I'm nuts because I squeeze my eyes shut as she places the bowl in front of me. I open my eyes once I hear her move away, and a genuine smile stretches across my lips. Steam is swirling off brilliant red sauce, intertwined between long noodles and funnel-shaped chanterelle mushrooms.

"Yes!" I shoot my fist in the air. "Grybas are mushrooms."

I twirl the noodles around the fork tines and moan as the taste of rich garlic and peppery mushroom explodes in my mouth.

I demolish the massive bowl, as does Dejah.

After lunch, we visit the lagoon side of town, then get lost wandering the relaxing streets. Scarred by our long search for a place to eat, we opt to buy groceries for dinner and get our usual bread, cheese, pickles, and red peppers for sandwiches.

Dejah pops a George Michael tape in the ghetto blaster. We set up a picnic on the table between our beds as his soulful voice fills our small space. We eat, tell jokes, talk about nothing, and sing along with George.

Being here is nice … but it's also *slow*.

I kick back on my hard single bed and pull out my journal. I pause my pen over the half-filled page struggling for the right words. I want adventure, but this isn't busy or wild enough to be classified as one. I bite the tip of my pen. Does an adventure have to be edgy and wild? Or can you have a quiet and slow one?

And more importantly, what do I need? Wild with friends is all-consuming and makes me forget. But quiet gives me space to think and reflect—churning up my carefully guarded sorrow. My stomach sinks as it dawns on me why I prefer to cram my days with action. Because it hurts too much otherwise.

I THROW my cards on the table after our fourth game of War, then finish my last few mouthfuls of coffee. We played it safe and returned to yesterday's café for lunch as we know it's good and open.

"It's sad," I say. "I played so many card games growing up, but the only ones I can remember are Crazy Eights, War, and Go-Fish. I feel like I'm in third grade."

"Sorry, mate, I've got nothing to contribute because we never played cards growing up. But I'm keen to play anything you remember. Should we mix it up today, with grybas omelets?"

I run my fingers through my hair and tug the ends.

"Oh my God, we have to leave this region. It's nice, but the lack of excitement and the same food is driving me mad." And all this downtime is forcing me to *think*. I need to keep busy because I'm not ready to do a deep dive on myself just yet.

"Maybe they have a sandwich like the one from Vilnius here?" She bites her bottom lip as she scans the menu.

"Ugh, I'll eat stale bread any day than one nasty brown bite of that again." I recoil.

"How about an *exciting* grybas omelet then?" Her eyes shine, and her lips quirk.

"All right." I sigh as I shuffle the cards. "Go-Fish this time."

After lunch, we visit the tourist office to determine how we get to Poland. The only way is via Vilnius because we need a visa, which we can't get without an invitation from a host in Russia and a trip to the embassy for the faster route through Russia.

Bummer. Looks like we're going to have to backtrack.

We stop at the shop and due to a lack of options, we buy the same food for dinner as we ate last night.

"Do you call this *exciting*?" Dejah holds out a small jar. The white label has mystery words and a smiling cartoon squirrel holding a nut.

"Yes, it is." I grin as she adds the chocolate nut spread to the metal grocery basket.

"Is it sad that I can't wait to crack into that fake Nutella?" I smack my lips as we stroll back to our room.

"Nah. I'm looking forward to it too. Why's he standing in his garden in a trench coat?" She slows her steps as we approach a man in the center of a well-manicured lawn.

It's odd since it's warm out.

"Oh no, not again." I slap my hand to my forehead.

Lawn Man's eyes light up at our attention. He flings his coat open with a gummy grin. His sunken naked chest is as blindingly white as the rest of him.

"You wanted excitement." Dejah flings her hand at Naked Lawn Man.

"Not what I meant." I rub my temples.

His narrow wrinkly hips thrust back and forth, lassoing his floppy wiener. We should walk away, but I can't take my eyes off his shriveled penis knocking his saggy balls in different directions.

"I'm so glad we're leaving the Baltics tomorrow." I sigh as he gyrates. "At least he's not yanking it like the old dude in Pärnu." The 'not masturbating at me' benchmark for acceptable human behavior is still a thing. "He's gotta be getting tired."

"Mate, I can't." Dejah snorts.

"His balls are almost to his knees. I wonder if they ever get tangled?" I giggle.

"Stop." She doubles over with laughter.

Even during the down times, we make our own fun.

And I'm glad because at the rate we're going with old-man penis sightings, there's probably more to come.

I JUMP out of bed and race down the hallway to the communal shower, excited to visit the dunes and wide beaches before we leave Nida.

I strip off my sleep clothes, happy to see my concealed bruises from *the encounter* are now deep green with yellow edges. And the angry red circle around my belly button is almost gone. Thank you, Juanma, Dimples Noah, and Beady-Eyed Austin for the diagnosis. There's just a bit of yellowish crust around the gold ring that should clear up with a few more days on antibiotics.

I crank the shower tap, and a trickle of water drips from the shower head. But it's warm, so I embrace it and hope my hair doesn't look too greasy from the soap I won't be able to rinse out.

We store Barney and Hulk at the tourist office, and just before ten, we visit our usual café for toast or a muffin. Our familiar server shakes her head. They have no bread. It's bused in from Klaipėda, and today's delivery has yet to arrive.

"It's pretty here, but I couldn't live in a town so small, remote, and dependent," I say as we exit the café empty-handed.

"Let's see this beach then." Dejah shrugs.

We head west. The paved road ends, and we pick up the worn trail cutting a path up a tall honey-colored sand dune. I'm thankful to be wearing pants because the knee-high sharp grass lining the trail bites when it brushes against bare skin.

I suck in air as I climb, and it tastes like sea salt. I rest my hands on my hips at the peak of the dune and enjoy the sweeping views of rolling sand and majestic green trees, sandwiched between the salty Baltic Sea and the freshwater Curonian Lagoon. The spit's so narrow, it's like I could reach out to touch the sea and lagoon at the same time. No wonder this town's tiny; there's no land for anything else, but I figure a bakery is something they should consider.

"We could probably tiptoe into Russia. It's like a kilometer south of us, with no border," I say.

"Sure, then what? We would never get out." She tuts.

"It was bad enough leaving Russia when we had the right paperwork." I wince at the memory. "Sneaking into Russia is more excitement than I would like."

"We'll just stick to old man willies." Dejah chuckles.

"I'd like to opt out of both. We saw enough of Russia and I've had enough random penis sightings to last me a lifetime," I say as we ramble down the dune then follow a path through a dense forest of spruce and birch trees.

"I hear the crashing waves," Khadejah shouts as she leads us toward the beach.

We burst through the trees, and I gape at the wide, empty beach. The pristine shoreline goes on for as far as I can see in each direction. Violent waves start far, far out in the eerie dark Baltic Sea, and crash onto the fine sand. I race toward the water. The rain from yesterday has washed up loads of shells and green sea glass. It's like I have a private appointment to be the first one here to pick through the sea's latest gifts. I pocket quite a few to add to my pile of things I need to mail home at some point.

I reach for a stone resting in the sand beside my boot. I rub my fingertips over the smooth contours before I launch it into the sea. It disappears in the angry waves. I wonder how long it will be before it ends up back on shore. Or will it go somewhere different or maybe get buried beneath the sand for years—

I gasp as cold water from the latest wave soaks my hiking boots.

But I stay glued in place, watching the wild sea batter the quiet beach. You know, I think an adventure can be wild, edgy, busy, quiet, slow, or reflective. And I'm going to need a mix of all types to find the peace I'm searching for.

THE MONEY GAME – BUS STATIONS ALL OVER LITHUANIA

There's no room for our big packs under the bus leaving Nida, so we put them on the seats next to us. The short bus fills with passengers from the handful of sleepy towns we stop at on the slow journey up the spit to Smiltynė. I end up squished between Barney and a man in jean overalls clutching a metal bucket of muddy grybas on his lap.

I sigh as I lean my head against Barney. This is going to be a long day. Morning in Nida, lunch in Klaipėda, dinner in Vilnius. Overnight on the bus through Lithuania and Poland, then breakfast tomorrow in Gdańsk.

We catch the short ferry from Smiltynė to Klaipėda and head for the good grocery store we discovered when we stayed here. My lips part as six tall guys with sharp features and short haircuts march past. At the next corner, four guys with broad shoulders and blond hair laugh over a shared joke as they exit a café.

"Is it just me, or are there loads more hot guys around than a few days ago?" I ask Khadejah as another hot-guy group passes.

"Nope, there're heaps. Check that out." She points to the banner strung between two buildings over the narrow street above us.

Baltic Challenge '98
Peace Military Exercise
5000 air, naval, and ground forces from eleven countries

"You know, before I flashed Juanma and the guys my belly button, they said something about a peace mission. That must be what they're here for," I say as we enter the store to buy food for lunch.

I keep my eyes peeled for Juanma as we trek to the bus station carrying our packs and groceries, but he's not around.

I'm not disappointed because it's not like it would come to anything, but it would have been nice to see his abs through his tight T-shirt one more time.

I glide my fingertips across the clean plush seat of our afternoon double-decker bus to Vilnius. We score two seats to ourselves opposite each other and spread out. This ride is an unexpected luxury after the squishy trip up the spit, but I already miss the sea as this view out the window is a repetitive bore of yellow haystacks on flat prairie fields.

The bus speakers crackle as the small screen at the front of the bus fills with brilliant white.

"A movie?" I lean forward as the familiar tinkling movie introduction tune fills the air. The screen pans out to a woman holding a torch in a white gown on the top of a grand staircase.

A monotone male Lithuanian voice blares through the speakers. My brow wrinkles as Monotone Voice dubs over the previews and Lithuanian-izes the stars' names in the upcoming movies to Brados Pittos and Nikos Nolta.

Dejah's boisterous laughter rings through the bus.

"Are Brad Pitt and Nick Nolte hard to pronounce?" I ask.

"I reckon," Dejah says. "If yah listen super closely, you can make out the English in the background."

I lean back, munching on a hunk of crusty bread from the shop, as *My Best Friend's Wedding* starts. I listen past Monotone Voice for the English as he dubs *every* character in the same flat and empty way, which is disturbing when the film characters laugh and holler.

The frowning money, the lifeless dubbing, and the lack of interesting food—no wonder no one smiles here. This place lacks joy.

After the movie, we crack open our guidebooks to plan our stops after Gdańsk.

I'm super pumped to visit Poland; it's steeped in tragic WWII history, and I'm keen to see everything with my own eyes. I thumb the pages to Kraków. It has a great square and a castle. I love a good town square. That's enough for me to want to visit.

"I want to go to Kraków," I say to Dejah across the aisle.

"Oh, yeah," she says. "I like the look of Zamość."

I flip to the pages about the small town. Hitler fancied it a good spot for the home of the Third Reich.

"Must be something to see if Hitler wanted to keep it intact." Dejah shrugs.

"Add it to the list." I nod.

I read about Zakopane, in the Tatra Mountains. The Polish people like to holiday there, and it must be good if it's a local vacation favorite. "What about Zakopane?" I ask.

Pages flip, then she reads.

"Yes. Want to skip Warsaw?" Dejah asks as she glances up from her book.

"Oh yeah, my guidebook says it's an armpit." I crinkle my nose.

"Our most logical route after Gdańsk is Zamość, Kraków, then Zakopane before we go to Prague." She trails her fingers along the map in her *Let's Go!*

"Works for me." I smile as I snap my book closed.

As simple as that, we have a plan from the tidbits of information in our travel guides.

Dejah mumbles under her breath as she scribbles on a piece of paper.

We needed to go through the Baltics to overland out of Russia, but it's been a difficult place to travel, and in hindsight, we should have spent less time here. I'll be sure to pull the pin earlier if we don't jive with a place. I'm hoping the hard yards are behind us now as we'll be traveling to more populated places that are used to tourists.

"It's July twentieth. Spending a few days in each place will put us in Kraków about July twenty-sixth. Then in Prague anywhere from August fourth to seventh depending on how long we spend in Zakopane," she says.

I grin as I count the days out on my paper pocket calendar. I'm excited for Poland, but I can't freaking wait to get to Prague. I've heard nothing but good stuff about it, the buildings, the history, the nightlife—bring on the wild adventures.

"That leaves about five weeks until we need to meet the girls in Istanbul," I say.

Dejah and I are meeting my old London flatmates Gwen and Stella mid-September in Istanbul. From there, the four of us plan to travel through Turkey, Syria, Lebanon, Jordan, Israel, and Egypt for two months. Excitement flares in my chest. The Middle East will be vastly different from anything I've ever experienced. I desperately want a Turkish massage, and visiting the pyramids is at the top of my must-see list. But we have loads to see before then.

"After we spend time in Prague, Vienna, and Budapest, even with a few other places, we'll have heaps of time to visit Croatia." She quirks an eyebrow.

"Yes, we sure will." A burst of energy zings through my body tingling my fingertips. I love that we have a plan. But what I love even more is that we can change our minds anytime we want—like adding in Croatia. I just hope it lives up to Keith's hype.

MY STOMACH DROPS, and I tremble as the ghost of *his* fingers scald my skin when the bus pulls into *the* central bus station in Vilnius after dark—where *the encounter* occurred.

I ball my hands and focus on my nails biting into my palms.

"You can do this," I whisper.

My blood roars in my ears as my eyes dart around the open space while I stumble behind Dejah toward the ticket kiosk.

He's not here.

Relief surges through me as I blink away my unshed tears while Dejah buys tickets for the overnight bus to Gdańsk from a dour-faced woman.

I straighten my spine and repeat to myself, *I'm safe. I'm safe. I'm safe.*

Tickets in hand, we stand to the side of the booth and combine the last of our grumpy-faced Litas to see how much money remains for food as we ate all our groceries on the bus coming here. A woman dressed in a baggy brown dress passes me a two-for-one Big Mac coupon as Dejah counts our meager cash.

"Does this help?" I pass Dejah the small paper with yellow arches on the front.

"We have just enough to buy one meal deal with an extra Big Mac. Looks like we have supper plans." She flaps the bills and coupon.

"Keith wouldn't be impressed," I say as I follow her out of the station to McDonald's across the street.

Big Macs aren't my favorite, but I'll manage. After the coin fiasco leaving Latvia, we've been more cash-conscious. Now we calculate how many days we plan to be in the country before we withdraw money. This way we stay on budget and avoid exchanging the same cash over and over, losing value each time. We didn't get it right in Russia, Estonia, or Latvia, but in Lithuania, we're leaving with zero local currency.

I send out good vibes to the universe as I chow down on my Big Mac. May there be nicer weather, friendlier people, and better food and places to stay in Poland.

ARMPIT BOOK - LITHUANIAN AND POLISH BORDER

The bus grinds into gear after the Lithuanian police exit. The two policemen were quick; they spent five minutes stamping all fifty passengers out of the country.

"That was easier than leaving Russia," I say as we bounce through no man's land to Poland.

"Everything is easier than getting out of Russia," Dejah says.

The Polish border policeman's serious blue eyes scan the bus as he boards with a little book tucked up tight in his right armpit. His posture is perfect, but I don't know if it's him or the starchy black uniform that looks like it could stand on its own. His brow is drawn and his lips are turned down in a deep scowl as he scrutinizes the Polish and Lithuanian passports of the people in the front rows.

He tips his chin as he reaches our seat in the middle of the bus.

Khadejah goes first. Mr. Serious holds her sketchy Irish passport up to the light, then pulls out his Armpit Book and quickly flicks through it. He stops at a page and studies it. He looks at her, the passport, her, the passport, and back to his secret book. Nods. Unclips the metal stamper from his waist belt and smashes it on a page. She's in.

I open my passport to the Polish visa I paid thirty pounds for before I left London and smile as I hold it out to Mr. Serious. His frown deepens, and I didn't think he could get more frowny. He barks at me in Polish. It sounds guttural like he's shouting and shooshing at the same time.

My mouth parts as his jaw grinds, waiting for a response.

I have no idea what he could want, then my lips part as it hits me. The Polish embassy gave me a separate piece of paper with the visa when I got it back. They never *said* I needed it later, but then again, no one spoke English at the embassy. I threw it away in London because why would I carry a piece of paper in my passport for months?

A flush of red peeks out the top of his stiff collar as he continues to scream at me in Polish, getting incrementally louder with each word. I sigh. Like I'll somehow understand him if he talks louder.

Dejah faces the window to hide her laughter.

I widen my eyes and shake my head trying to look like I don't know what he's saying. Which technically I don't—since I don't speak Polish—but I'm pretty sure he's looking for the mystery paper I tossed a month ago.

He stops yelling. His nostrils flare as he studies me. He looks at my passport, flips through Armpit Book, compares my passport to Armpit Book, looks at me, looks at the book, looks at me. Then stamps me into Poland.

I slouch in my seat as Mr. Serious moves to the people behind us.

"I'm glad I got that visa in London. I doubt the bus would have waited while they processed it," I say. "It's always a drama with my passport. I don't get it when yours looks like you crafted it yourself."

"There's nothing wrong with my passport." She chuckles, and I roll my eyes. "Maybe it's *you,* mate. Suspicious Spice strikes again." She bumps my shoulder.

"My Spice name is beginning to feel like a self-fulfilling prophecy."

ARMAGEDDON - GDAŃSK, POLAND

Layers and layers of immovable filth grip the gray walls and linoleum floors in our dorm room in Gdańsk. Hundreds of flies buzz as they circle the blinding yellow ceiling light. I throw Barney next to a rickety metal bunk bed and curl my nose at the stained mattress that reeks of smelly feet.

So much for things getting better in Poland.

This is our worst lodging to date.

My eyes gape at the young woman, around my age, chatting in Polish to her pre-teen son while she neatly places their clothes in the grim dorm room cupboards.

I give Dejah the wide eyes, and she gives them right back.

I couldn't imagine bringing a child to stay in a room like this. My tongue sticks to the roof of my mouth as I unzip Barney. God, I sound like a huge snob. What do I know about their situation? Nothing. So I should pack away my judgy-ness. As each day passes, I appreciate how incredibly lucky I am to have grown up with the advantages I did.

I remove my wash bag and cringe at the odor of stale sweat clinging to my skin. I traipse past the mother and child to the bathroom to wash away my stink. Water gushes from the shower head, and I throw myself under the warm spray, ecstatic to be able to fully rinse my hair after washing it for the first time in weeks.

We leave the hostel just before the mandatory day lock-out begins. We've not faced one yet, but it's not unheard of. And this place is gross so I'm not terribly sad about being barred from hanging out here from ten to five.

The sun is throwing out its warmth as we step outside to start our day. It's a welcome reprieve after the Baltics because aside from the hot day in Pärnu, even our beach days had an edge of chill.

"This feels like summer." I smile as the heat seeps off the cobblestone streets into the souls of my plastic Teva sandals.

"Sure does." Dejah pulls on a ballcap and directs us to the center of town as she's back up as tour guide. "There are three parts to the city. Main City, Old Town, and New Town. It was hit hard during World War II, and Main City was rebuilt as close as they could to its original Renaissance and Baroque design."

A wide smile spreads across my face as I cast my eyes up the tall, narrow row of buildings with symmetrical windows and different pitched roofs.

"It's like Amsterdam," I say.

The wide streets are a colorful trip to the past and just what I was hoping to see when I left home.

"Yeah, the book says it has Dutch and Flemish influences. But I reckon we should save sightseeing for tomorrow." She closes her book. "We should chill and ring home today."

"Oh, yeah." I'm all about a down day now, and I haven't spoken to my dad since I left London last month. I miss talking to him, and I'm sure he's wondering where I am.

At the Main City information office, we get a map. At my sixth bank machine, I manage to withdraw cash, taking a mental note of the bank name where my card worked so I can get more when I need it. And then I buy a phone card from a shop on the first floor of one of the rows of tenements along Długi Targ, the main pedestrian street.

On the embankment of the muddy green Motława River, we find two yellow phone booths with a view of The Crane—a dark wooden attachment between two brick towers—boasting to be the biggest Middle Ages port crane.

My tummy flutters as I pick up the phone receiver and slide the phone card into the slot to get a dial tone. I flick through my address book and search for the laminated call reference card I taped on the back. Each country has a different code to call Canada collect. Calling is expensive, so any calls I make to family I charge to my dad. He's cool with it as long as I don't call too often.

I press the unique number sequence for Poland and frown at the harsh repetitive beep droning in my ear. I try Dad three more times with the same result. I dial my brothers in Vancouver. Pete, the youngest, is living with our older brother Kev this summer. My heart twinges when the same shrill tone crushes my hopes of connecting with family.

I slouch onto the pavement beside Dejah's phone booth, sulk, and smoke four cigarettes while she gabs to her parents in Australia.

"Mum's winter garden is in full bloom," she recounts her conversation as we walk toward the place Dejah has picked for lunch.

I stop in my tracks.

"Look." My fingers tingle as I point to the Internet sign in the shop window.

I haven't emailed since Riga ten days ago. And after my failed phone calls, I'm desperate for some news from home. I peek through the glass and see orange price tags on shelves stacked with monitors and tall computer towers.

"Oh man, it looks like a computer shop. I'm going in anyway." I tug the glass door open.

The rat-a-tat-tat of guns from a computer combat game rings in my ears. The lone guy behind the counter by the cash is jabbing the keys on his keyboard, eyes focused on the screen. I bite my lip. Dude has pit sweat soaking his thin T-shirt stretched over his round gut. I can smell his body odor from the doorway, but he has *Internet,* so I'm not deterred.

"Hi." I bat my eyelashes and take four strides so I'm standing in front of him. "We saw your Internet sign in the window."

"It's for staff only," Pit Sweat mutters in English.

"Do you think we could use it?" I lean over the glass counter. "Just for a few minutes?"

Pit Sweat frowns and pauses his game.

I flash him my best smile and minimal cleavage as Dejah twirls her long dark ponytail, gazing up at him adoringly.

He presses a few buttons.

"You can use it quickly." Pit Sweat moves out from behind the counter.

I pounce on the keyboard and boot up my Hotmail while Khadejah asks questions about the shop inventory to keep Pit Sweat occupied.

After *forever,* my email loads, and the screen fills with unread messages. My eyes widen. I have so many. Ten for sure, maybe even fifteen! I scan the senders, and my breath catches when I see Josh's name. *Twice.* With a shaky click of the mouse, I open the oldest one first. The screen blanks as it takes precious minutes to load.

I miss you and want to meet up with you,

Josh xo

I wipe my damp palms on my shorts and wait just as long for the second one to open.

Let me know when you're in Czech and I'll be there,

    Josh xo

I blink. Holy shit. He really wants to meet. Never in a million years would I have thought Dejah's and my *dreams are free* ramblings of hypothetical reunions could come true. My heart hammers at the prospect of seeing him. Because despite how badly it hurt when he dumped me, I miss his friendship *and* the physical ... *wait* ... does he want to meet for a hook-up or to travel together?

I huff. Great sex or not, I would never leave Dejah for him.

Pit Sweat taps his finger on the glass countertop, impatience radiating off him.

Damn the freaking slow connection. I wasted five minutes opening Josh's two short notes, and I'm out of time. Dejah needs to check her mail, and we're pushing the limits of Pit Sweat's goodwill. I stare longingly at my *many* unopened messages, then shut down without replying to anyone or reading other notes.

"Is there an Internet café in town?" I ask as I swap places with Dejah.

"No." Pit Sweat crosses his arms.

My shoulders slump as disappointment seeps into my bones. I don't know how I'm going to respond to Josh about a Czech rendezvous, but I yearn to spend hours online immersing myself in notes from home. They're like food for the soul, and even though I don't want to be at home, I love hearing about it.

"This town is lovely. Have you lived here all your life?" I ask, flashing him a big smile.

"Yes." Pit Sweat grunts as he stares at my chest.

For once, the boob staring is working in our favor. I pepper him with questions, giving Dejah time to tap out a quick message.

After lunch, we trudge through the hot streets in the late-day sun and wilt a little more with each sticky step.

"We've been traveling in cold weather for so long. I'm not used to this type of heat." I take a long drink of warm water from my water bottle, then bunch my hair into a ponytail to air my neck.

"Check it out." Dejah stops in front of a long glass window with an orange movie poster of Bruce Willis, flanked by Ben Affleck and Liv Tyler … and the Space Shuttle.

"*Armageddon*." I read the title arching above the actor trio. "Never heard of it. What do you think it's about?"

"Who cares?" Dejah shrugs. "It's in English with Polish subtitles, and I bet it's air-conditioned in there."

"True. Plus, no monotone Lithuanian voice-over and it has Bruce Willis and Ben Affleck. I'm in," I say as she pulls out Ken to pay for our movie tickets.

I fall into my seat and the cool air in the theater pebbles my skin. The film is outrageous and cheesy, but I love every ridiculous minute. It's a stellar break from the heat and a few hours of escape, just like a movie should be.

We race back to the hostel and slip inside before the ten o'clock curfew. Yes, they have a daily lockout *and* a curfew. They can't be bothered with you during the day *and* don't want to wait up either.

Mom and her son are snoring, and the only other person in the room is a skinny blond guy with rosy skin lazing on the bunk next to mine. Dejah rushes to the shower, but I'm too tired to care about the dried sweat on my skin.

"I noticed the Canada flag on your backpack." The skinny guy swirls his finger at Barney, leaning against my bed.

"Yeah, hey." I introduce myself and fall onto my fusty mattress. I try not to move too much to avoid creating more pongy stink or disturbing the lingering flies on every surface since their overhead-light-entertainment is off.

"Patrick, from Toronto. College and Young area," he sing-songs. "I just went to Hel. It's a short boat trip, and I *totally* recommend it for a great beach day." He claps his thin hands in front of his face.

"Thanks for the recommendation. We'll check it out." I close my eyes as tiredness sweeps over me from my lack of sleep on last night's overnight bus and traipsing around in today's heat. "Hey, do you know Right Said Fred's other song after 'I'm Too Sexy'?"

"No." He tuts. "But I just love Poland. It reminds me of home. Did I tell you I'm from Toronto …"

I only half-listen to Patrick Thin Hands. My other half is thinking about Josh. I *would* love to see him again, but doubt swirls at the base of my spine, making me question if meeting him would be the best thing for *me*.

THE NEXT MORNING, the hostel receptionist informs us that she has a double room available, so we nab it. Our new room is only marginally cleaner, but the mattress is less whiffy, and it's nice to have our own space with fewer flies.

I hand wash some underwear and a few T-shirts while I'm in the shower, then string them on my travel clothesline at the bottom of our metal bed frame. I wrinkle my nose at my *kind of* clean clothes as they drip on the dirty floor. We need to find a real washer soon as we haven't done it since Tallinn. But it won't be today because it's sightseeing day.

Dejah marches us through Old Town, stopping at St. Catherine's and St. Bridget's churches then on to an old mill.

"This is the Monument to the Shipyard Workers," she says as I glance up at the forty-two-meter-high cluster of three crosses.

"It commemorates those who died during the protests in December 1970. It's a symbol of opposition to totalitarian—"

"Hi, I heard you speaking English," a guy working a dad bod says as he appears beside us. "I'm Simon from Canada. Where are you girls from?" The wrinkles around his eyes deepen as he smiles hopefully.

He's probably about ten years older than us, and I get a good vibe from him.

I share our details as he cleans his glasses on the bottom of his rumpled T-shirt.

"Nice. I'm traveling alone." Simon scratches his glistening pale cheek.

I feel for the guy. We haven't met many people in the last month, and if I were on my own, I would be desperate for some company and conversation too.

"Want to join us for a coffee?" I ask.

"I would love to." A bright grin transforms his plain face. "I passed a café with a nice patio on my way here."

"Lead the way," Dejah says as she places her guidebook in her daypack.

Our small wrought iron table wobbles on the uneven cobblestones as we sip on milky lattes, served in small white mugs in the late morning sun.

"I'm here on my own because my wife, Wendy, is at home studying for her final law exams. I'm taking this European holiday to give her some space to study. I'm a divorce lawyer and know you need full concentration on the books for the final push." His lips tip downwards, and his eyes lose their sparkle. "It's also nice to get away from the broken people I represent."

"How do you mean?" Khadejah asks, sitting back in her seat.

"As a divorce lawyer, women come to me broken and defeated. Not always from violent relationships; some are from verbally abusive ones. It takes the last of their energy to get through the divorce proceedings," he says.

"I know that feeling." I take a slow sip of my warm, creamy

coffee, knowing all too well what it's like to be broken because of a man. My long-term relationship in Toronto before meeting Josh was devastating.

"*Mate*?" Dejah asks, and they both turn to me.

"Not a *divorce*." I bite my lip. "But I was with someone abusive for two years. It was all verbal, not physical. Piece by piece, he chipped away at me. Even after all this time, it still boggles my mind that someone I thought cared about me could make me feel smaller and more insignificant each day." I swallow past the knot in my throat. "It wasn't easy, but I managed to get away from him."

Another reason I latched on to Josh; he lit up my life, rather than snuffing it out.

Simon sighs and gifts me a soft smile.

"Candace, I've seen many a guy like him in my time. I'm so glad you got out before he demolished your spirit."

"I wish I'd had someone like you to talk to back then because I blamed myself for a long time after that breakup," I say as I circle the rim of my mug with the edge of my thumb.

Maybe it was because I was already in a fragile state over my mom's death that he was able to walk all over me. I sigh. Either way, that relationship was another dent in my spirit, dragging me deeper into myself. I wipe my nose with my napkin as Simon asks Dejah about Australia, and they thoughtfully give me a moment to recover.

Piece by piece, I've been broken down.

I squeeze my eyes closed and square my shoulders.

And piece by piece is how I will put myself back together.

WE SAY goodbye to Simon because he's already visited the part of town we're exploring next. There are a lot of churches listed in the guidebook, and we visit them all. I light a candle in each one for my mom. I talk to her in my head and see her as a butterfly on occasion but lighting them along the way is my beacon for her to follow us on our trip.

We finish our tour at St. Mary's Church, the largest brick church in Poland. It boasts amazing views from the top of its four hundred and five step tower.

We start the climb.

Twelve steps up the narrow, steep, circular stairwell, my heart starts to pound.

Thirty steps.

My hands start to shake.

Fifty-seven steps.

My damp palm slides up the guide rope, and my throat wobbles.

Ninety steps.

The stale air is stifling. Spots line my vision. Behind me, there's an endless press of people and in front of me are hundreds of legs. I flatten my hand over my mouth so I don't throw up.

"You go on. I'll see you at the bottom," I mumble to Dejah.

Like a salmon ready to mate, I shoulder my way through the one-way oncoming traffic. Shouts in foreign languages jar my ears as I pinball everyone I pass. I ignore the voices and focus on counting each stair as I descend.

When I finally get out, I throw myself on a bench under a shady tree and suck back deep gulps of air. I slide my hands down my shirt to dry them, but they only get wetter from the sweat that's accumulated on my clothes. Ugh, no wonder my stuff is so gross. I make a mental note to add this outfit to my must-do laundry list.

I'm *almost* back to normal as Dejah casts a shadow over my slouched form on the bench half an hour later.

"I'm not good at tight spaces or heights," I say.

"No kidding." She snickers.

"No more climbing towers for me."

"Probably best." She hums. "How about we put off going to Westerplatte till this afternoon and go for lunch. Pizza?"

"You know the way to my heart." I leap off the bench.

BACK IN GDAŃSK after a depressing hour-long boat ride through container ships to visit Westerplatte, I enter one of the handful of pay phones around town to try my luck calling home.

My breath catches when the phone clicks and starts to ring.

"Hello." My dad's voice makes my knees buckle.

"Dad." I lean against the side of the phone booth. "It's good to hear your voice."

I share only the good stories about Russia, Estonia, Lithuania, and Latvia, leaving out masturbation stories and *the encounter* details so he doesn't worry.

"I'm glad you girls are having fun." He tells me about my brothers in Vancouver making bagels at my older brother's bagel shop. "I had the willow tree in the backyard cut down because it was growing into the power lines."

My stomach dips. My mom loved that tree. She planted it twenty-five years ago when it was no taller than me and the width of my index finger. It's a heartbreaking reality that time moves on, with or without you in the world.

I jolt at the sound of fists banging on glass. I turn, and my head jerks at the crowd of ten people glaring at me.

"Oh man, I have to go, there are loads of people waiting to use the phone."

I smile as I pull the door open after our goodbyes. A woman with wild eyes screams at me in Polish as she shoves past, reaching for the phone. I shrug. She can be as pissy as she likes because nothing is going to squash my excitement from my conversation.

A sliver of the moon hangs in the twilight sky as I wander alongside Dejah toward our hostel.

"Girls," Simon shouts and waves from a table outside a bar in Długi Targ Square.

I chuckle as he wraps us each in a warm hug. We just met this morning, but it's like crossing paths with an old friend.

"Join me for a drink?" he asks, pointing to the empty seats beside him.

"We have two hours until our curfew," Dejah says as she takes a seat and orders a beer.

I tap my toe to the dance music spilling out from inside the bar as Simon chats our ears off. After two Diet Cokes—as I'm still on antibiotics—I know everything about Simon's wife Wendy because every conversation circles back to her.

It's not annoying—it's super sweet.

My lips curl into a frown.

I crave what Simon and Wendy have. The memory of Josh's gleaming smile and twinkly blue eyes slides through my mind. Josh, who I've been trying to avoid spending every moment thinking about since I read his email. Josh, who I'm positive isn't singing my praises to anyone he's with at this moment.

God, how am I going to respond to his note?

"You know, I reckon Simon deserves a Spice Girl name." Dejah outlines our game. "And I already know what it should be … Wendy Spice." She smacks her hand on the table.

He chuckles as he holds up his beer to cheers.

"Hey, how about we meet up again in Kraków?" I say as we clink glasses.

He's leaving town tomorrow via a different route south through Poland, and it would be great to see him again since we all get along so well.

"Good idea." Dejah nods.

"I would love that." He beams.

"We can't rely on the Internet," Dejah says as she cracks open her guidebook. "Let's pick a place to meet."

Simon gets out his book, and we pick a restaurant in the Jewish Quarter of Kraków.

"Let's meet at six on the twenty-seventh and twenty-eighth of July. In case either one of us can't make the first night," Dejah says.

"I'll be there," he promises and notes the dates next to the restaurant in his book.

I smile as the stars twinkle overhead in the night sky. There's something about backpacking, the openness of it that swiftly forms fast friendships. It takes mere hours, sometimes even minutes, to develop the kind of camaraderie and ease I feel with my family, making it easy to disclose personal information that you might never share in everyday life.

And it's this kind of real honesty that's healing my heart a little bit more each day.

ECHELON OF BAD - HEL, POLAND

Based on Patrick Thin Hands from Toronto's glowing recommendation and because of the scorching weather, we're having a beach day. My bruises from *the encounter* have faded to a light brown and are not as noticeable, so swimsuits are a go. We book in for another night at the hostel, stop at the market, buy a heaving bag of food, then hop on the morning ferry to Hel.

The large white boat has twenty rows of wooden benches on deck. We settle in a spot near the railing. Dejah lays out the snacks, and I shuffle the cards. The warm salty breeze off the Baltic Sea rustles my hair as the boat's horn blasts when we depart Gdańsk.

This is going to be a great day.

"IS IT JUST ME, or is this boat going slow?" I ask hours later as I collect the cards off the bench between us.

"I could swim there faster," Dejah says as she lights a cigarette.

I take a swig from my water bottle and groan.

"I'm so sick of warm water." In this heat, the water in my Nalgene bottle ends up tasting like stewed plastic. "I would give a lot for a cold drink or ice cubes."

"Ditto." Dejah holds up her similar reusable bottle.

"We should be there soon, right?" I ask as I scan the wild green coastline with no town in sight.

"I'm going to ask around." Dejah heads off while I watch the bags.

She stomps back muttering under her breath.

"The boat doesn't arrive in Hel for another two hours." Her arms fly as she slumps on the bench. "I can't believe I didn't ask how long the trip was when we bought the tickets."

"*What?*" I blink. "It's a four-hour boat trip—e*ach way*?"

"Yeah." She huffs.

"But Patrick Thin Hands said it's a short day trip." I furrow my brow.

"He lied." She crosses her arms.

"Why would he do that?" My mouth falls open.

"He probably wanted other people to do this trip because *he* got sucked in," Dejah growls.

"What a punk." My nostrils flare. This is the second word-of-mouth side trip—mud baths—that's been crap. "I'm not lovin' Patrick Thin Hands right now." I can sit on any mode of transportation for hours on end if I have to, but without mental preparation, this type of trip can be soul-crushing. "At least we have food. I would be super pissed if we didn't."

Dejah cracks open a Diet Coke from the food bag and passes me one.

I snap open my can and take a sip. My taste buds twist as the warm fizzy soda hits my tongue. I'd hoped it would be a bit cooler because it was sitting in the shade. But even though it's warm, I take another drink because I need a caffeine hit after that news.

"This sucks." I sigh as I kick off my shoes.

"Would you rather eat *the sandwich* from Vilnius or be on this boat?" Dejah asks.

I cough and choke on my syrupy drink.

"Slow your roll, lady." I wag my finger. "Let's not get hasty. That brown grease features in my nightmares. But …" I glance at the cloudless blue sky. "I would rather sleep with Beady-Eyed Austin who we met in Klaipėda than be on this boat." I wrinkle my nose as I recall the chewing gum hanging from his lip. "But only if he doesn't chew gum … or talk, like at all."

"*That* would be shorter than this trip," Dejah says.

"Yup." I giggle. "A few minutes, tops."

"Right." She chuckles. "I would rather sleep with Austin than be on this boat too. But I would rather be on this boat than sleep with Keith."

"Ugh." I rub my forehead. "You just made me go there in my head with Keith. And it was bad enough with Austin." I shiver. "I would hang with Keith anytime. But sexy times? Hard pass. Seeing his naked chest at the pond and beach was enough."

Dejah's eyes shine as she laughs.

"What's worse, sleeping with Keith or eating *the sandwich*?" she asks.

"No question. Eating *the sandwich*. You?"

"Yeah, same." She twists her lips.

"So there we have it. The official hierarchy of bad." I tick them off on my fingers as I go. "Bad—is sleeping with Austin. Very bad—is being on this boat. Very, very bad—is sleeping with Keith. The worst—is eating *the sandwich*."

She grins and nods.

"So it could be worse." I lean back on the bench and take another sip of my warm soda. "You know, this echelon of bad puts a situation into perspective."

My skin is tight when the ferry docks in Hel; I'm positive I'll be burnt to a crisp in the morning. We traipse down the main drag through the throngs of people—some of whom are smiling —toward the beach. The path is lined with colorful stalls selling rainbow air mattresses, plastic bat and ball games, mystery cookies, chips, and soft drinks. Everyone's dressed in bathing suits and coverups, and there's a light, relaxed vibe in the air. After the dour locals we've encountered, this atmosphere is good for the soul. I'm taking it as a positive sign for our time in Poland that people smile here slightly more than in the Baltics.

"We need a beach game." I bounce in front of a stall with blue, green, and red frisbees stacked on shelves behind a vendor with neatly trimmed blond hair and mirror shades.

"Only on the condition that you carry it for the rest of the trip," Dejah says.

"Done." Barney already weighs a ton, and adding one plastic frisbee isn't going to make a difference.

I motion to Mirror Shades that I want one.

"Duży?" He holds up a large blue frisbee in his left hand. It looks like a donut as it has a hole in the middle. "Mały?" He flashes a smaller red one in his right.

"Duży." I stab my finger at the big blue one, Ken pays Mirror Shades, then we continue our trek to the beach.

"Look at us learning new words. Duży means big and mały means small," I say as I twirl the frisbee around my wrist. "You know, I should give *Lonely Planet* some feedback. The Polish words they have in there about tickets and hotels have been zero help. I would love more practical stuff like beer or—"

"How about—you're a bitch, ticket lady, for selling us a day trip to Hel." Dejah huffs.

"We know a word for that ..." My mouth sours. "Kurwa."

My breath stalls as I'm thrust back to the bus station in Vilnius.

His panting.

His tongue.

His touch tainting my skin.

God, why can't that memory fade away like the bruises did?

I swallow the oily memory and shove it back into its box.

"I was thinking more like big, small; you know—nice

words." I flex my shaky fingers and focus on the happy chatter of the crowd.

She chuckles and shakes her head.

The road ends at a worn dirt path leading through a thick pine forest. The sound of laughter, dance music, and waves crashing on sand lets us know we're on the right track.

We break through the trees, and I intake a breath. Kite surfers are flipping over waves in the sparkling blue sea. Bodies are lining the white sand on bright towels. People are playing volleyball or drinking in bright promotional tents. Smoke is billowing from burgers sizzling on a massive open grill. And a DJ is spinning records on stage in the middle of it all, stirring up the party vibe.

Patrick Thin Hands is a weasel, but he was right about one thing; Hel *is* a lovely beach town. *But* it's not worth the boat trip *or* sleeping with Keith to experience it for two hours.

FOOD INSTEAD OF BOOBS - GDAŃSK, POLAND

First thing the next morning, I slather cream on my tender red skin and pack Barney. I'm ready to move on, specifically out of our grim hostel.

We hoof it to the train station to buy tickets to Zamość with hopes that the rave reviews don't disappoint and we get to experience the hyped beauty of this remote Polish town.

"We have a few hours before departure. Should we see if Pit Sweat will let us use the Internet?" I ask as I pocket my ticket.

"Yeah." Dejah taps her lips. "But we should stop on the way and buy him something."

"I do love your conniving evil side." I smile as we exit the station.

Pit Sweat's head drops when we burst inside the empty shop. I waltz to the counter placing a Coke, chocolate bar, and a bag of chips in front of him.

"Can we use the Internet for a few minutes?" I ask.

He scowls.

"Please." Khadejah bats her eyelashes and passes him a vanilla ice cream cone.

Pit Sweat sighs, takes the cone, and moves away from the computer.

Dejah uses it first.

Pit Sweat jams the ice cream in his mouth, then pops the can of Coke.

I wring my hands and contemplate how to respond to Josh as Dejah clicks the keys.

Dejah and I discussed it on the long ferry ride back from Hel last night. We'll be in Prague for a while, and she's cool if I spend a few days with him as there's loads to keep her occupied in town. She reinforced that everyone deserves a second chance, and at her words, all I felt was relief because I *want* to see him again. My stomach clenches. I know I'll pay the price in heartache and regret when our time is done, but—

"All yours, mate." Dejah closes her email as Pit Sweat unwraps the chocolate bar.

I take my place behind the counter and open my email. My heart pinches at the long list of messages I have no time to read. I straighten my shoulders, open a new note, and outline our intended dates to be in Prague.

I stab the send button, and the email swooshes away.

I've officially given Josh a second chance.

I just hope I haven't made a huge mistake.

FANTA LIMON MAKES IT BETTER - WEST TRAIN STATION, WARSAW, POLAND

We're at the doors wearing Barney and Hulk on our backs and our daypacks strapped to our front when the train pulls into West Warsaw station. We only have ten minutes to catch our connection for Zamość and need to move fast if we have any hope of making it.

The doors beep and swish open.

We leap out and dash along the platform and down the stairs into the station to check the large black departure boards. Even with the same alphabet, we can't reconcile the train names because the cities listed on the board are the final destination, and we're getting off before the end of the line. But … platform three has a train departing at the connection time on our ticket.

We take off, sweat racing down the back of my legs with each heavy step.

My chest is heaving when we reach platform three.

We wait, but no train arrives.

"Are we on the wrong platform?" I flap my arms to air my sticky armpits.

"No idea. You watch Hulk, I'm going to ask around." She drops her bag at my feet.

Ticket in hand, she approaches various passengers on the platform. The frown lines on her face deepen with each person who turns their back on her.

"That was pointless." She tuts. "But it doesn't matter now; we've missed the connection. There's a ticket window at the end of the platform, let's ask about another train."

We traipse over.

"Zamość?" Khadejah slides our tickets under the small slit in the bottom of the window to the pinched face lady behind the glass.

She glares at our tickets, snips at us in Polish, and shoves the tickets away.

Dejah narrows her eyes and leans into the window.

"Wait." I place my hand on her arm. "Maybe those Polish words in the *Lonely Planet* will come in handy after all."

I pull my guidebook from my daypack along with a pen and paper. I flip to the page that has Polish words with English translations. On a scrap of paper, I write:

Peron Zamość Proszę

"This should totally solve our communication problems." I grin as I slide the paper to Pinched Face that reads—*train platform Zamość, please* in Polish.

Pinched Face sneers, turns, and disappears into a back room.

"That's it. I'm totally writing *Lonely Planet* a letter. These words are useless." I wrap my fingers around Barney's straps to ease the weight on my shoulders. "What now?"

"You're going to stay here with the bags while I get a phone card." She tips her chin to a bench in the middle of the platform. "I'm going to ring the tourist information office or find a helpful ticket lady." She dumps Hulk at my feet and stalks off.

"Right, I'll just wait here then," I mumble as I drop Barney beside Hulk.

My back clicks as I collapse on the bench.

Sometimes it doesn't seem worth the blur of trains, buses, and miscommunications for a few hours of seeing a busy tourist destination. I snort and roll my eyes. I'm so full of it. Of course it's worth it. I like it on the road. This trip is more than rushing around sightseeing—every step, laugh with Dejah, and time spent watching the miles slide past the window—is my life now. And I couldn't imagine living any other way or changing places with anyone.

I drum my fingers on my thigh as I sing "Ice Ice Baby" by Vanilla Ice and fantasize about a cold drink. My eyes water as the choking stench of someone who hasn't bathed in a long time swamps my senses.

I twist my neck and gasp. Sprawled on the ground behind me is a man in torn, dirty gray clothes and mismatched shoes. His face is swollen with blood leaking from his left eye and nostrils. How did I not notice him before? And now I'm stuck because Dejah is meeting me here, and I can't carry both our bags anywhere.

I risk another peek over my shoulder.

He's not moving.

"Oh God, is he dead?" I squeeze my eyes closed.

A dead guy is not the adventure I'm looking for.

Maybe I would like to change places with someone after all … like Dejah.

Next time, *she* can watch the bags.

He rasps, and I exhale. Not dead. A rattling cough bursts from his chest. I cover my nose with my forearm to escape the new smell of stale liquor. He groans and rubs his face with his palm, smearing blood across his cheek.

I squeeze my eyes shut.

This is *so* not cool. I mean, it's better he's alive than dead, but I have no idea what he's capable of, or how he got his ass kicked, or if he's violent. I would have to abandon all our stuff to escape him—

The clunk of heavy boots marches toward us. Two glowering armed police dressed in dark uniforms each grab one of Blood Face's arms. They heave him off the ground, dragging his feet as they haul him away.

I sink back on the bench. I dodged a bullet there.

My jaw grinds as Blood Face stumbles along the platform toward me ten minutes later. What the heck? Did the police just let him go? He limps past shouting in Polish, stopping at a dark corner behind the ticket kiosk. He sways as his words get louder and harsher.

I squint to see what has him so upset.

My mouth gapes. A woman is curled in a ball at his feet. Her dark clothes are unkempt, and her hair hangs listlessly by her bruised face.

I clench my hands. Nobody helped me in Vilnius. So maybe I should help her?

Her violent shouting joins his. Nah, looks like she knows him and she's got this. I tug Barney and Hulk closer to my legs, clutch my daypack to my chest, then scan for Dejah.

Nothing.

Just me and the quarreling couple. At least they're more interested in fighting with each other than interacting with me.

My jaw aches from clenching, my butt hole is puckered, and I've lost my sense of smell when Dejah waltzes up looking super relaxed and carefree half an hour later.

"The lady at the tourist office rang the train station, and the next train to Zamość is at midnight. Our tickets are valid for it, so we're set," she says, flipping her hair.

"Whatever." I leap off the bench and toss Hulk at her. "Can we get the fuck out of here now?"

She steps back. Her eyes flick behind me, and she hisses at my platform pals. Blood Face and his woman ran out of steam a few minutes ago and are passed out side by side.

"Oh. Sorry, mate. Let's re-group." She leads us off the platform.

"I need a cold drink, and Diet Coke isn't going to cut it," I say as I follow her down the stairs. "This situation calls for a full-sugar Fanta Limon."

"Fair." She orders two at a drink stand in the station.

I snap open the bright yellow can and whimper as the cold, tangy lemon liquid splashes my tongue. Like a magic elixir, each sugary gulp washes away my stress and frustration.

"Okay." I smack my lips, feeling human again. "Where to next?"

"We have seven hours to kill. I reckon they'll have luggage lockers at Central Station, and it's one stop away," Dejah says. "We can lock up our packs and go out for some food. I'm sure downtown isn't as bad as we've read."

I twist my lips. Our travel guides didn't have nice things to say about Warsaw. And I won't be singing its praises based on my first few hours in town. I can't wait to get out of here.

PLATFORM KILL - CENTRAL TRAIN STATION, WARSAW, POLAND

Thirty people rush the door as we try to exit the train at Central Station. Dejah rams her shoulder into my back, and I use the momentum from the push to jump. But as I'm mid-air, with the ground rushing toward me, I realize the lack of foresight in my actions. What was my plan? Crowd surf with Barney on my back?

I yelp as I splat on the platform.

The weight of Barney on my back presses my stomach into the dirty floor.

My recently healed belly button pulses with spicy shots of pain.

I groan as someone steps on my hand.

"Are you okay?" Dejah crouches to peel me off the floor.

"Not the best idea." I shuffle to standing. I gingerly lift my top, and my heart drops at the ragged line of blood, with my gold belly button hoop hanging at an unnatural angle. "The antibiotics just healed it."

"It doesn't look bad." Dejah bites her lip.

"Liar." I sigh as we make our way toward the luggage lockers. "After I clean this up, I'm going to need another sugary beverage *and* greasy food."

"I got your back." Khadejah nods as we load Barney and Hulk into storage.

Outside the station, there's a strip of fast-food options. I get KFC, and she opts for Taco Bell. We eat our food in silence leaning against the brick wall of the train station.

"Guess what?" she asks as I wipe the greasy chicken from my face. "The *Let's Go!* recommends a nice little Irish pub not far from here."

"Thank gosh for that." I roll my eyes as I throw my empty wrapper in the trash. "I was going into Irish pub withdrawal."

"I'm ignoring your snark because I know you're still salty about your belly button." She chuckles. "I have even better news than the pub. There's an Internet café we can hit along the way."

"You better not be joking." My stomach quivers with excitement at the prospect of the unread messages waiting in my inbox.

"Nah, mate. Would I do that to you?" She places her hand over her heart.

"Yes." We both crack up.

She directs us from her travel book to the café. The heavy block buildings lining the streets are decent, and generally the town seems clean.

"You know, Warsaw's not *so* bad," I say.

"My book says it got the crap kicked out of it during the war. It has a similar feel to St. Petersburg," she says, and I agree.

"Plus, they have Internet," I say.

We each score an hour before the café closes. I tap the tabletop of the scratched desk as the computer beeps and churns, taking precious minutes to open Hotmail.

My heart fills with happiness as my notes load. I count them. *Twenty-two!* I don't think I've ever received that many before. Nothing from Josh, but I only emailed him this morning, so that's not a surprise.

Forty minutes go by in the blink of an eye as I revel in each email. I use my last twenty minutes to bang out an upbeat group note with a few small fibs to keep it light.

From: Candace

To: My Friends

Date: July 24, 1998

Subject: Hello from Poland

I love, love, love getting your emails - they have made my day. But Internet cafés are rare, and the dial-up connections are painfully slow so please accept this one letter as I don't have enough time online to reply to everyone individually.

Before I get into my travel update, I have a question. Does anyone have the Right Said Fred album in their collection? Can you tell me their hit song other than "I'm Too Sexy"? We and no one we've met knows it and it's driving us crazy not knowing.

Now for the travel. Our first stop after my last email was Vilnius, the capital of Lithuania. The city is packed with lovely churches and has loads of interesting food. Our next stop was Klaipėda, on the coast of Lithuania where we met American Red Cross Navy guys, who were in town for a military exercise. I learned from them that backpacking sounds better than living on a ship with a bunch of stinky sailors. From there we took a bumpy bus trip to Nida near the Russian/Lithuania border. Nida has wild, empty beaches and a fascination with mushrooms. I even got a sunburn on my nose (it has been cold and raining for the last month, so a sunburn is something to report).

After an eighteen-hour bus trip, we arrived in Gdańsk, Poland. It's scorching hot but luckily, it's a stunning place to get lost in on a hot afternoon. We took a boat trip to Westerplatte—where Germany initiated WWII on September 1st, 1939.

This morning we caught a train from Gdańsk for Zamość in southern Poland. But we missed our connection in Warsaw and are stuck here for a few hours. But it's a happy accident as it's a nice place to visit, with friendly locals.

Everywhere has been quite safe and we've been having a great time.

I miss you all so very much.

Candace xoxo

I STEP into the night recharged and looking forward to a beer now that I'm finished my antibiotics.

Lilty fiddle music pours out of the pub when I swing open the glass door. The long bar has shiny brass taps with beer names I recognize from the trip to Ireland I took before I left London. I zero in on my favorite, Kilkenny. I smile at the bartender. Point to the tap. Do a pulling motion. Hold up my thumb and index finger indicating two and nod.

The bartender rests his tattooed forearms on the bar and smirks.

"Two pints of Kilkenny then, love?" he asks in an Irish accent.

My shoulders dip as Dejah barks out a laugh.

"Yes please." I sigh—every time one of us puts on a superior mime show, the person we're performing for speaks English.

Irish Guy slides my pint across the smooth bar top as I park my butt on the stool beside Dejah.

"Cheers." Dejah holds out her dark pint.

"Cheers to finding unexpected happiness in Warsaw." I clink her glass and moan as the bitter and creamy taste of Kilkenny glides down my throat.

This has been one weird-ass day. A few hours ago, I was miserable. But not anymore. Maybe we're getting better at this, maybe we're desensitized to the crap, maybe it's a positive outlook, or maybe it's Fanta Limon and beer. But somehow, even our bad days turn out pretty good.

"Here's to an uneventful night train to Zamość," Dejah says.

"Oh man, don't jinx it." I drop my head on the bar.

CHAPTER 4
HOT DAY CHILLS

SATURDAY, July 25, 1998

BE FUCKING CAREFUL – CENTRAL TRAIN STATION, WARSAW, POLAND

It's midnight, and we're the only two wearing backpacks on the packed platform. Even though we've perfected our get on the bus and train routine, we step back, having no desire to tangle with the locals after being platform kill this afternoon. The mob are vying to get close to the tracks to be the first on the train—all except one guy.

"Short blond dude's checking us out," I whisper to Khadejah as I tuck my hands under my biceps to ward off the night chill.

"That's an understatement. He should take a bloody picture." She scoffs.

Breaks squeak as the train glides to a stop and the doors glide open. The crowd elbows and shoves inside while we wait behind the chaos. Once the mob boards, we follow, and traipse through five train cars until we find an empty compartment for ourselves.

My belly button throbs and I'm fuzzy from the three pints of

Kilkenny I drank at the Irish pub. I'm past ready to spread out and get a few hours' sleep before we arrive in Zamość. Dejah hops on one of the two blue pleather benches, and together, we hoist Hulk onto the upper luggage rack. The door rolls open just as we position Barney on the rack at Hulk's side.

The short blond dude from the platform strolls in, shadowed by two bulky guys each carrying a case of beer.

"My name is fucking Chris," Blondie says in English with a swooshy Polish accent. "Where the fuck are you fucking from?"

"Uh …" My eyes go wide as Dejah and I step off the seat to the floor.

The three guys huddle in the middle of the compartment and confer in rapid-fire Polish.

"Oh my God, this day," I say as I drop on the bench.

"Technically, it's a new day—it's after midnight." She smirks as she sits beside me.

I flip her the bird.

The Polish conversation stops abruptly. Blondie takes a seat beside Dejah near the compartment door as the two bulky guys place the beer cases on the floor. They sit on the opposite bench, spread their legs, and take up the entire space.

There go my plans for sleep.

"You jinxed us at the pub," I whisper in Dejah's ear.

"This is fucking Andrew. He's a bouncer at a fucking club." Blondie indicates to the guy seated near the window, who's more fat than muscle with receding blond hair. "The other fucking guy is a cop named Dorek. They don't speak fucking English, but I fucking do." The cop seated near the door is more muscle than fat with light skin and dark brown wavy hair.

I share our details.

"Looks like you're the official compartment translator." I fake smile at Blondie.

"You better fucking talk slower then. Because you talk fucking fast, and I have trouble fucking understanding you." Blondie crosses his arms over his small but strong chest.

My lips part. He should talk; those words flew out of his mouth. And why is he using the word *fuck* so much? I glance at Dejah, and she shrugs.

"Piwo?" Fat blond bouncer holds up a beer.

I nod. Might as well. It looks like it's going to be a long night.

For an hour we laugh, smoke, and drink piwo as we share stories about living in Poland, Canada, and Australia through Blondie.

"You know, you don't need to describe everything with the word fuck," I say.

"You don't fucking know what you're fucking talking about. I've been to fucking New York and that's how everyone fucking speaks English there." Blondie shakes his head like *I'm* the strange one.

"It's not, mate." Dejah snorts so loud I think she's choking on her spit.

"Truly." I cover my mouth with my fingertips as I erupt in giggles.

Dejah and I debate him, but there's no changing his mind. So 'fucking this' or 'fuck that' is how Blondie is going to embrace English. We roll with it because aside from his potty mouth, he seems like a decent guy, and it's funny as hell.

"Where have you fucking been?" Blondie asks.

"We left London a month ago," I say. "We went to Russia—"

The three men erupt, their arms in the air as they shout in Polish.

I rear back in my seat.

"We fucking hate Germans." Blondie's normally friendly face is a cloud of thunder. "But we really, really fucking hate Russians. We fucking can't believe you fucking went there, it's fucking dangerous."

I blink. I should have known better. After visiting Gdańsk and Warsaw, cities permanently scarred from the war, it makes sense the people would be too.

"Have you been?" Dejah asks, Blondie translates, and they all shake their heads. "It's not *that* bad."

"You fucking have to be fucking kidding me." Blondie grips his short blond hair.

Gruff, shooshing Polish shouting continues between the men. Dejah and I stay quiet. I press my lips together. Good thing we never said Warsaw reminds us of St. Petersburg.

The mood is heavy when the Polish conversation wanes.

The rhythmic roll of the train wheels on the tracks consumes the space.

Bouncer cracks two cans, shotguns them in succession, then burps.

Cop glares as he guzzles his beer.

Even Blondie's quiet.

I swipe my clammy hands along my shorts.

Wait.

The one thing my phonetical Polish words from the travel guide are good for is entertainment. I pull out the book and read to the disgruntled Polish men. My butchering of their language gets a few laughs and lightens the prickly mood.

Note to self: don't talk about Russia or Germany in Poland. But especially Russia.

Piwo cans litter the floor of the compartment, and it smells like yeasty feet and stale cigarettes. There are five unopened cans from the forty-eight Bouncer and Cop arrived with. Dejah, Blondie, and I have each had three. Bouncer's eyes are glassed over; he's beyond wasted, and Cop isn't far behind. Cans rattle as Bouncer scoops an armful off the floor and shouts as he tosses them out the window.

I wrinkle my nose at his unnecessary littering.

Cop snaps at Bouncer in Polish and pulls him away from the window.

I shift in my seat as they whisper and leer at us.

"I would rather have sex with Austin and Keith on the boat to Hel than be on this train right now," I say in Dejah's ear.

126

Her shoulders shake as she nods.

"What about *the sandwich*?" she asks.

"Nope." My stomach revolts at the thought. "I would rather be here than eat *the sandwich*. It has to be like travesty level bad for that."

"It's not all bad then." She chuckles.

The train conductor enters our compartment just before three in the morning and yammers in Polish. Dejah and I swing our heads to Blondie.

"The fucking train is going to be fucking split and sent in different fucking directions at the next stop. You have to fucking move cars."

"Oh, thanks," I say.

Blondie for the win tonight. Who knows where we would have ended up without him?

"Fuck." He sighs as his forehead creases. "I'm going in the fucking other direction; you two are going the same fucking way as *them*." *Them* being Bouncer and Cop. "They've been fucking talking. And not fucking good talking about you two. Be fucking careful."

"Zamość better be pretty," I huff.

This fucking trip—I'm stealing Blondie's word—across Poland has been one situation after the next. And now we have to deal with *them*.

"I'm way too tired for this." Dejah rubs her hand down her face.

"We'll be okay." Together we can figure it out.

The train stops somewhere in southern Poland to split.

"I'm fucking serious. Be fucking careful," Blondie warns as he leaves the compartment.

My eyes are heavy as Dejah and I pull on our packs then trudge down the hall to a different part of the train.

"I don't think we can ditch them," I say as Cop and Bouncer trail us.

"Fat chance of that." Dejah enters a compartment that has

two guys wearing army uniforms. "It's our best bet. Safety in numbers."

"Good call," I say as Bouncer and Cop stumble in behind us and exchange words with the army dudes like they know each other.

I huddle into my seat next to Dejah and hope the next few hours pass quickly.

A ticket guy enters and barks in Polish as he examines ours.

"Aw shit." I sit up straight at the sound of his rough voice. "I miss Blondie. At least he could translate." I hope Ticket Guy doesn't try to make us pay extra money or kick us off the train—

Cop snaps in Polish, his stern cop voice leaving no room for argument.

Ticket Guy's shoulders dip, and he sheepishly hands back our tickets.

"At least the drunk twins are good for something." Dejah smiles at Cop.

Bouncer and Cop rattle a paper map in front of us. They point to a town not far from Zamość. Then point to us, them, the map, and nod like bobbleheads.

"They want us to *visit* with them." Dejah crosses her arms. "Tempting, but no thanks."

"How do we get out of this one?" I grumble.

WORTH THE TRIP - ZAMOŚĆ, POLAND

Dust plumes as Dejah and I jump off the train into the dirt next to the tracks. The early morning light casts an eerie glow over the surrounding dense pine forest. A small white sign with black letters reading *Zamość* beside a tiny hut and a winding gravel road are the only indication we're in the right place.

No one else disembarks.

Bouncer and Cop are hanging out the window waving, and we wave back as the train pulls away. We got out of their 'visiting' offer by playing dumb and using the language barrier to our benefit. I'm liking how this goes both ways. So many times we're ignored, and it's nice when avoidance works for us, too.

"This is so cool." Chills race up my arms. "It's like a spooky spy drop point."

"You're extra chipper." The muscles in her cheeks twitch.

I bite back a laugh. She's snarky because after Ticket Guy left, I slept, leaving her to stay awake to watch over us for the last two hours of the trip.

I ignore Miss Grumpy and inhale the cool, fresh forest air once the train is out of sight. I can already tell. This place is going to be awesome.

"I'm up as tour guide." I reach into my bag and pull out my *Lonely Planet*. "And, according to the map in my book, we're …" I slouch. "Off the map." I step onto the plush green grass weaving between the railway tracks and eye the road. "We have to use *The Force*. What do you think, left or right?"

Sometimes we have to guess, but we prefer to call it *The Force* since it's more fun. Dejah points to the right, and we start down the gravel road toward what we hope is the town square.

The sun moves higher in the sky, and birds are chirping and swooping between the tall, leafy trees hugging the road. My lips part as a huge bird with a sleek white stomach, gray tips on its wings, and a long, orange beak lands in a nest of tangled branches high in a pine tree.

"A stork." Dejah smiles for the first time since we got off the train.

"It's beautiful." It stretches and ruffles its long wings before it settles in the nest.

This impromptu forest hike is a gift after the stuffy train compartment.

My eyes widen at the bold green, yellow, red, and blue ornate buildings positioned above white-arched arcade-covered walkways in the Zamość town square. The only other people here are five older ladies on the perimeter of the square wearing aprons with hair tied back in a triangular scarf sweeping the cobblestones with brooms made of tree twigs.

"I feel like I've walked onto a Disney movie set." I spin in a circle and soak in the welcoming, homey feeling. "We just need talking bluebirds—"

A dog barks and growls as it charges Khadejah from gosh knows where.

He's brown and scruffy and weighs maybe five pounds all wet.

"Or this yappy mutt." Dejah marches to a nearby bench as the dog barks and bounces around her ankles.

"He doesn't like you." I smirk as I drop Barney next to the bench. The dog trots off to the other side of the square once he corrals us on the bench. I take a seat on the wooden slats and open my guidebook.

"My book says there's a cheap hotel around the corner," I say.

I leave Khadejah with the bags—in a much nicer place than I was left yesterday—and walk to the swishy beat of the sweeping twigs scraping stone. I exit the square and follow the written directions in my book three blocks to the hotel.

I yank on the door, and my shoulder jars when it doesn't budge.

I double check the address.

I have it right.

I try the door again—still locked.

I hang my head. I would have loved a bed right now, but it will have to wait a few hours. I retrace my steps to the square. Dejah's splayed out asleep on the bench. I curl up on top of Barney on the ground—not that I think anyone is going to steal him, but it's my best bet for a comfortable rest. I close my eyes and let the heat from the sun warm my tired bones.

I wake with a start and rub my bleary eyes.

The blue clock on the town hall tower looming over the square reads seven-thirty. I stretch my arms over my head, rouse

Dejah, and we traipse back to the hotel. Thankfully, it's open. Our room has two big windows, high ceilings, seven single beds, and no flies. We're already better off than the hostel in Gdańsk. I shower, then nap, and I'm not sure what pleases me more.

We search for food. Reading any menu proves to be far too difficult because again, we don't recognize any of the words. So we go to the grocery store, buy our staples, then return to our bench in the square and prepare sandwiches. There are only a handful of people passing through the space without taking pictures or gaping in awe at its beauty.

"I think we're the only tourists in town," I say, then take a bite of my sandwich. The bland white bread and flavorless cheese curbs my hunger but does nothing for my taste buds. "I would love a prepacked sandwich from England right now."

"Out of everything, a sarnie is what you want to eat?" She chuckles, and her crumbly bread flops between her fingers.

"Oh, no, I didn't realize we could have *anything*. I want my dad's burgers." My mouth waters as I imagine the meat grilling and sizzling on the barbeque in his backyard.

"I want anything made by my mum. She's the best cook ever." Dejah sighs.

I rub the pang of homesickness that throbs in my chest. But my heart brightens as the sun shimmers off the lineup of symmetrical windows on the colorful buildings.

"A home-cooked meal would be nice." I nudge her shoulder. "But sitting in this square is way better than all right."

"It is." She smiles.

I swipe the crumbs from my shirt onto the cobblestones, then grab my guidebook.

"So Zamość has a long, sad history," I extrapolate as I read. "In World War II, the Nazis renamed it Himmlerstadt. Must be after that evil Himmler guy. They expelled all Polish inhabitants from the town and around it. German colonists were placed here. Hitler envisioned this place as an eastern power city of the Third Reich. *Fucking psycho.* On a happy note, the historical center of Zamość was added to the World Heritage List in 1992."

I begin the city tour at the long, beige Zamoyski Palace. It's large but not as ornate as the palaces in Russia. Not that I would ever tell anyone in Poland. I feel ghosts slide around me as we pay our respects at the Rotunda where the Nazis executed 8,000 residents. Then we visit the Collegiate church. The decorative inside is glittery gold magic for the eye, and *this place* rivals any church we visited in Russia.

We return to the town square and stop at the one touristy shop for postcards. I pluck ten as I turn the metal postcard stand. I can't resist; they're all so beautiful and they're my backup. In case the film I mail home gets lost, the negatives don't turn out, or my pictures are crap. This reasoning also helps justify the stack of cards in Barney that's now an inch thick.

I run my finger down the plastic box front at the restaurant next door, searching the menu for our safe word—grzyby— which we know is mushrooms in Polish because it's close to grebes in Lithuanian. Honestly, the *Lonely Planet* needs to add some food word translations—

"Can I help you?" someone from behind us asks in English with a slight accent.

I turn to the short man with kind blue eyes behind his thick glasses.

"Yes." I dig around my daypack for paper and pen, delighted for the help. "Can you help us with food words? Like fish and chicken?"

"Okay." Thick Glasses' mouth is slightly gaped as he takes my pen and writes the words in Polish.

"Thanks for this." I rub the paper between my fingertips. Something so simple as being able to recognize the words for food we like—not just mushrooms—means so much.

"What are you doing here?" Thick Glasses' forehead scrunches.

"We came here because—" I stop myself before I say we read

LIFE STRIKES BACK

two lines in our travel book that said Hitler fancied this place as the home of the Third Reich and we figured it must be something to see. "Because …"

My stomach dips. He has a point. Why *do* we put ourselves through this remote travel for a few moments spent sitting in a pretty town square?

I *want* to visit secluded towns; only then in my mind are you a traveler and not a tourist. But it took us forever to get here. Then there was Blood Face in Warsaw and the drunk guys on the train. We can't speak the language, have no idea what anything is most of the time, and have been existing on the same dull sandwiches for most meals.

My lips tip up as I recall the majestic stork landing in its nest or at my aching gut from laughing at Blondie's liberal use of the word fuck. It's the things that happen along the way, not necessarily the sites shining bright in my memories.

"Because we heard it's beautiful." My chest flutters with pride. It's not easy, but we're doing it. And it's all the more rewarding when we work our asses off to achieve it.

ENDLESS FLAT GREEN FIELDS - BUS STATION, ZAMOŚĆ, POLAND

My legs ache with each step of our early Sunday morning hike to the station to catch a bus to Kraków. We pass a white-steepled church; the heavy wooden doors are propped open. The drone of the service is blaring on loudspeakers for the overflow of people spilling out onto the steps and manicured green lawn. Everyone looks so nice, not a hair out of place, dressed in freshly pressed suits or flowing summer dresses.

"Ugh, I feel like a vagabond." My cheeks heat as I glide my hands down my rumpled green pants and a gray T-shirt with the lingering blood stain from my platform kill incident in Warsaw.

"Technically you *are* a vagabond." Dejah smirks, and I scrunch my face. "You have no job, and you're wandering from place to place."

133

"Dude." I frown. "Seriously?"

"Deadly." Her laughter dances on the breeze.

I shake my head and grin. Even poking fun at my sore spot of being unemployed, she lightens my mood with a quick quip.

The dapper crowd on the lawn sway in unison as they start singing a hymn in Polish, like the Whos from Whoville around the Christmas tree after the Grinch stole their gifts.

I breathe in the warm morning air, flooding my senses with the rich smell of wildflowers, fresh cut grass, and their melodic voices. I savor this bright moment because our days are a spin of the *chance wheel*—you just never know what's coming next.

I climb up the bus steps and drop onto the firm bench. Dust rushes up from the threadbare seat, making me sneeze. I shift my bottom, trying to find a comfy position, but there isn't one. The *chance wheel* has spun, and this is going to be an uncomfortable trip.

My body jerks as the bus driver hits the gas. We jolt forward over the bumpy roads. Coast. Slow to an almost stop. He stomps on the gas. We coast. This happens again. Again, and again, and *again*.

"This is going to be a long ride." Dejah's cheeks have a green tinge.

"If I don't barf it's going to be a miracle," I say as I press my hands over my rolling stomach. Great—double the fun: uncomfortable *and* nauseating.

"I reckon being able to drive properly would be a skill a bus driver would need to get this job." She huffs.

"Not in Poland." I sigh.

Writing in my journal or reading is not an option because I'll lose my breakfast, so I watch the lush green fields glide past the window. There's a massive metal pipeline running parallel to the road. It's propped up above the long grass and daisies bent on the breeze with a backdrop of birch and willow trees. There are a few black and white cows dotting the landscape but not a lot of animals relative to the vast space.

I brace myself on the seat ahead of me as the bus pitches forward. My back jars as we hit a pothole, and my head fogs from the smell of diesel flooding the bus. I focus on the little square houses along the road with tipped brown roofs. Their front gardens are bursting with pots overflowing with bright pink impatiens, black-eyed Susans with their soft yellow petals and dark centers, and sunflowers turning their sunny faces to the sky.

Maybe I overreacted. It's not so bad to sit and watch the world out the window.

RUNNING TO THE CONVENT - KRAKÓW, POLAND

My vomit splats in the gutter behind our bus at the Kraków station. I wipe my mouth with the back of my hand, then drain the dregs of my warm water. No view out the window could help that trip. It was a brutal eight hours of bad driving, toxic smells, and non-existent suspension shocks to travel three hundred kilometers.

"Better?" Dejah asks, dragging Barney and Hulk along the pavement she retrieved from the under bus storage.

"Yeah." I nod and swing Barney on my back.

Aside from the rough entry, I'm looking forward to this town. It's big, and we'll be able to go out, enjoy the nightlife, see some cool stuff, and hopefully run into some other travelers to mix things up. I love Dejah's company, but it's also nice to meet new people, have new conversations, and gain different perspectives.

"On the bus, I was reading about places to stay. How about the Convent of the Norbertine Sisters?" Khadejah asks.

"Pardon?" I blink. "Did you say convent?"

"How many chances are we going to get to stay in one?"

"I don't *know*?" I enjoyed *walking past* the church this morning but have zero desire to mingle with ladies in habits. "I'm not—"

"Great." She claps her hands. "We need to catch a tram."

I tip my head to the twilight sky, then trudge along behind her. I have no better hostel options since I didn't do any pre-reading on the queasy bus trip, so convent it is.

It's a long ride out of town, followed by a longer trek through the dark streets where we get turned around three times. Sweat's dripping down the side of my face by the time we ruck up to the tan building adjacent to the Vistula River.

One point against the convent: it's far out of the city center.

"This just feels wrong on so many levels," I say as we approach the eight-foot heavy oak door with an iron grate in front of an eye-level peek-a-boo window. I feel like a poser standing here. My grandmother used to gripe at my mom that my brothers and I didn't know the words to "Jesus Loves Me."

"Shouldn't we save the beds for people who go to church on the regular?" We were not big on church in my house. Occasionally we'd go to a Christmas Eve service. My mom would belt out every carol, and if you were in her vicinity, you'd be dazed by stale tea breath. I have a lot of fond memories of her, but those aren't ones.

"Nah, it'll be fun." Dejah presses the doorbell, and my shoulders tense at the harsh buzz.

The mighty door creaks on the hardworking metal hinges.

I step back as the surly-faced nun sweeps a skeptical eye over us. I cross my arms over the bottom of my unwashed T-shirt to hide the blood stains from my belly ring. She huffs and spins on her heel, her black veil and floor-length tunic swishing as she strides away.

Dejah shrugs and follows her along the worn dark wooden floorboards to the check-in desk. I smile as she asks for less than five dollars a night each. Maybe this isn't so bad after all. Cheap accommodation means more daily budget allocation for drinking.

The nun taps the sign tacked on the wall in English.

Eleven o'clock curfew.

I groan.

Second point against the convent: no late-night drinking and dancing because we'll have to leave as the fun's getting started.

We climb the wide mahogany staircase to our dorm room on the second floor. The walls and floor are the same wood as the staircase with high ceilings, crown molding rosettes around the lights, and twelve sturdy bunk beds.

I dump Barney next to one of the last empty beds and flinch at the chatter of young children speaking French. I grimace at the mom, dad, and *four* pre-teens across the room.

Third point against the convent: we're in the middle of another family holiday. One I have zero desire to witness, knowing it's not something I'll ever have again.

We need to cut our losses—in this case, five dollars—and leave.

"We gotta go." I grab my book, thumbing the pages to find a new hostel.

"What's that?" Dejah's smile is blinding as she organizes her pajamas on her bunk.

She loves this place. I close my book and press my fingertips to my temples as two kids squeal when they race past. Her excitement wipes out all the negative points. Even the tightness in my throat as I watch one of the kids sink into their mom's warm embrace.

"I meant, we gotta get ready to go out. I need five minutes." I unzip Barney, grab my toothbrush, and stomp to the communal bathroom resigned to our convent living.

My back's a sticky mess as we enter the vibrant Kraków Old Town main square after a brisk forty-minute walk from the convent. It's a vast space, surrounded by medieval buildings with opulent roofs and a Renaissance-style market arcade dominating the center of the square. The imposing red brick church on the east corner has two different towers flanking the entryway. One is oddly taller with an extra circular level topped with a loftier spire.

The humid summer night has brought out the crowds. Lively

outdoor cafés along the perimeter are brimming with people drinking under large tan umbrellas. The hum of chatter and music fills the air, giving it a party atmosphere.

We score prime seats at an outdoor table and order two large —duży—beers. The server with slicked-back brown hair, a pointy nose, and pale skin places two pints of clear golden lager on our round metal table. Beads of moisture trickle down the side of my drink as Dejah pays him from Ken.

"Cheers." She holds out her pint, and we tap drinks. "These seats are top-notch for people-watching." Dejah points at the woman our age in a bright lilac ruffled skirt and pointy black flat shoes with white ankle socks as they saunter past the café.

"Wow," I say pressing my lips together. "Oh, and Madonna's here." Three wannabes dressed in layered black tulle skirts and fingerless gloves strut by with a bounce in their step.

"*Early* Madonna." Dejah's eyes shine as she takes a drink of her beer. "Check those ones." Two girls flick their voluminous locks of hairspray curls as they teeter along the cobblestones in skyscraper heels and acid-wash jeans.

"Right, so I get I'm wearing this." I flick my bloody T-shirt I didn't change out of since I have no clean options and tap my plastic Teva sandals. "I'm the last person who should be commenting on how people are dressed. But I feel like an '80s prom party is about to kick off. Or a Van Halen concert."

"It's all the rage." She tips her head to the patrons around the café with big bangs, off-the-shoulder tops, and oversized pleated pants.

"Did they miss fifteen years of fashion? I wore those clothes in my early teens."

"Same. But all the women we've seen since we left London are behind in fashion," Dejah says as she holds up her thumb and index fingers to Pointy-Nose Server asking for two more beers.

"Ugh, except the women in Moscow." I frown at my empty glass. "I've never felt so frumpy and ugly in my whole life. I'm a swampy mess, and I feel better about myself now than I did next to those skinny beauties."

"I hear you," Dejah says.

Feeling less than your best compared to the locals who have access to a full wardrobe and a hairdryer is one of the hard parts about traveling. Always settling for being kind of clean. Trying to eke out a decent look in your basic overused clothing and limited makeup is a constant struggle. It's a knock to your confidence even when comparing yourself to the '80s wannabes strutting the square.

"Sixteen zlotys," Pointy-Nose Server says as he places two new beers and a paper receipt on the table.

"We paid eight for our last two," Khadejah says as she examines the receipt.

"You did *not* pay anything," Pointy-Nose Server says in English with a thick Polish accent.

"We *paid* for the first two." Dejah's jaw clenches as she opens Ken and counts the money inside. "We had one fifty note in here, and there's forty-two left."

"The receipt clearly says you need to pay for four," he sneers. "I've been working at this café for two months, and I *never* make a mistake."

"Well, yah have now." Dejah grips Ken, refusing to hand over one more zloty until we get this sorted.

I sigh. This totally sucks. With no receipt for the first two beers, it's us against the word of the never-mistaken Pointy-Nose Server.

"Puis-je t'aider?" A gray-haired Polish woman from two tables over asks in French if she can help.

The buzz of the café stalls, and all patrons' eyes turn our way.

I explain to gray-haired Polish woman in French what happened.

My cheeks burn as she loudly translates the story in Polish to Pointy-Nose Server and the hundred or so other people —dressed in their '80s wear—listening in on our drama.

A different server swoops past and whisks away the two new untouched beers that were in front of us.

"We're out." Khadejah's Australian accent thickens with frustration. She narrows her eyes on Pointy-Nose Server as she stands. "Better luck on your scamming next time." She marches out of the café to the center of the square as I double-time to keep up. "They were trying to rip us off because we're foreigners." Her hands fly around her face. "No way was I backing down. It's the principle."

"I know. It's cool. I support you," I say in a soft, even tone. "They didn't stop us from leaving because they *were* scamming. And probably do it all night. The worst is that we lost our prime seats to watch the impending Poison MTV video shoot."

"It could have been Bananarama." She chuckles as the tension slips from her shoulders and neck. "Or George Michael."

"Now if it was George, we would have paid the scammers." I shrug.

"Anything for George," she says, and we both crack up.

My heart blooms with warmth that I can bring her calm and make her laugh in a crappy situation like she does for me. And I love that after our day full of *chance wheel* ups and downs, we can still find something to smile about.

I SIT on the edge of my bunk in our dorm room and combine my clothes into one heaving plastic bag as Dejah does the same with hers. I jostle the handles to compress the contents, and my throat constricts from the smell of dirt and foul salty sweat. There's no going back now. Once stale socks and dirty underwear mix with everything else, it has to be washed, and no hand washing will do.

The only launderette listed in either of our guidebooks is on the outskirts of town, but we have no idea exactly where, as it's off the small maps in our books. And since we rushed to the convent last night, we didn't stop to buy a full city map. We try asking the nuns. They're no help with directions or anything as none of them speak English. Our best option is to hoof it the forty minutes into town to the tourist office and buy a map to locate the launderette.

No problem; we'll have these dirty clothes dropped off in no time and enjoy the rest of the day.

Heat ripples off the pavement. My plastic bag is glued to the insides of my arms as I carry it like a baby, and my only clean outfit, my blue mid-thigh sheath dress, is stuck to my lower back from a layer of sweat.

"It's barely nine in the morning. How can it be so hot already?" I ask.

"Reckon we stop for breakfast?" Dejah tips her chin to an unassuming café with vibrant green ivy clinging to the white sandstone bricks around dark brown wooden doors.

Instead of answering, I hoist my heavy bag on my left hip and reach for the door handle with my right hand. Cool air hits my face. My taste buds twitch with longing at the smell of rich ground coffee. Happy chatter of the other patrons blends with the sultry lyrics of "Iris" by the Goo Goo Dolls.

"This place is a dream come true." I pull out a metal chair at a table in the center of the busy room and we both drop our bags on the floor.

One side of the bright café has exposed red brick walls; the other has a soft garden mural, with pastel pink and yellow flowers popping up between large pale green leaves. A server glides through the tables with two plates of food. My lips part at the grill marks on the side of the bread oozing with cheese and vegetables she drops at the adjacent table.

"They have proper squishy panini sandwiches." Saliva floods my mouth.

"And juice served with actual ice cubes." Dejah blinks.

"I never want to leave. The only way this place could be better would be if it had a washing machine in the back."

"Bad luck, mate. I can't see one," Dejah says before she places our order for sandwiches and drinks with the server.

I sink my teeth into the savory bread and sigh as spicy salami goodness bursts on my tongue. I reach for my drink, and the ice cubes tinkle as I bring the bright orange juice to my lips. I whimper as the cool sweet liquid glides down my throat. Laundry services or not, this place has started this day off right.

This *has to* be a sign. Nothing but good things ahead. I'm sure of it.

We pry ourselves away from the café and continue the trek to the tourist office. We buy a map, and the tourist office lady unfolds it and marks a laundry place ten blocks away. My shoulders straighten. Usually getting basic stuff done takes ages, but not today. Map in hand, I happily lug my sticky bag of dirty clothes with Dejah at my side.

My arms are going to fall off and my ankles are puffy from the heat after many kilometers of walking when we reach the quiet leafy street where the tourist lady marked the map. Dejah's thick hair is wet at the temples, and her skin flushed as we stride past a row of gray and brown sandstone buildings with storefronts and signs over the doors written in Polish.

A hardware store, corner shop, flower shop. It must be the next one, then we'll be able to ditch these bags. I stand beside Dejah and peer through the last shop window, and my heart lurches like I've caught my lover on a romantic date. Not a washing machine in sight. A bald man behind the counter at the till hits a button on the wall. Crisp white dress shirts and flowing dresses individually wrapped in clear plastic whizz around on the ceiling hanger conveyor belt. It's a *dry cleaner*.

"*No.*" The slick white bag slips in my grip, but I manage to hold on to it before it hits the sidewalk.

I want to throw myself on the ground and pound my fists against the pavement.

"Well, fuck." Dejah purses her lips. "Let's re-group on the bench in the shade and go back to the *Let's Go!* recommended one." She points to the leafy area at the end of the block and starts walking. A warm breeze whispers across my skin and the calming smell of lavender floods my senses as I slump beside her on the bench.

"This sucks." I pout as I toss my bag at my feet. "I'm going to melt."

"I'll check the map to see how far it is." She holds out her palm.

My hands are … empty? But I *was* holding the map when we walked down the street. My eyes search the ground. Nothing. My bag. Just clothes. I pat my sides, but there's no pockets in this thin sheath dress.

"I lost it." I drop my head.

She reclines on the bench, crossing her feet in front of her.

"Your penance for losing the map is to search for a new one and buy us two Lemon Calippo ice lollies while I wait here," she says as she laces her fingers behind her head.

I nod sharply, accepting my fate because after everything we went through to get the freaking map, I should have taken better care of it. I leave her with our rank laundry while I search for the items. I retrace my steps but can't find the one I dropped. The corner shop near the stupid dry cleaners has everything I need, including a new map. I frown as I pay for the items. We're such dorks. We should have tried a corner shop near the convent to see if they had a map before we trudged all the way into town to the tourist office. But then we might not have found the café with air conditioning and paninis.

I slurp my tart icy Calippo as I return the short distance to the bench. Dejah takes a bite of her popsicle, then unfolds the paper map, stretching her hands wide.

"Ugh." She drops her arms to her lap, crushing the map. "You're not going to believe this; the launderette is near the convent."

I blow out a frustrated breath. I need to pee, I stink like salty dirt, and I'm beyond pissed for wasting this beautiful day.

We catch a tram, then haul our smelly bags six blocks until finally we find it—*five hours* after we left the convent this morning.

They will process it in three hours.

"Want to try and find the Internet café listed in my book while we wait?" Dejah asks as we exit the launderette.

"Does a bear shit in the woods?" I bounce on my toes.

"What?" Her face scrunches.

"Sorry … does a kangaroo poo in the … *outback*?" I ask, trying to recreate the popular saying from home meaning 'hell yes.'

"Still not getting you."

I roll my eyes—at myself. If she hasn't heard of the original expression, then she probably won't know what I mean if I make it *local*.

"Internet would be great." News from home and hopefully Josh is as exciting as ice cubes and just what I need to turn this day around.

THE BLUE SCREEN on the boxy monitor flickers as the painfully slow dial-up rings and wails. I light a cigarette and take a deep drag. The screeching stops, and I type Hotmail in the search engine. The beige computer clicks and churns as I wait.

And wait.

I stub out my cigarette as my inbox finally loads. I slouch as disappointment tangles in my stomach when I don't see Josh's name. But it's only been a week since I emailed him agreeing to meet in Prague; he could be struggling to find Internet cafés too.

I scan the names in my inbox with fresh eyes. My lips split into a huge smile at Vasilii's name. This is the first note I've received from him since he emailed the day after I left Russia sharing his plans to meet me in South Africa. I click on his note and hum as I wait for it to open, excited to see what he has to say.

"Oh my God!" The blood drains from my face as I read the first line.

"What's wrong?" Concern fills Dejah's eyes from her seat beside me.

"Katrine, Vasilii's mom." A sob rips from my chest. "She passed away unexpectedly from a heart attack six days after we left Moscow."

Dejah leaps out of her chair and rushes over.

Sorrow twists beneath my skin and nausea overwhelms me.

"There was no indication she was unwell. It came as a complete surprise," Dejah reads from his note.

She died.

Six days after we had tea with her in her cozy sitting room.

Six days after she gave us that thoughtful care package of golden cookies.

Six days after she gave me the best hug before we left her apartment.

My body trembles. Black spots blur my vision. I have no idea if a quick, unexpected death is worse than the long drawn-out one my mother had. But both end up in the same place. Devastation, loss, and crippling grief.

"I'm just sending Vasilii our deepest sympathies." Dejah taps at my keyboard as I rock in my seat.

"What are he and his sister Nastasia going to do? How will they live?" It's not the same in Russia as at home. They live in a luxury apartment by Moscow standards, and I don't think the two of them can afford to stay there without their mother's support. And their dad's not in the picture.

"I don't know." She shuts down my computer then hers.

"It's too close." The anniversary of my mom's death is days away. "I know what he's going through ... and it's debilitating. I wish I could do something for him."

Grief floods my chest and coils around my heart.

"I know, darlin'. I know. I wish we could too." Dejah guides me out of the café toward the bus stop as tears flood my eyes.

This fucking day has plummeted past the worst level of the Echelon of Bad—like I would rather eat *the sandwich* level bad.

"My soul aches from the inside out from missing her." I lean into Dejah for the long bus trip to the launderette then another bus to the convent, too distraught and heartbroken to say anything else.

———

I SOOTHE MY SWOLLEN, tear-stained face with my fingertips as I roll out of bed the next morning. The ache in my chest throbs for Vasilii and for the memory of my own loss. I tip my chin and gather my toiletries from Barney. This pain will not win. I'm going to do what I always do when I'm overwhelmed. I shove my hurt down and coax myself to take one step. Then another. Then another. And push through.

"Shower's free," Dejah says as she saunters into the room and shuffles through Hulk, looking for her hairbrush.

I study my feet, willing myself to move. But I can't.

"The water's hot. Better get there before the family does." Soft steps pad toward me. Her palm gently settles on the middle of my back. "Come on. Shower. You'll feel better."

My lips quiver. Grief, you complicated asshole.

Compartmentalizing and taking one step at a time has helped me get through most days. But it hasn't *healed* anything. I still can't talk about my mother without blubbering. Or hear about death without crumbling into a messy heap.

Being on this trip and experiencing everything keeps my mind busy and gives me space to reflect in the quiet times. But it's not enough because I can't crawl out from under this pile of grief.

I suck in my bottom lip and focus on Dejah's reassuring hand on my back.

I need help.

I know how to ask for logistical help, like how to get somewhere or what's on a menu. But how do I get deep, complicated emotional help? And how can I ask someone to take that on when I can't handle it myself?

LAUGH WHERE YOU CAN - WIELICZKA SALT MINE, WIELICZKA, POLAND

The wind howls, and the slanted rain soaks through my yellow slicker, drenching my newly clean clothes as we hustle to the central bus station. This miserable weather makes it a perfect time to visit the underground Wieliczka Salt Mine, a must-see, according to our guidebooks. And I'm looking for any busy distraction I can get today, so I'm all in.

Wet drops roll down the sleeves of my jacket as I hunch and shuffle down the aisle of the short bus. The windows are steamed up, and the air smells like wet dog. With limited free seats, we can't sit together. Dejah snags a seat in the back, and I sit two rows ahead beside a guy with slight shoulders and light brown skin. I slide off my hood, then smooth my hands over the pigtail braids Dejah did for me this morning.

My head tips to the side as my right braid is tugged. The skinny guy at my side hasn't moved. Must be someone behind me. Pain pulses at the base of my hairline as my left braid is yanked. Male snickers fill the air. I whip my head around and glare at the two baby-faced white guys at my back.

"You better tell your friend to stop before I lose it," I growl at a skinny guy.

"Oh. I'm not with them," he says in a strong Australian accent. His big brown eyes shine as bright as his smile as he holds out his hand. "I'm a dentist from Sydney, name's David. But everybody calls me Dude Davo."

"Candace." I shake his delicate hand. By the wrinkles around his eyes, he must be my age, if not older. I know I was hoping to meet new people my age in town, but this guy's lame. What grown man willingly goes by dude? Besides *The Big Lebowski.*

"So glad to meet you." He runs his fingers through his thick black hair. "I'm here on my own, and now I have a friend to visit the mine with."

"Ye-a…h." What the heck? I have no desire to hang with this guy—or should I say, dude. My nostrils flare as I recognize the snickers at my back. Dejah. She's enjoying this way too much and thinks this is funny. Well, hang on.

"Not just one friend." I jab my thumb backward. "Wait till you meet Khadejah. She's big on dental hygiene, and she's from Sydney too. I'm sure you'll have loads to talk about."

Her snickers stop and mine begin.

The three of us catch the first available guided English tour of the mine. Our group of fifteen circle a dizzying number of steps to descend over one hundred meters underground. Soft yellow lights illuminate our path through a narrow slate-gray tunnel. I glide my hand across the salt wall surface; it's smooth, almost soft, leaving the tips of my fingers damp. I blink rapidly as we pass detailed carved gnomes with jaunty hats and human-sized religious figures in flowing robes organized in a mock service.

We came here on a whim because of the rain, and I've done zero research on this place. I had no idea they had carvings; I thought it was just a mine.

"Kraków is my first stop on my month-long trip away," Dude Davo says as we trail the group through another long tunnel.

I clench my fists as he natters about his fiancée back at home and his jogging club. Dejah's smartly a few steps ahead and missing his soliloquy. I roll my eyes. He probably hasn't spoken to anyone in days, so I'm getting his backlog of words.

Our tour guide wearing a polyester brown shirt says something about churches that I can't hear because of Dude Davo's incessant chatter.

I huff. I hate missing facts.

"What was that?" I shout to Polyester Shirt Girl.

"There are four churches here, and our next stop is The Chapel of St. Kinga," Polyester Shirt Girl says in English with a thick Polish accent.

Dude Davo stops talking, and my lips part as the tunnel opens into an enormous space. Twinkling crystal chandeliers hang from a twelve-foot ceiling, casting a soft glow over the elaborately carved gray salt floor larger than a basketball court. My head tips and twists as I take in the intricate cross carvings around the room. It's magnificent. And Dude Davo is blissfully silent. So I love it even more.

The hour tour complete, Polyester Shirt Girl leaves us in a dimly lit passageway behind a group of people to wait for transport to the surface. I pop on my tiptoes and can just make out metal doors over the fifty heads in front of us.

We inch forward.

The babble of the crowd and Dude Davo echoes in the tight space over the clang of metal and the whir of an engine as the elevator transports the latest group up and out.

The elevator groans as it returns to our level. My throat tightens at my first good look at it through the thinning crowd. It's a two-level enclosed metal cage with a folding security door on the front. Twenty people in front of us cram into the top compartment like they're livestock ready for transport. The usher slams the folding door closed, and the metal cage grinds as it rises ten feet.

We're next.

My heart thrashes as the three of us shuffle across the salt floor and squish inside the bottom cage. I'm jostled to the center as more bodies press inside. I jump when a bag pokes into my back. I shuffle closer to Dejah and Dude Davo. The metal gate slams, and the attendant folds over the lock with a mighty bang.

I hate small spaces.

The lights flicker. We're blanketed in darkness.

My stomach drops to my feet as the cage rockets upward, rattling as it speeds us one hundred thirty meters to the surface.

I clench my eyes shut and hum "Club Tropicana" by Wham!.
Dude Davo is muttering about dental needles and fillings.
And Khadejah's laughing and whooping in delight.
We jolt to an abrupt stop, the car bouncing from the force.
I teeter out on shaky legs.
"Best part of the tour." Dejah beams.
"New Spice Girl name for you." I jab a trembling finger in her face. "Morbid Spice."
"Aces, mate." She rocks on her toes with a smile.
I roll my eyes. Of course, she loves it.

WE CAN'T SHAKE Dude Davo, so he joins us to meet Simon in the Jewish Quarter at the predetermined restaurant we agreed on in Gdańsk. We missed our first rendezvous last night because I was too distraught over Vasilii's news. Hopefully, Simon will be here tonight. I've put on a brave face today, but I'm struggling with my weighty emotions, and he has a calming presence in a big brother kind of way that I could use right now.

I push the white door of the restaurant open and step onto the mosaic-tiled green floor. I squint as my eyes adjust to the dark room. A man with a bushy gray mustache is playing a graceful song of longing on a violin from the far corner to the handful of customers. My nose wrinkles because none of them are Simon.

We sit near the door so he won't miss us and order three pints of local lager.

"Can I get a Spice Girl name?" Dude Davo asks as I watch the door. "I heard you give Khadejah the name Morbid Spice."

I chuckle. He *wants* a Spice Girl name. Dejah tips one eyebrow as we share a look, asking for my opinion. I shrug and lift my chin, giving her the go-ahead. I know we said we'd only give Spice names to people who have meant something to us. And in a weird way, he has, as he's been a decent distraction from my sadness today. It's hard to forget a dentist who's the size of Dejah and likes to be called Dude Davo.

"Okay, how about this." Dejah taps the table with her fingertips. "Hair Removal Spice, because you do your fiancée's waxing."

"I love it." Dude Davo flashes his perfect white teeth as he gives us a double thumbs-up.

I roll my lips. That's her worst Spice name yet.

"This has been so fun, let's make a plan to meet in Prague, since we'll be there at the same time," Dude Davo says.

We're all in now with a Spice Girl name, so we might as well meet again. Dejah nods as I flip through the pages of my guidebook. We pick a random bar close to the center of town near the hostel we intend to stay at and agree on the same time for three nights in a row.

"I reckon we should order food." Dejah sighs with less sparkle in her eyes than usual. "Simon's a no-show."

"Right." My jaw stiffens as I study the menu.

"I'm sad too." Dejah taps my forearm after we order food.

"I know, I just didn't think *he* would stand us up." Josh, yes—Simon, no.

Elbows on the table, I rest my head in my cupped palms.

"I'm sure he's not in town." Dejah flaps her hand in the air.

"You're right. He would show if he was here." Since he promised he would.

"It's time to show you my secret party trick," Dejah says.

"Don't bother. I know all your tricks." I shake my head with a budding smile.

"Not this one." She cracks her knuckles. "Ready?"

"Hold on." I reach down and pull my small black pocket camera from my backpack beside my chair. "Go on then." I poise it at the ready.

Dejah tips her pint glass that's resting on the table toward her. She opens her mouth and lowers her face to the rim of the glass. She uses her free hand to edge her lips over and around the circumference of the glass until they encompass the entire pint.

"How on earth?" My eyes bulge as I click away with my camera.

"Wow," Dude Davo says in awe.

My laughter drowns out the sound of the wistful violin and my heavy heart. Dejah removes the glass, her eyes shining with mischief. I endure a thousand emotions every day, swinging from happy to sad with the flick of a switch. And it's exhausting. But with Dejah, we usually end with a smile even during the direst of times.

I just hope we can keep it up. Because as we approach the anniversary of my mother's death, each day seems more challenging than the last. And tomorrow will be no exception as we're visiting Auschwitz.

WILDFLOWERS - AUSCHWITZ AND BIRKENAU, POLAND

I clutch my white polystyrene cup filled with Dunkin Donuts coffee as I fidget at the bus stop in the center of Kraków. My stomach twists as I scan the somber faces of the twenty people we're waiting with for the bus to Oświęcim, the closest town to Auschwitz and Birkenau.

"I have mixed feelings about today." I rub my fingers across my chin. "I want to pay my respects and get educated. But I'm also torn because it feels wrong to visit a place of horrific genocide."

"I feel the same." Dejah tugs the straps on her daypack. "But we're going with an open heart."

I reach out and squeeze her hand.

I drain my drink; the contrast of sweet cream and bitter coffee soothes my nerves. I've mentally prepared for today—as much as I can—and our team of two is strong. And maybe in some small way, our visit will help ensure the victims and survivors are never forgotten.

"No. Way," I say when I spot a tall guy with blond flowing locks prancing toward the bus stop with three men in tow. "It's Patrick Thin Hands we met in Gdańsk."

Dejah growls.

"Girls! Hey." Patrick Thin Hands frantically waves.

"Oh, sure. Mister *visit Hel, it's so great* is happy to see us." I toss my empty cup into the overflowing trash and prop my hands on my hips.

Patrick Thin Hands' arms open wide when he reaches us.

I slap his hand.

He gasps, followed by a high-pitched shriek.

"Seriously?" I shove my index finger in his face. "You *forgot* to mention that it's a four-hour boat trip—*each way*—to Hel when you raved about it being the perfect day trip."

His three friends' eyes wrinkle as they throw looks at each other.

Patrick Thin Hands purses his lips and wiggles his hips.

"It was kind of a long trip." He sighs and scratches behind his ear. "Not the nicest. *Sorry? Forgive me?*"

I sigh, and Dejah rolls her eyes. The one good thing that came out of our day trip to Hel was the Echelon of Bad. It's funny and allows us to take everything with a grain of salt. Patrick Thin Hands is annoying, but *he* doesn't rate anywhere near the boat ride, sleeping with Austin, Keith, or eating *the sandwich.*

"Pretty please?" He bats his eyelashes.

He's doing the same day trip. There's no avoiding him without being extremely awkward. Plus, he's hard to ignore in his pink T-shirt and purple cords.

"All right." I shrug, and he throws his arms around me.

"These are my friends," he says after he hugs Dejah. "Garth from Toronto, Sam from Korea, and Darren from Australia."

"Hey." I shake hands with Garth, the vanilla clean-cut chino and polo-wearing white guy. Then smiley Sam with jet black hair who speaks very little English.

"G-day. I'm from Darwin." Darren's palm is callused, and his accent is deep and twangy.

I bite my bottom lip to stifle a laugh. He sounds like Crocodile Dundee and looks like an Australian poster child with a blond mullet, green rugby shirt, and white short shorts.

"Great to meet a fellow Aussie," Darren says as he pumps Dejah's hand.

"You've no idea, mate. I've been with this Canadian for ages," Dejah jokes.

Dejah's and Darren's eyes dance as they exchange stories about Australia. Her Australian accent has softened over the last month, and after one minute of chatting with him, it's back in full force. Her enthusiasm isn't because she fancies him; he's not her type—or mine; none of them are. She's just happy for a connection to home, and as amusing as he was, Dude Davo didn't count because he talked to us, not with us.

"Here we go," Chino Garth says as the bus arrives and a somber blanket is thrown over our banter.

"We got this," I say.

"We do." Patrick Thin Hands nods.

All the seats are taken by the time we board, so we stand in a unit in the center of the bus. And just like that, our team of two grows to six. And I'm glad for it. Dejah and I have each other's backs, but today isn't going to be easy, and I welcome the extra partners.

The driver hits the gas, and I cling to a pole so I don't tumble from the jarring potholes on the road as crippling anxiety swirls in my gut.

Pre-mom-death I was hyper-tuned to moods. But since death day, that part of me has been absent. But on this packed bus, I'm absorbing everyone's dark and suffocating mood like a sponge.

Maybe my empathy's not as broken as I thought.

And what a time to realize it.

I SQUINT at the brilliant sun as I step off the bus in Oświęcim. The sky is a cloudless blue, the hot air is thick with the smell of fresh cut grass and summer flowers … but it tastes heavy and off.

Our group is silent as we follow the signs to our destination.

I stop in my tracks before the infamous black metal sign over the entrance to Auschwitz that I would consider aesthetically appealing under any other circumstance.

Arbeit macht frei—it says in arched font.

"It means 'work sets you free' in German," Patrick Thin Hands whispers.

I tug at my necklace.

Australian Darren clears his throat.

I take a deep breath and proceed under the sign past the raised black and white boom gate. Seven steps down the gravel road and my heart hammers under my ribs. The imposing barbed wire fences at my sides and guard post towers looming at regular intervals are terrifying.

We enter the red brick buildings.

Pre-war, they were Polish Army barracks.

In 1940, Auschwitz was established to hold Polish political prisoners.

Then it evolved into a concentration and extermination camp.

The thirty prison blocks that survive today house the museum.

I steel my shoulders and take a step forward because it's time to pay my respects.

The six of us disperse to different areas of the museum to take it in at our own pace. I wander down the hallway to the block dedicated to the heroes who risked their lives to help people in the camp and get news to the outside world. I examine each face in the black and white photographs on the wall. Men. Women. Young. Old. I study the lines around their eyes. The tips of their chins. Their looks of sheer determination. So much more than ordinary; they were brave, fierce, and heroic.

I move to the next block holding the prisoners' personal items.

My steps falter as I pass through room after room of round wire glasses, simple combs, hairbrushes, and shoes, all stacked to the ceiling behind glass walls.

My chest throbs as I ghost my fingers across the glass.

Shoes. Small, heeled, men's ... so, so, so many. They would fill an Olympic-sized swimming pool, and these are *only* the ones the Nazis didn't have time to destroy.

Tears pool in my eyes as I enter the room holding suitcases. Rectangular and black, all stacked on top of each other, five deep. Gold monogrammed names and hometowns: Vienna, Warsaw, Prague, Hamburg. The list is endless.

The six of us meet at the exit of the museum. No words are shared as we make our way down the long street into the concentration camp.

My feet drag over the rough cement floor of the reconstructed gas chamber.

My stomach pitches as gloom slithers over my skin at the sight of the red brick ovens with open heavy black iron doors they used to dispose of the bodies.

I rub my arms to abate my prickling skin.

It doesn't help.

We walk three kilometers to Birkenau.

Birkenau is one hundred and seventy-five hectares, purpose-built, and *efficient* (word from fact sheet). It had over three hundred prisoner barracks and held up to 200,000 people at one time. It *boasted* (another word from the fact sheet) four gas chambers that accommodated 2,000 people at a time with electric lifts to raise the bodies into the ovens—so no one had to get their hands dirty (not in the fact sheet).

We follow the overgrown train tracks through the gate.

The tracks end in the middle of the camp.

I shiver as I stand at the selection site, and it's 30°C outside.

Long lines of meshed barbed wire and watchtowers

stretching nearly as far as my eye can see cage the rows and rows of identical barracks. The long wooden structures are surrounded by tall green grass interwoven with yellow, purple, and white wildflowers swaying in the light summer breeze.

I break off from the group and enter one of the barracks. A slice of sunlight spills through the uninsulated wooden wall slats. God, it must have been freezing in here in the winter. I glide my hand over the rough three-level-high sleep platforms and hiss as a sharp edge pierces my index finger. I pluck the sliver as anger churns in my gut. I wouldn't use these shacks to store *anything*, and this is where they slept?

I spin to exit but stop in my tracks at the sight of a black spider the size of a large coin resting on his intricate web over a small window above a high bunk. Dust particles float around him in the sunlight. I hate spiders, but there's something about this one and his defined web that's calming and safe.

Goosebumps pebble my skin.

It's because no one lives here anymore but him.

Back outside in the direct sunshine, I tug on my sweater because I can't shake the chill I've had since I entered the camp. I walk over to the ruins of one of the four gas chambers. At the stairway, I look down at the messy pile of blasted bricks. Five meters behind me is the barbed wire fence leading to the outside world.

I lean over and grip my thighs as sour saliva surges in my mouth. God, I think I'm going to be sick. No amount of mental preparation could have equipped me for these stifling emotions.

I close my eyes and focus on the good to unburden some of the heaviness in my chest: the new friends I met this morning, wildflowers tilting on the breeze, and the undisturbed spider. I send my love, hope for peace, and respect to the victims and survivors. And my promise that I'll never forget.

SO MANY PEOPLE HAVE EMAIL THESE DAYS - KRAKÓW, POLAND

My eyes widen at the sight of a familiar, short balding guy chatting to a pale, brown-haired girl at the bus depot in Oświęcim.

"Simon!" I scream as my sandals slap against the pavement. I sink into his open arms, ecstatic to see his kind face after this grim day. "We missed you at the rendezvous at the restaurant on Tuesday."

"I went on Monday," he says.

I frown as I step back. That was the day we got the news about Katrine, and I was in no shape to go anywhere but bed.

"I figured you weren't in town so I didn't go back." He shrugs. "And the food was marginal and expensive."

My stomach sinks. I thought we'd made a real friend connection with Simon. And I'm disappointed he broke his promise and didn't make the effort to swing by the rendezvous location on the second night to check if we were there.

"It's good to see you, mate." Dejah slides in for a Simon hug.

"You too." Simon gestures to the plain girl at his side. "This is my friend Carol from England."

There are murmurs and handshakes all around as we introduce Patrick Thin Hands, Australian Darren, Chino Garth, and Smiley Sam. A pang of dejection clinks in my chest as I shake hands with Plain Carol. Not that Simon owes us anything, and we're here with other people too, but she makes me feel easily replaced. I grip the straps on my daypack and move to the side of the group. It's great to see Simon again and I'll gladly hang out with him, but his lack of dependability when I pegged him as safe and reliable stings.

My mind's a chaotic mess as we board the bus. I don't know where to begin to process this day. And the swirl of black anxiety that was leaking off the crowd on our journey here has morphed into melancholy that pulses under my skin and swells in my gut. I rest my head against the window. A blur of green fields passes by as the blue sky turns to dusk. The two-hour trip is over in the blink of an eye, and I'm still a mess.

"I scouted a great underground bar last night. Who's up for a drink?" Chino Garth asks as we loiter outside the bus in Kraków.

Everyone's in. No one wants to be alone. And now we're a team of eight.

Chino Garth jogs down the worn stone switchback steps at an unnamed bar not far off the town square. The two mighty candles propped on iron candlesticks flanking the landing are taller than Dejah. The wicks flicker, liberally dripping onto the cumulative layers of colorful wax heaped on the limestone floor. A hallway lined with medieval metal armor suits leads to a smoky room with barrel ceilings and red brick walls. High brassy notes of a trumpet and a soulful voice singing in Polish quiet my sadness and release some of the tension riding my shoulders.

Plain Carol leads us to an empty long wooden table that seats about twelve. Our group lines the benches, and purple banknotes are tossed in a pile from each pocket. I reach into my daypack as Simon orders four pitchers of beer from the server. I pull out a deck of cards and hold it up. It's met with collective sighs and nods—everyone keen for a conversation distraction.

"Before we start," I say as I shuffle the cards, "does anyone know Right Said Fred's other song? The one after 'I'm Too Sexy'? We saw a sign for a gig they were doing in Estonia, but we can't remember what his other song was."

"Aw, I know it …" Chino Garth snaps his fingers. "It's …" He shakes his head. "Damn, this is going to bug me. I'll email a friend who'll know for sure."

"Great. Let us know if you figure it out." I smooth a crumpled receipt from my pocket, jot down my email address, and slide it to Chino Garth. "Does anyone else want to swap emails?"

Simon and Australian Darren have emails along with Chino Garth to share, and I exchange home addresses with the others.

The server drops the pitchers on the table. Simon and Plain Carol pass out the drinks as Patrick Thin Hands reaches for the cards and separates the deck into two piles.

"I'm going to Australia in a few weeks," Chino Garth says to Dejah and Darren. "Any tips?"

"I'm going to send my friend Desy a *treat*," Dejah whispers.

What? I mouth.

She swings her eyes to Chino Garth.

"Oh." He's not my type, but Dejah's beaming smile says he'll be Desy's.

"Garth, here's my friend's phone number. I know she would *love* to show you around Sydney." Dejah slides him the details.

He pockets the information and promises to reach out.

"What are we playing, Patrick?" It takes everything in me not to say *Thin Hands* after his name.

"Threes." He places one of the two piles of cards to the side. "We'll only use one to six cards of each suit. If you draw a three, you drink. If you draw a six, the person to the right drinks. A two is a social—everyone drinks. You get to make a rule if you draw a five. If you draw a four or a one, you get a pass."

"I don't understand." Smiley Sam's eyelashes flicker.

"Let's just play, you'll pick it up. I'll go first." Patrick Thin Hands flips over the two of spades. "Social."

We all reach for our glasses, and laughter floats around the table. I love this. Easy camaraderie and quick friendships are what make backpacking so special.

"Five," Plain Carol says after she draws a card. "My rule is no pointing."

Dang, I hate that rule. I clutch my fingers to resist my sudden urge to point.

Australian Darren draws a three and drains his glass.

"We're going to need more," I say as I fill Darren's pint, emptying a pitcher.

"On it." Chino Garth signals the server.

This light fun is just what we need after our heavy day. I have no idea when I'll process the depth of evil that slithered around that place. But what I do know is the more people, the better to support *the after*.

My spine twitches and the hairs rise on the back of my neck. I worry about asking for help with getting out from under my grief. But maybe I don't need to ask. Because out here on the road, support and friendship is given freely by the people I meet and choose to spend my time with.

Could my recovery be that simple?

"Social," Smiley Sam says as he raises his glass.

My chest fills with warmth as I grab my pint. I don't know if these new easy connections and the way I'm living my life is my grief solution, if it will be enough, or if anything will ever be enough.

But right at this moment, I'm so very glad for my chosen crew.

IT'S A SUNNY, warm day, so Dejah and I hit Kraków hard on the sightseeing front. We traipse through the winding streets in the Jewish Quarter, visit the museum packed with paintings, prints, and sculptures at the Renaissance Wawel Royal Castle on the top of a limestone hill, then climb down into the rocky Dragon's Den under Castle Hill.

Ready for a break from the heat, we return to the Internet café where I got the bad news about Vasilii's mom just days ago. We leave tomorrow for the Tatra Mountains in southern Poland, and we doubt there'll be email in the small town of Zakopane, so we need to get our time online while we can.

My throat dries as my email loads. Nothing from Vasilii, but Josh's new note is like a beacon in my inbox. This is what I've been waiting for, his reply to my second chance email I sent from

Pit Sweat's computer shop in Gdańsk. I hold my breath and click on his note.

I miss you; I want to meet you in Prague, and I'll try to do whatever it takes to make this work.

    Josh xo

My stomach swirls as I flip him a one-liner saying I hope he can make it because I would love to see him. I dig my fingernails in my palms to tamper my trip down excitement lane. I have zero idea where he is, and nothing is anything until it's right in front of me. So I can't get my hopes up because my fragile heart will be in tatters if I count on seeing him, and he doesn't do whatever it takes to get to Prague.

I sigh and open a new note, adding Simon, Chino Garth, and Australian Darren from last night to my group list. My 'To' list wraps around six lines. Holy cow, who would have thought so many people are using email these days? And check me out, I have *forty* friends and family who do. My fingers fly over the keyboard as I compose a new note. Next thing you know, everyone will have an email.

I scoff—what an outrageous notion.

From: Candace

   To: My Friends

  Date: July 30, 1998

Subject: Kraków is Wonderful

We've been in Poland since my last email. After Warsaw, we headed south to a beautiful small town near the Ukraine border called Zamość. It's steeped in tragic history as Hitler planned for it to become the eastern point for the 3rd Reich.

After a rocky bus trip, we arrived in Kraków. There's loads to see here, a castle, salt mine, endless cobblestone streets but best of all is the grandest town square yet. And on my first visit, I noticed the St. Mary's church has different spires out front. In 1200-something two brothers were commissioned to each build a tower in front of the church facing the square. One brother rushed and the other took his time. The one who took his time produced the better tower. So, Rushing Brother killed Take His Time Brother in a fit of jealousy. Rushing Brother later stabbed himself in the heart and fell from the top of the shorter tower. Could be true or a cautionary tale, either way, all the best town squares have a gory story.

And now for the heavy. Yesterday, we visited Auschwitz and Birkenau.

The Museum in Auschwitz is set up in the original buildings. There are rooms and rooms of prisoner personal items but what stuck with me was the hair. There were still piles and piles, even after they used it to line Nazi uniforms for warmth. I can't imagine how much there was to begin with. The last building in the museum is the Death Block. The punishment cell is one yard, by one yard, by two yards. After hard labor during the day, they put four people inside to stand, with no light, no air, and no food, all night. On average most people only lasted ten days.

We walked three kilometers to Birkenau. I stood at the place where they made the selection. Here they had four gas chambers with connecting crematoriums. The Nazis blew up three when they realized they were going to lose the war. The last one they kept going right up until the Russians came. One man I was with said, "They blew up the crematoriums, they had to know what they were doing was wrong, or why else would they do that?" With the sun shining, colorful wildflowers, and long grass bending on the breeze between the endless prisoner barracks, it's hard to conceive the horrors that took place at Birkenau. But I could feel it. It was 30°C and I wore a sweater as I couldn't shake my bone-deep chill. It's hard to say anything else after that so I'll end here.

Candace xoxo

CHAPTER 5
PRAGUE STUNNER

FRIDAY, July 31, 1998

YELLOW BUTTERFLY - ZAKOPANE, POLAND

I curl into my sleeping bag as beams of early morning light sneak past the flimsy dorm room curtains. I press the palms of my hands into my eyes as my chest explodes with anguish.

It's here. The fourth anniversary of my mom's death.

The crackling and popping of a plastic bag echoes in the still room.

"Bloody hell," Dejah grumbles.

The rustling continues as she searches for something in Hulk. The man in the bed above mine punches his pillow, and the bunk jiggles as he rolls toward the wall, while the lady on the bed beside Dejah tosses her arm over her ear.

"There's one in every dorm room," I whisper as a small smile tips my lips.

I take a deep breath, so grateful for Dejah's crinkly distraction, then crawl out of my cocoon because today we leave the convent.

Barney jars my spine with each step, but I'm thankful for the forty-minute trek through the quiet streets to the bus station to sort through my busy mind. We've spent most of our time since we started this trip dodging harassment, avoiding rain, and finding food with some sights in between. It's been exhausting, yet we've managed. But I don't know how to manage this annual torment.

"How many years is it going to take for this to stop being my most hated day?" My neck cracks as I tip it from side to side while we wait for the traffic light to change.

"No idea. But I'm here for ya," she vows as we cross the street.

"Thanks." Because this day blows, and I need all the help I can get.

We board the eight o'clock bus for Zakopane — *the* tourist destination in Poland, known best for hiking, skiing, and crystal clear postglacial lakes. And the perfect distraction for my limping heart. Dejah and I lean into each other and sleep for the hour's drive south to the promise of a mountain oasis.

The Zakopane bus station brims with expectation and excitement as folks bustle past wearing carefree holiday smiles. More smiles than I've seen all trip. Polish, German, French, and other shooshy words are spoken. A large circular information desk is smack in the middle of the station. Maps, shopping, and hiking information pamphlets are lined up in plastic display cases by language.

"They have English." My eyes widen at the sight of my native tongue on a colorful folded paper, something we haven't seen since *Klaipėda in Your Pocket*. I pluck a town map and information on hiking trails as the tourist woman smiles. *Smiles.* We haven't had a smile from someone at an information booth —ever.

"The youth hostel's not far," Dejah says as we exit the station.

Sweet mountain air fills my lungs. Clean sidewalks glisten in the sun. Brown flower boxes burst with pink pansies and yellow marigolds. And the rocky peaked Tatra Mountains jut into the sapphire sky behind yellow chalet-style buildings.

"Wow." My jaw drops.

"I've a good feeling about this place," Dejah says.

"Me, too." This *is* the ideal distraction for my worst day of the year.

We traipse across the worn green carpet to the cherry-stained log check-in desk at the hostel. We can't view the dorm rooms as they have a lock-out, but we figure it'll be decent because of the town's popularity. Besides, it can't be any worse than Gdańsk. We pay for three nights, put Barney and Hulk in their storage lockers, then hit the town.

The bi-fold brochure from the bus station recommends a tram ride up the mountain, so that's where we start. The door slides shut on the tiny red box car, and my back presses against the seat as we zoom off. The sweeping view of the tipped roofs of Zakopane with the majestic gray Tatra Mountains gets more breathtaking as we climb higher along the wire toward the top of Gubałówka.

We exit the stuffy tram steps away from an outdoor market. Bright crocheted blankets, small paintings of the mountains, postcards, and other handicrafts are displayed at stalls around the perimeter of the flat area at the top of the mountain. Loads of people are milling from table to table enjoying the sunny afternoon. The smell of corn draws us to the food stalls on the other side of the bazaar. We each get corn on the cob, park on a bench, and soak in the lively atmosphere.

Past the market, there's a line of people waiting for a turn on the nine-hundred-meter shiny silver toboggan run built into the mountain. It's like a water slide and a luge had a baby but without water or ice; this is ten loopy turns down smooth concave metal riding a plastic sled.

"We've got to do that," I say as I toss my cob in the trash and wipe the butter from my sticky fingers.

"We really don't." Dejah shakes her head.

"Come on, you love these things." I rub my palms together.

"Only for you," she says as we join the short line.

Ahead of us is a nun dressed in a black habit, with thick slouchy wool socks and white sneakers. I'm roasting in shorts, a T-shirt, and sandals, but her face isn't even shiny. She hops into the red sled, and her smile's blinding as she takes off. Her habit flaps in the wind like a superhero cape as she peels around corners. She's fabulous. My first nun experience in Kraków was a chilly one. But this lady brings the fun to nun.

Our turn.

Dejah and I pile in the same sled. I'm in front, in charge of the combined steering and brake. Inspired by Fun Nun, I ignore the brakes. I squeal, and my hair whips in front of my eyes as we take a corner way too fast. Dejah's laughter fills my ears. With each turn, the wind blows away the heaviness in my shoulders. My body jolts as we screech to a stop way too soon. The attendant snaps a T-bar to the front of the sled, and it drags us to the starting point.

My mom would have loved this. She made everything fun. Even the worst chores were an adventure. We never went without growing up, but there was never spare cash left at the end of the month, so we had to cut corners where we could. We had cords of wood delivered to the house for the fireplace, but we would 'source' our kindling. And our source was the nearby construction site.

Early Saturday morning, she would tell us to pull on our old clothes. My brother Kev and I would race upstairs shedding our superhero Underoos for flood jeans, then leap into the back of her yellow and veneer-brown station wagon next to an empty cardboard box. Five other neighborhood kids would catch wind of my mom and the box and rush over in their old clothes too, knowing good times were ahead.

We would sing along with Dolly Parton blaring from the cassette deck in her Vega. Then we'd pick through the off-cuts of two-by-fours lying on the dirt in front of the half-built houses.

Everyone would have at least one splinter by the time the box was full, but it didn't stop us from searching for treasures in the debris. An oddly bent nail, a long screw, a cool box, my mom would *ooh* and *ahh* over every find. One time I hit pay dirt and found a yellow water capsule that must have fallen out of someone's level. I put my prize on the shelf next to my coveted doll collection. So yeah, she would have gotten a kick out of this day, and I know for sure she wouldn't have used the brake on her sled either.

It takes a lot not to spin and sing "The Sound of Music" as we traverse across the Gubałówka ridge. Maybe Julie was on to something when she sang about how the mountains were her place to go when her heart was lonely. Because the soaring peaks all around us make me feel protected and safe. One thing we have that Julie didn't are rows upon rows of eight-foot-tall haystacks. The stacks are shaped like bullets, neatly lined and spaced like lamp posts.

"How do they not blow away?" I ask as I snap a photo of the loose hay mounds.

"No idea." Dejah shrugs.

I gasp as a little yellow butterfly sweeps down the slope of the hay and flutters in front of my face. My insides warm as I reach out to touch it. But it dances just out of reach.

"Your mom's here." Khadejah stands at my side as it disappears behind a haystack.

"She is." This really is the perfect place to be today. "Look what I brought." I pull the blue Frisbee we bought in Hel from my bag.

"Only you." She jogs ahead, holding out her hands, ready for a pass.

The blue disk spins in the air and lands nowhere near her. We miss more than we catch and spend most of our time scrambling through the haystacks after the damn thing, but we laugh. People throw wide-eyed looks at us as they hike past. But I don't care. I'm so over worrying about what people think. It's tiring, and I'm tired enough. I need to *just do* to feel alive again. So I'm going to play frisbee on the edge of the mountain and do whatever the heck else makes me happy.

I swing my feet as we ride the rickety two-seater Butorowy Wierch chairlift to the base of the mountain, then merrily hike forty-five minutes back to the hostel. Lockout's over, so we collect our bags from storage and find our dorm room.

I freeze in the doorway. My nose burns at the pungent, rotting smell of mildew. I breathe through my mouth like Darth Vader, and rush to the one window. The wood frame around the glass creaks as I shove it open. But there's not one whisper of air to dissipate the smell. The bunks are pushed together, making every top and bottom bed into a double. I'm glad I have Dejah; it would suck sleeping next to some random.

"I thought Gdańsk was bad. But this is worse than the smelly room in Pärnu." I sigh as I place my fists on my hips.

"So foul. Our beds are over here." Dejah places her hand on our assigned mattresses in the center of the room. She flinches and takes a step back.

"What is it?" I groan.

"Best to feel for yourself." She shudders.

Wetness floats to the surface as my fingertips press into the small space without dark stains. "What the hell?" I yank my hand away. "It's like someone poured a bucket of water on it."

Ten people trickle into the room. Slack-jawed, they go through the same routine with the same result. It must be everyone's first night by the look of horror on their faces.

"So where are you staying tomorrow night?" the petite brunette Aussie in the bunks above us asks.

"Not here," Dejah says.

I hang my head. Death day started in a swirl of sorrow, had a great middle in the mountains, and is ending on a wet mattress. But at least it's over.

CURLER COMMANDO - ZAKOPANE, POLAND

Dejah's raspy cough wakes me the next morning. The right side of my body pressed to the mattress is damp. But so is my stomach. I hiss as my fingers slide over the slick, hot, bumpy ring around my belly button.

"*NO.*" Under my soaked T-shirt is a seeping red bullseye. "I have cellulitis—again."

I jump out of bed and rummage through Barney for my medical kit. I frown as I rattle the bottle of diminishing red and white antibiotics. I have two remaining treatments with a lot of road left to travel. I hate using the drugs for something small like this, but it won't get better without it.

"Maybe you should take the ring out." Dejah rubs her bloodshot eyes.

"Bite your tongue." I'm not taking it out. Ever. "We gotta get out of here."

"No shit, Sherlock." She blows her nose.

I pop a capsule. Then we pack.

I hang back with the bags while Dejah argues with the front desk lady. She's fired up and manages to get a partial refund on the nights we paid for in advance.

"They should pay us not to blab all over Europe about this shit show," she says as she stomps out of the hostel toward town.

The clean and bright tourist office has even more information than the bus station. And bonus, the blond lady with sharp cheekbones behind the counter speaks perfect English. Cheekbones picks up the heavy black receiver off the rotary phone, dials a private establishment, and yapping in Polish, secures us a room for two nights a block away.

Fir trees shade our walk with the Tatra Mountains lining the treetops like a movie set backdrop. My boots crunch along the flat gravel path, startling a red squirrel. His floofy auburn tail twitches as he races up a rough trunk. This walk is stunning, but it's hard to enjoy because my belly button itches like first-day chickenpox blisters.

The trees open to a clearing with a simple, rectangular, flat-roofed two-story home surrounded by emerald green grass. Three concrete stairs lead to the one large door at the long end of the building facing the pathway. On the landing is a compact woman in bright orange pants with three rows of curlers tightly containing every gray hair on her head.

She shouts something in Polish and waves us inside. She's old but fast. I hoof it to keep up with her to the upper level. The second-floor hallway runs down the middle of the rectangle with a window at each end and four closed doors on either side. Curlers opens the first door on the left and scurries inside.

Clean, dry air fills my lungs, and I smile. Cheekbones did us a solid. It's like the inside of a Keebler Elf tree with unfinished pine wood paneling on the walls, floors, and ceilings. It has two single beds on opposite walls, a closet, a tiny desk and chair, and a Juliet balcony overlooking the mountains. *And* it only costs sixty złotys a night—about eleven dollars each.

"Nice and cheap," I say as I drop Barney on the floor.

"I reckon we should stay three nights instead of two," Khadejah says.

"Totally. I'll ask."

I wave at Curlers, point to the room, count out *two* using my thumb and index finger on my left hand. I do a dramatic circular motion with my right hand then pop a third finger on my left —tapping it with my right finger.

Curlers' forehead creases as she grumbles under her breath. Then she nods and holds up three fingers. We give her our identification and one hundred and eighty złotys. She mumbles something, then leaves with our passports and cash.

"I'm going to shower and wash a few bits." Khadejah digs through Hulk.

"Cool, I'll go after," I say as she heads off to the communal bathroom across the hall with an armful of socks and underwear.

I unzip Barney and frown at the waft of bitter mildew clinging to my clothes. They're damp from being *inside* him at the shit-hole hostel. It's gutting after the hassle we went through in Kraków on laundry day. I pile the worst impacted stuff, two T-shirts, my green pants, and three pairs of underwear on the floor to bring with me when I shower. I strew the rest around the room to dry out and am hanging my sleeping bag over the balcony when the door wooshes open.

"How was—" My head rears back.

It's not Dejah. Curlers strides inside with our passports and jingling keys.

She didn't knock.

Khadejah—hair dripping and carrying an armful of wet clothes—bumps into her as she enters. Curlers' eyes bulge and screechy screams fly out of her mouth as her tiny fists punch Dejah's dripping socks.

I wrinkle my nose as Curlers storms out, slamming the door.

"Guess she's not keen on hand washing." Dejah shrugs.

"Too bad for her." I risk Curlers' wrath and sneak out with my contraband laundry.

Every inch of the bathroom is covered in spotless powder blue tiles—floor, walls, and ceiling. There's no shower curtain, just a shower head on one side and a sink on the other. I crank the circular shower handle and sigh as hot water rushes out. I pop the shampoo bottle and scrub my clothes and body—leaving my hair for later. Despite Curlers' yelling and waltzing into our room unannounced, this place is a thousand times better than the hostel.

Finally, we got it right.

———

I TUCK my hands in my shorts pockets as we step onto the main pedestrian street in search of phone booths to call home. Wooden gingerbread buildings with scalloped white trim house the restaurants and touristy shops along the main cobblestone strip.

This town is delivering on all it promised to be, but something is … off.

With me.

Each step is work, and it's taking everything I have not to burst into tears.

Death day has wrung me out, and the aftermath has stirred up my ugly insecurities. Namely my go-to hot button: what happens when this is over and my bank accounts are drained? If I fail to secure a job, I'll have to live in the death house. I'll be an unemployed, almost middle-aged spinster living with my dad and a ratty purple backpack.

"There." Dejah slants her chin to three glass hexagon phone booths past a pizza restaurant.

I rush inside the center one, then pinch the yellow phone receiver between my ear and shoulder. I punch in the numbers to reach Montreal, confident my dad will have sage advice to shake off my worries. At the very least, he'll be able to commiserate on death day.

"Hi, Can."

I close my eyes and sigh, so happy to hear his voice.

"Where are you today?" he asks.

I tell him about Poland. He makes idle chat about the weather and his work.

"Dad?" I trace the numbers around the keypad with my index finger. "Do you think I'm doing the right thing? Being here, traveling, and not being at home working?"

Please have words of wisdom, please have words of wisdom, I beg in my head.

"When I tell people what you're doing, they think it's great," he says.

Silence.

That's it.

Not *he* thinks it's great, or *you're living your dream*, or *where's this coming from?*

"Okay," I whisper and rest my head against the phone booth wall.

"I guess we're all done here. It was good to talk. I love you." He hangs up.

The buzz of our disconnection drones in my ear. That's all he has for me. No insight. And no mention of Mom's death anniversary. My heavy heart wilts. He forgot. Or avoided the topic—since we never talk about it.

I fling the door open and bite back a scream.

"Pizza?" Dejah asks as she glides out of her phone booth.

"Sure." I spin my back to her because her blinding smile churns the self-pity chewing up my insides.

We pull out chairs on the patio of the nearby restaurant and order a large pepperoni and two Diet Cokes. My foot taps under the table as Dejah raves about her phone call: how much her mum supports her and is proud of her, how her brother's doing in school, what her mum's making for dinner, and how much she misses her. I'm happy for her, but I'm so freaking jealous I can barely see straight. Because she got everything I wanted in her call home.

The server delivers an eight-slice pizza that takes up most of our table. Heat swirls off the slice I jam in my mouth. I snarl as the bland bite hits my tongue. I drop it on my plate and chug Diet Coke to clear my throat.

"That's terrible." I push it away. "This is the worst. Pizza is always supposed to be kind of good."

"I can usually eat anything, but not this." Dejah plucks a pepperoni off her barely touched slice.

A boy whose head just clears the top of our table thrusts his hand out and says something in Polish. He wants money. Dejah shakes her head. His scruffy sneakers kick the ground as he rubs grubby fingers down his red shorts. He points to the pizza. Blue eyes bulge as I place a slice in his outstretched palms that extends down his forearms. He vibrates with excitement then chomps off a massive chunk. Pizza sauce smearing his cheek, he grins, takes another bite, and skips away.

"For a reaction like that, we should have given him the whole pizza," Dejah chuckles.

"Yeah." I wince. "We should have."

Something I dismissed is a treat for him.

My eyes sting. I don't need my dad or anyone to tell me I'm doing what's best for me. I can do that myself. But on the days I'm drowning in doubts, I need a boost to get me back on track. And today it's a little boy in red shorts who lights up over a crappy slice of pizza reminding me how lucky I am to be sitting here in this beautiful mountain town, experiencing things I used to only dream about. So what if my time out here isn't progressing my career. It's progressing *me*. And I'll keep going —even if I end up a penniless freeloader when this trip is all said and done.

BACK IN OUR ROOM, I dump the remaining contents of Barney on the floor as Dejah changes out the roll of film in her 35mm camera. I stack spare travel books for the Middle East and Africa, organize my ticket stubs, and shake the dirt lodged in the seams of my bag. It's the first time I've done this since London, and it's like a spring clean reset.

"I'm going to ask for the handle," I say.

Curlers burst into our room clutching the circular shower tap like *my precious* after my shower this morning. Now, like naughty children, we need to ask for it if we want to shower.

"Good luck with that." Dejah scoffs as she grabs her journal.

I skip down the stairs to Curlers' door beside the main entrance. Before I can knock, the diminutive woman's door flings open.

"Shhhhh." I raise my hand above my head, fingers pointed down—imitating water.

Curlers huffs, slaps the handle in my palm, then slams the door.

I snag two dirty T-shirts and my shorts from our room, then spend ages figuring out how to re-attach the shower handle. I toss my clothes on the pristine tile floor and stomp on them like squashing grapes while I wash my hair. I smile at my ingenuity as I rinse and wring out the clothes.

I peek out the bathroom door. Blissfully empty. I trot across the hall in my towel and deposit my wet bundle on the desk.

Curlers pushes past me before the door closes.

I blink. Man, she's fast. Where did she come from?

Short gray hair bounces around her wrinkly face as she shouts. She snags my bicep in her freakishly strong grip and drags me —in my towel that barely covers my ass—to the bathroom. She kicks the door with her flowered slipper, then hollers and points at the water dripping down the blue tiled walls.

I sneer. It's a wet room without a curtain. It's going to get wet.

Her nails dig into my triceps as she stabs her finger at the few puddles on the floor still draining.

I'm done listening to this. I twist out of her hold and back away.

"Sorry," I say as I shut the door with her on the other side.

I jump back as the door swings open. Water drips off my hair onto the floor as she screams in Polish to Khadejah, who's lying on her bed biting back a smile. I roll my eyes—since she's not facing me—assuming she's ranting about the state of the wet bathroom or how long I took in the shower to Dejah.

Curlers tosses her arms in the air, then storms out.

"Mate, you're in *trou-ble*," Dejah chuckles as the door latches. "See if she gives you the shower handle again."

"She scared me half to death when she came out of nowhere

like a freaking ninja." I slump on my bed and dip my toe in my hair drip puddle.

"A ninja until she opens her mouth." Dejah cackles. "You know, I reckon Curlers isn't enough. We need to change her name to Curler Commando."

"Way better than Curler Ninja," I say as I hang out my contraband laundry.

Curler Commando hums Mendelssohn's "Wedding March" as she waltzes into our room—without knocking, again— carrying two wine glasses a short while later. My shoulders fall as I stare at the lock we forgot to twist on the door handle. Keys jingle in her green apron pocket as she thrusts the tall red beverages in our hands. I sigh. It didn't matter if we locked the door or not; she was coming in.

The sharp smell of fermenting fruit stings my nostrils as orange slices bob in the glass. "A wedding drink peace offering?" I ask Dejah through a fake smile.

"Or poison," Dejah mumbles.

Curler Commando settles on the wooden chair by the desk and flicks her hands for us to drink. I take a sip, and my eyes water at the salty bitterness. Not poison but not sweet sangria either.

"Thank you." I tip the glass toward her.

"Disco?" Curler Commando twirls her finger on her palm.

"Uh, no." Dejah shakes her head.

Curler Commando's face falls.

"I think she's disappointed we're not going out," I say.

Heavy silence hangs in the air as we stare at each other.

Curler Commando leaps up and murmurs soft Polish words as she gives us each a hug *and* a kiss on the cheek before departing.

"This lady needs to choose a lane." I place my full wine glass on the desk and drag the chair in front of the door. It won't stop her, but she won't be able to surprise us.

"Reckon she'll come back?" Dejah deposits her glass next to mine.

"I hope not." I sit cross-legged on my bed and shiver. "I was getting teenage flashbacks of my mom busting into my room without knocking."

"My mom always knocked." Dejah shrugs.

"Lucky you." For as awesome as my mom was, she wasn't perfect. Not big on privacy and a guilt trip expert with a hot temper was the Yin to her fun Yang.

"How can we get rid of the drinks without her noticing?" Dejah lies on her bed.

"We'll put them in my water bottle and dump it in town," I say.

"Nice one." Dejah smiles. "Reckon there's a disco here we missed?"

"Hardly. She was just trying to make nice for screaming about the bathroom."

I suck in a breath. Oh my God, Curler Commando's just like my mother. Up in our business, coming in without knocking, yelling at us one minute then cozying up the next like nothing happened. Turns out I didn't need to commiserate with my dad about missing my mom because her Yin doppelganger lives downstairs.

I giggle as I climb under the covers. Curler Commando will have to find someone else to holler at tomorrow because we'll be out enjoying a highly recommended cruise along the river border between Poland and Slovakia.

I fluff my pillow—one perfect day coming up.

MODERN TALKING - DUNAJEC RIVER GORGE, POLAND

I dump the fruit and salty wine in the trees behind the station, then fill my Nalgene bottle at the tap near the bus stop. Sweat drips down my face as I slump into a seat beside Dejah on the packed bus. It's already a thousand degrees outside, the windows don't open, and there's no air conditioning. Excited foreign chatter bubbles around us. The driver says something over the crackling speaker in Polish as he navigates the long vehicle on narrow roads through the mountains.

"I expect he's talking about the stops on the tour." I sit statue-still to not create more heat.

"Who knows?" Dejah rests her head against the window.

We booked this tour the same day we got the room at Curler Commando's because Cheekbones from the tourist office said the must-see Pieniny mountain range is best experienced from a raft. So we're here for the one-way Dunajec River Gorge trip, but since there's no English translation, and we never asked at the tourist office, we have no idea how many sites we'll visit before we get there.

Our ride screeches to a stop in Dębno, which according to my travel guide boasts one of the best timber Gothic churches in Poland. The medieval church resembles an old cottage with a steep gray roof encircled by a wooden fence and high trees. Like in Zamość, there are loudspeakers out front, and the congregation is spilling out the broad wooden doors onto the grass. Everyone files off the bus to take a photo. We can't get near it. I snap a shot from a distance, with little hope it'll come out.

Next, we visit a house with a stork's nest on the roof holding two squawking chicks. I grin. I've never seen a stork before in my life, and this is my second sighting in a week. Gnarly twigs are woven tightly together in a circle, keeping them snug in place. Mama stork swoops out of the cloudless blue sky, landing in the nest with her long orange beak full of food for her babies. My camera clicks as she drops lunch in one chick's open mouth.

We stop at some ruins. Dejah and I loiter and smoke behind the group as the driver yaps in Polish while pointing at a crumbling wall of dark stones. I return to the bus without wasting my film.

At the next stop, people shove and surge to the front.

"This must be where the boat trip starts." My teeth rattle as I'm elbowed by a family rushing down the aisle.

"What gave that away?" Dejah huffs as two blue-rinse grannies shoulder-check past.

We're herded behind the pushy masses down a switchback gravel path leading to the raft loading station. This is it, the extraordinary boat trip we've been waiting for, cruising through the three-hundred-meter-high rock walls dividing Poland and Slovakia.

"What?" I stop in my tracks on the bank of the dark green river.

Dejah cackles and slaps her thigh.

There's barely a ripple on the surface of the shallow water. This is good because the endless parade of identical boats snaking down the river and the fleet behind us waiting to be filled barely look seaworthy.

"This is like a bad amusement park ride," I say.

A man straddles the rocky shore and a dodgy flat rectangular wooden raft—akin to Tom Sawyer's. Straddling Man reaches out to help passengers from our bus board and lines everyone up on the flat wooden benches precariously perched on the wobbly boat base. The long sleeves of Straddling Man's white shirt are rolled up to his elbow, and there's zero chance his embroidered, white-flowered blue vest will close over his enormous belly. Sweat runs down the back of his neck under his wide-brimmed felt black hat as he lifts the two blue-rinse grannies from the shore onto the boat.

We're next, securing the last two seats on the edge of a row of six.

Once the thirty seats are full, we're only millimeters above the waterline.

"I'm sure if we add one more person we'll sink," I say, as Straddling Man picks up a long black pole and stands at the back of the raft.

"We can swim if we need to." Dejah lifts one shoulder as he pushes us away from the shore like a gondola driver in Venice.

We travel at a snail's pace, flowing through the wide curves of the deep ravine. The green trees and rocky cliff face on the shores are stunning. But I'm melting. Side by side, skin to skin, with the boiling mid-day sun beating down on us is killer. My bra and underwear are soaked with sweat. Straddling Man rips off the vest, his carpet of black chest hair visible through his now transparent white shirt.

"Having fun yet?" I curl my nose at sweaty Straddling Man.

"It's riveting." Dejah fans her face because there's not a breath of wind.

The puffs and grunts of Straddling Man sound painful as he propels us down the river. People along the shore dip their feet in the water, but no one swims since it's prohibited in the National Park.

"My ass is killing." I shift on the wooden slat seats.

"Yeah." She rolls her eyes. "So relaxing."

I snort, then covertly dip my hand in the river and hiss as the icy water shocks my sweltering skin.

We disembark in Szczawnica two hours later. The only route to the bus is a ten-minute shuffle through a pathway lined with shopping stalls. Pushy vendors shout in Polish as they rattle key chains, itchy T-shirts, and postcards under our noses. I lean into Dejah. This is not the day of dreams I anticipated when Cheekbones raved about it.

The bus door slides closed, locking us inside the sweltering metal tube. I cover my nose with the back of my hand as fifty passenger funks unite like a rank blanket. The driver slides in a cassette and hits the gas, layering the smell of diesel on top of body odor.

My shoulders sag as kitschy Europop disco blares through the speakers. The passengers cheer when "Cheri Cheri Lady" by Modern Talking cues up. My mouth gapes as everyone bar Dejah, myself, and the driver—only because the roads are twisty and he needs his hands on the wheel—partake in a rousing coordinated clapping routine to the song.

He rewinds the single.

"Kill me." I smack my head against the seat as the crowd whoops and claps three times to the whiny chorus.

"Reckon we can learn the routine?" Dejah asks.

"Pass." My skin hurts. I ran out of drinking water ages ago, and it tasted like sour wine. And I've sweat so much I've run out of that too. "I'm thirsty and grumpy *and* have no interest in figuring out the clapping routine when I would normally be all over that."

Just like the mud bath and the boat trip to Hel, we got sucked into something that was supposed to be great and wasn't. But we have to take a chance on recommendations because our only source of information is guidebooks, information offices, and word of mouth from other travelers.

"From now on, we need to ask way more questions before we commit to an excursion," I huff.

"If we can get past the language barrier." She passes me her water bottle.

"Ugh, stupid languages." I take a big drink. "But seriously, this day was lame."

Muddling through is our way out here, and we don't always win with our plans.

"Would you rather eat *the sandwich* than be here?" she asks as I pass her water back.

"No." I cringe. "But I would ride the boat *and* Austin for a do-over."

"Ditto." She frowns as the song starts again. "I reckon I'd root Keith as well if they'd turn off the bloody music."

"Not *the sandwich* level bad then." I giggle.

Tomorrow we're hiking to a beautiful lake, and it *will* be a better day. I have to believe it because we're bound to get it right at some point.

DAY IN THE CLOUDS - LAKE MORSKIE OKO, POLAND

The ancient bus grinds as it struggles to climb the steep Tatra Mountain roads to Polana Palenica, the closest stop to Lake Morskie Oko. Oppressive heat weighs on my skin as I step off the bus into the gravel parking lot. We're a dizzying 1,400 meters above sea level. Narrow pine trees thin out as they climb the steep rocky cliffs a further 1,000 meters into the brilliant morning sky. It's almost like I can reach out and ball the fluffy clouds overhead. My chest swells as I inhale the clean air.

This is *our* day. I can feel it in my bones.

"Motorized vehicles are prohibited past this point due to road erosion," Dejah reads from her *Let's Go!* "We can either take a horse carriage or hike to the lake."

"How far is it?" I study the gradual incline of the endless road.

"Nine kilometers." She grimaces. "Each way."

"Ugh. That's farther than I thought." I pinch my lips. "That incline is going to suck in this heat."

Hooves clack against the pavement as two black horses labor past with five girthy passengers relaxing in the cart they're pulling. I recoil. It's just past nine and their fur is already soaked with visible lines of sweat. I startle as the driver's whip cracks over the horse's ear.

"We're walking." I turn to Dejah.

"Yes, we are," she agrees.

Pine trees on either side of the road shade our walk.

"This is good for us after sitting on our butts all day yesterday," I say, already feeling the burn in my thighs.

"Speak for yourself." Dejah scoffs. "It was hard work sitting on that boat. My ass still hurts."

"I'm not surprised. It *is* quite flat." I chuckle as she flips me the bird. "What *was* really hard work was listening to the music on the bus."

"Nah, that was the punishment for using too much water at Curler Commando's," Dejah says.

"Bet she knows the clapping routine," I say as a warm breeze slides across my skin.

"She probably made it up." Dejah cackles.

"Over a nice glass of wedding wine." I smirk.

My hiking boots drag along the worn pavement in the center of the road.

"How are you feeling about Prague?" She takes a drink of her water, then pops it back in her daypack.

"I've read about how awesome it is and can't wait to see it." I blow out a breath and wipe my brow with the hem of my T-shirt.

"That's not what I meant." She narrows her eyes.

"I know." She's talking about Josh. My heart pounds at the mere possibility of seeing him in Prague. "I doubt he'll show." I have to keep telling myself that because my heart is barely hanging in there and can't deal with the crushing disappointment of him letting me down—again.

"What if he does?" she asks quietly.

"He won't." I blow out a breath. "But if—and that's a big if ... I'll see him."

I flex my shaky fingers as I walk.

Dejah turns her face away.

"Listen." I stop in the middle of the road as loathing burns in my gut for wanting to see him so badly after how horribly he ended things with me. "I'm not leaving you for him. Not happening. It's you and me going all the way to Cairo."

"You're sure?" Her eyes are wide.

"Positive." I hug her tightly.

We resume our hike.

I refuse to leave her *or* blow up our plans ... but that doesn't mean I'm not going to benefit from the full Josh experience if he shows.

"But I might go missing for a few nights in Prague." I shrug.

"I'll manage." She smiles.

"I know you will." I grin back.

It takes two hours to reach the pristine glacial lake bordered by the snow-capped jagged mountains. We find a shady spot next to the clear blue lake, take off our shoes, and sigh as we stealthily dip our feet in the icy water. I lie on the rocky shore and smile as I prop my hands behind my head. I have no idea what will happen with Josh, but I do know that brushing shoulders with the clouds makes for the perfect day trip we deserve.

DUŻY PROBLEM - ZAKOPANE, POLAND

My muscles ache in a most delicious way from hiking eighteen kilometers in the baking heat to the lake. But I smell like a teenage boy who's gone days without deodorant. I desperately need a shower, but Curler Commando is out and has re-confiscated the handle. I sneak downstairs to use the *other* shower, then spread out on my bed and write in my journal while Dejah uses the washroom.

"Duży problem," Curler Commando screams as she stomps in our room behind Dejah, whose hair is dripping down the back of her T-shirt from her shower.

"Oooooh, it's your turn to be in trouble." I smirk as I look up from my journal. "Legit *big* trouble since we learned from buying the frisbee in Hel, duży is big."

Dejah rolls her eyes as Curler Commando rants and paces between our beds.

She points to her watch. And to us. Then out the window.

"Did she expect us to be gone?" I wrinkle my nose.

"We paid for three nights and tonight is our third." Dejah holds up three fingers in Curler Commando's face and points around the room.

My shoulders tense as harsh words roll off Curler Commando's tongue. She's been mad before, but this time, anger is radiating from her. *And* it's not because we used the downstairs shower. She jabs her finger at me then Dejah, clenches her fist in the air then slams the door on the way out.

"How did we get our wires crossed so badly? We paid for three nights." I frown.

We joke around about her, but her lashing scorn smarts because it feels undeserved. But what makes my heart blue is that this interaction has clouded our perfect day. I sigh. It's always up, down. Up. Down. Up. Down.

"No more hugs and kisses for us." Dejah wraps her hair in her towel.

"Nope. She's chosen a lane. And it's the one that doesn't like us." I hop off the bed.

"I reckon there'll be no more wine." Dejah grins as she applies cream to her face.

"Thank gosh." We laugh as I unzip Barney to pack.

Expecting a perfect day is a lot to ask. Instead, I need to hang on to the perfect moments like we had at the lake. Then laugh and puzzle our way through the trying ones. Thankfully, the latter we do very well—otherwise, I would implode like Curler Commando. I can't wait to leave for fun Prague tomorrow morning, and you can bet your ass I'll be taking one very long shower before I do.

ENOUGH - KRAKÓW, POLAND

Squeaky clean, we escape Curler Commando's at the crack of dawn and roll into the Kraków bus station as the sun climbs over the city. We lumber to the train station, buy night tickets to Prague, and store our bags for the day.

"The flowered café with paninis is calling my name," I say as I shove Barney in a locker.

"I'll lead the way." Dejah opens to the map page in her book.

Cars roar past. My jaw tenses as we march down the busy sidewalks dodging pedestrians. This harried vibe is jarring after quiet Zakopane. I fist my hands, focusing on the goal: soft music, ice cubes, and crunchy sandwiches. And coffee. I need one of those.

"I can already taste it." My mouth waters.

"Maybe we can try a new sandwich. How about chicken this time?" Dejah taps her chin.

We cut through a park block. Birds sing happy tunes. The paved path is edged with grass and leafy beech trees. The air tastes fresher and my shoulders slacken.

An old man parked on a bench next to the walkway glares as we approach. His clothes are frayed, and wisps of greasy gray hair flop into his dirty face as he twists his stained fingers. His lips snarl as harsh Polish words roll out. My shoulders ache with deep fatigue from the ongoing vicious verbal harassment we receive at least twice a day. And not just from Curler Commando. Local men in small or big towns share their leers and jeers liberally.

"I genuinely think they feel it's their job to harass women tourists," I say as my eyes flick around the green space. No one else is around. It's only the three of us within earshot.

"Is it bad that I'm used to it?" Dejah lifts one shoulder.

"Used to it or not, it still sucks." I huff.

Old Man's rants gear up as we approach. At least it's daytime. Bile rolls in my gut because I know firsthand from the bus station in Lithuania that sunlight doesn't make anything safer. But I'm not alone today. Plus, Dejah has a sneaky side; between the two of us we can take him if he tries anything.

"Just ignore him." Dejah tips her nose and hastens her stride.

Deep loathing drips from Old Man's taunts as we pass in front of him.

"Kurwa," he sneers.

My body locks. That. *Word.* Slut, bitch, whore, all rolled into one. Rage bubbles in my blood because kurwa is how I felt after *the encounter* with the ticket agent in Vilnius.

I turn and narrow my eyes on his. Unlike on *that* day, I can control this moment. And even if it's just a word, I refuse to be a victim again. I lean into his space, sucking in the reek of his unwashed skin.

"I know what kurwa means." My voice is strong, forceful, and steady. "And you have *no right* to use that word on us, Old Man."

Foul breath hits my cheek as his mouth gapes, but I don't move away.

He drops his gaze and says nothing more.

"Weak asshole." I stomp out of the park.

"At least he wasn't wanking," Dejah says, chasing after me.

"Small mercies."

I need a cigarette and a panini. And I need to leave this country. I also need to dance, drink, and meet fun people. Josh or no. Prague better live up to the hype of being awesome. Because no amount of inside jokes will stop me from going into Curler Commando mode if it isn't.

TWO HOURS - PRAGUE, CZECH REPUBLIC

Bright and early, I traipse behind Dejah down a deserted street to a four-story sandstone building a short ten-minute walk from the Prague train station. The sun shimmering off the valanced rosettes over the symmetrical sash windows on the hostel is picture-perfect but all I care about is having a shower. The night train was heaving with passengers, and I ended up draped over Barney outside the ripe toilets barely sleeping for the ten-hour journey.

"That train trip was brutal," I say. "They should monitor how many tickets they sell."

My knees crack as we lumber down six steps to the basement-level entry of the Twilight Hostel.

"We're *not* talking about it." Being closer to the commode, her hand was stomped on twice, and she was kicked four times by people using the facilities during the night.

"At least we got here quick." I flick my wrist to check the

time on my cheap black watch and smile as she yanks the oversized wooden door. "Off the train, map, money, and here in forty-five minutes. Our fastest time yet."

Check us out; we totally have the hang of organizing ourselves quickly in a new city.

"So far, so good," Dejah says.

The smell of cigarettes, beer, and vomit stings my nostrils as we step inside.

"Ugh. Spoke too soon." I cover my nose with my fingertips.

The door latches behind us, and I squint to adjust to the dark room. Long tables with bench seating line the length of the space under the low whitewash barrel ceiling. Twenty cheap liquor bottles line the shelf behind the square bar in the corner that doubles as reception. A dozen backpackers are lined up to sign the clipboard on the bar top wedged between two brass beer taps.

"Reception opens in two hours; we need to add our names to reserve our spot for check-in," Dejah says as I dump Barney next to an empty table, then we join the line.

The two white guys with dark hair queuing ahead of us are chatting in English. The taller one turns to the side, and I intake a breath when I see the circular Molson Dry logo stretched across his broad chest. He *has* to be Canadian because that's a popular beer exactly nowhere else. I tap him on the shoulder. "Are you from Canada?"

"Yeah. I'm Evan from Toronto." He flashes me his straight white teeth. "And this is Aaron." He thrusts his thumb at his buddy with bushy eyebrows.

"Thought so, the shirt gave it away." I share our names and where we're from.

"Montreal?" Molson Dry Evan lets out a booming laugh. "We go to Bishop's U."

A tight ache tugs at my chest. When it was time to choose a university, my mom was enduring yet another risky operation followed by a crushing round of chemotherapy. It was my fondest wish to go away, but my stack of acceptance letters from around the country—one being from Bishop's—I tossed in the trash. I attended a local university and lived at home so I could help care for my mom. I gulp past the knot in my throat. Another dream I gave up. But looking back, it was the right choice. I only got twenty-two years with her, and I would have lost four of them if I'd gone away for school.

"My younger brother goes there," I say. "Pete MacPhie, do you know him?"

Mom died a month after Pete finished high school, so even though the reason was devastating, I'm happy he's able to attend any school he wants. Bishop's, in Lennoxville, is two hours from my dad's—close for visits, but far enough that you need to live on campus.

"We were in the same dorm first year," Eyebrows Aaron says.

"I know him too. Nice guy." Molson Dry Evan nods.

My insides light up.

"Hear that, Dejah?" I bounce on my toes. "They know Pete."

"That's great, darlin'." She squeezes my forearm.

After we sign in, Eyebrows Aaron and Dejah pop out to get coffees while Molson Dry Evan and I grab a seat at one of the tables and watch all the big packs.

We smoke and rapid-fire names at each other to see who we know in common. And it's a lot. Because of our mutual friends, it's like being with Pete, in a *Six Degrees of Kevin Bacon* kind of way. And this easy connection to home is like a warm hug after the stress of getting through death day.

Dejah returns with Eyebrows Aaron and slides me a cappuccino and bagel as she tosses her leg over the bench. I sip my frothy beverage as we gab about things to do around town. Dejah flips her hair and giggles at the guys. I tip my head to the side as I crumple my sandwich wrapper. Maybe these two will be good for more than just a connection to home—like maybe a *love* connection … not for me—they're friend-zoned for being too close to my brother—but Dejah seems keen.

A white man with a high hairline, shaggy gray hair, and a mustache waddles behind the bar. He looks like David Crosby, the '70s music guy from Crosby, Stills, Nash and Young. With chubby fingers, he picks up the clipboard and calls the first name.

"Evan. Aaron," Crosby shouts after finding beds for the first backpackers on the sign-in sheet.

"We'll catch up later." Molson Dry Evan slings his bag over his shoulder.

"Cool." I wave. "Which one do you like?" I ask Dejah when the guys are out of earshot.

"Neither." Dejah rolls her eyes.

"Oh, come on." I scoff. "You were giggling, and you never do that."

"Okay, they're cute—"

"Candace and Khadejah," Crosby hollers as the guys wave before they disappear through a door past the bar.

"You're not off the hook." I wag my finger, then we rush over to Crosby. "Hi, do you have any double rooms?"

"The guys before you took the last one." Crosby sighs.

"Rats." I frown as I pick at the fraying veneer around the bar with my thumbnail.

"You want the attic dorm room with sixty beds?" Crosby taps his pen on the clipboard.

"Uh ..." My eyes bulge. Sixty beds? In the attic, in the height of summer? "No thank you. What else do you have?"

Crosby grumbles as he shuffles through his wide paper reservation book.

"The Green Room. It's a dorm room with six beds, across the hall from the last two."

"We'll take it," I say.

Whether Dejah *likes* them or just likes them, it will be good to be next door to Molson Dry Evan and Eyebrows Aaron because they'll be fun to hang out with while we're here.

I heave Barney up two flights of stairs to our narrow room

with three sturdy wooden bunk beds along one side and a window at the opposite end. I grunt as I toss my stuff on the bottom bunk by the door, and Dejah takes the empty bed over mine. I make a hasty exit to wash away last night's train journey. I sigh as hot water pounds my shoulders then enjoy the perks of hostel anonymity and no Curler Commando monitoring my water usage as I linger under the spray.

"I checked at the front desk; they have a guided walking tour that costs two hundred koruna and leaves from here in half an hour," Dejah says as I enter the Green Room.

"How much is that again?" I've got my second wind after the coffee, shower, and fresh clothes but my gut is a tangle of nerves because I don't know if Josh is coming to Prague or not.

"It's ten dollars and a good way to see the city. Want to do it?" She taps her toe.

I purse my lips and drag my brush through my wet hair. The Internet café in Kraków was closed yesterday, so I was hoping to check email this morning to see if Josh sent word. But we *are* here a day before I told him we would be. *And* this tour will give us a lay of the land without us having to play tour guide.

"Why not?" I zip my toiletries into Barney and hook my daypack over one shoulder.

I'm sure one more day without email won't make a difference.

Lukáš, our lanky tour guide with bright blond hair, leads fifteen of us—Molson Dry Evan and Eyebrows Aaron opted out to catch up on sleep—from the hostel to our first stop outside the Neo-Renaissance National Museum on the south end of Wenceslas Square.

"This square was called the Horse Market in 1348," Lukáš says as he gestures to the sunny space that's more like a Roman chariot racing circuit than a square, filled with trendy shops and cafés. "Tanks rolled down the cobblestones in WWII, and ten years ago"—his throat bobs—"I marched here with my parents and a quarter of a million other protestors to end the Communist totalitarian regime."

My heart wavers at the raw passion bleeding from his voice. Ten years is not a long time … I wonder how his life has changed since then.

"Moving on to the Old Town Square." He strides away, leading us to our next stop, leaving me to ruminate on my question that I have no right to ask.

Tight pristine buildings give way to a vast cobblestone square the length of a football field in each direction. Lukáš files us past the elegant buildings along the perimeter of the Old Town Square to the brilliant blue Astronomical Clock on the Town Hall stone tower in the far corner.

"When the clockmaker finished making it, the commissioners plucked both his eyes out so he couldn't make anything more beautiful anywhere else. The clockmaker later climbed to the top of the tower and threw himself into it. It took fifty years to get his body parts out and get it working again," Lukáš says.

Most cities we've visited have an iconic site with an ominous and bloody story drawing the tourists' attention. The Seven Sisters, identical buildings built over downed WWII German planes in Moscow, the Jealous Brother's church in Kraków with different towers, and in Prague, it's the Astronomical Clock.

The sun glistens off the rich blue Vltava River as we cross the medieval stone arch Charles Bridge. I adjust my sunglasses to counter the dazzling glare as Lukáš names the thirty statues of Catholic saints perched along the walls of the pedestrian bridge.

I sigh. This place couldn't be more romantic if it tried. I glide my fingers across the smooth stone ledge and fight the longing in my chest wishing I was here with someone special. Dejah's the best, but this place begs to be holding hands with a lover and canoodling at a sidewalk café. I wonder if it would be like that with Josh—

"Time for lunch," Lukáš says as we step off the bridge in the Malá Strana neighborhood.

I grit my teeth. There are lots of people here. The hostel has a sixty-bed dorm room and four floors filled with available options. I don't need Josh to make my romantic wishes come true.

I crack the menu at the sidewalk café and moisten my lips. It's in English, and they have cheese as a main course. Who needs a man when there's cheese? I smother deep-fried camembert on chewy French bread and decimate the small wheel by myself.

After we eat, the tour continues up the switchback steps to Prague Castle, whose ornate spires soar into the blue sky and can be seen from all over the city. Our last stop is the St. Vitus Cathedral boasting vibrant stained-glass windows, then Lukáš returns us to the hostel.

I stomp up the steps behind Dejah to our room. The tour was totally worth the ten bucks. I know my way around town, which was the goal, but my biggest takeaway, even with the cheese—is I need to get laid. And this is the perfect place to do it. I will choose someone. Just *after* I check email. My fingernails cut into my palms. I loathe that even with a bevy of alternatives, Josh is still my first choice. But this is it. If he's a no-show, I'm picking the hottest man I can find and getting it done.

The conversation of our four roomies halts as Dejah and I enter.

"Hey." She introduces us as we collapse on my bottom bunk near the door.

"I'm Baz, from New Zealand," the guy with glasses says in a thick Kiwi accent from the bottom middle bunk. "Dan and Spencer from Missouri." He points to the white-faced, rolled-shouldered duo sitting on the middle and far top bunk with their gangly legs hanging over the edge. "And Jan from Oz, who's got the shits." He tips his chin to the girl with springy red ringlets hugging her knees on the bottom bunk by the window.

"Ew." I wrinkle my nose.

"Not literally." Jan sighs. "Someone came through the

window while I was in the shower this morning and stole my daypack."

"Aw, man. That's terrible," I say.

"They got my camera, glasses, alarm clock, and Swiss Army knife." She twists her freckly fingers on her lap.

"Sorry, mate," Dejah says. "Did they get your passport?"

"No." She shakes her head, and her curls bounce. "At least that's something."

"We need a drink," Baz says as he stands from his bunk.

"Count us in," I say as the Americans leap off the top bunks and Jan unfolds herself from the corner.

I tap on Molson Dry Evan and Eyebrows Aaron's door, but they don't answer, so the six of us venture downstairs to the hostel bar where we checked in this morning to commiserate with Jan. Bluesy guitar riffs fill the room from the corner stage opposite the bar. One dude is strumming an acoustic B.B. King solo; the drum kit, bass, and microphone are unused.

"It's open mic night," Baz shouts over the twang as we slide to the end of a long table with ten people occupying the other side.

Giddy excitement zings in my chest as Baz and Dejah go to the bar to buy drinks. I wanted to meet fun people, and this boisterous table is overflowing with them. And I'm pumped to make new friends.

"Hi." I grin at the guy on my right with wide shoulders and a red sunburnt nose. "I'm Candace."

He slumps and scowls. "Jacob," Mr. Frowny says in an American accent.

Okay. I shift my back to him. So maybe not everyone is fun.

Dejah takes the seat on my other side and pours me a draft from the pitcher. I clink glasses with the gang from our room. Icy, hoppy beer glides down my throat, and I wiggle in my seat. Mr. Frowny's not fun, but they are.

Look at me ticking off my Prague wish list. Fun people *and* drinks.

Well, only one as I'm still on stupid antibiotics for two more days from the cellulitis I got at the hostel in Zakopane. The button is still painful and healing slower this time, but it should clear up soon.

"Jacob, we're up," a sinewy guy at the other end of the table shouts.

Mr. Frowny lights a cigarette, lumbers toward the stage, and plants himself behind the drums. Sinewy Guy slings the guitar over one shoulder, adjusts the microphone, then plucks the opening chords for "Given to Fly" by Pearl Jam. His fingers glide over the strings, head bobbing as he shouts the lyrics. The tip of Mr. Frowny's cigarette glows orange as he taps out a steady beat on the snare drum.

"How's he doing that?" I poke Dejah and tip my chin to Mr. Frowny, whose cigarette is dangling from one side of his mouth as he sucks in air through the other, then exhales smoke through his nose like a fiery dragon.

"No idea." Dejah cackles.

Our animated group is leaning in, elbows on the table and sharing stories. I just need a dance floor to complete my list. Oh, and to identify my perfect candidate for action. My eyes dart from one face to the next around the table. Too short, dirty fingernails, lame, slouching, weird eyes. Nope, nope, nope. For now, I'll enjoy the laughs and company.

"Jacob, wow that was impressive." I clap when Mr. Frowny returns. "You didn't miss a beat or touch your cigarette for the entire song."

Dejah mimics his drumming movements with a lit cigarette between her lips.

Mr. Frowny's nostrils flare as he glares.

"How did you do it?" I ask as he retakes his seat.

"We're the Mac Daddy in the States, that's how," Mr. Frowny shouts as he stubs out his cigarette. "You two are idiots."

Conversations halt as all eyes swing to us.

"What?" My mouth opens and closes. "I thought it was impressive."

Sure, it looked funny, but it was kind of cool.

"Oh, mate, I think we went too far," Dejah stage-whispers.

My cheeks burn, and Mr. Frowny shifts in his seat under the heavy stares. People mock me for the big Canadian flag sewn on Barney, but it's times like this that reinforce why I don't want to be mistaken for an American.

"My cousin ran over my grandfather with a tractor and killed him," he blurts out.

Jaws around the table gape. Everyone *except* Khadejah's. Her head is tipped back, spilling out laughter with her palm pounding on the table. Nothing gets in the way of fun for Dejah. And I love her for that.

MY BODY JOLTS at the crackling of plastic bags.

"Not again." I moan and duck under my sleeping bag that I crawled into a few hours ago after dancing with the Green Room gang at a bar beside Charles Bridge till dawn.

I ticked dancing off the to-do in Prague list last night too. Nothing more, though.

"Sorry, guys," Jan says as she zips her bag closed. "Top night, but my train for Vienna leaves in an hour, so I gotta run."

I wave as the others in our room shout goodbye.

Jan's riot of red curls bounce as she clicks the door closed.

"I hate plastic bags," Baz from New Zealand says.

The top bunk creaks and Dejah's long black hair cascades over the side.

"It's not just us," she says.

"Nope." I snicker, and it turns into a full fit of giggles.

"Dude, I'm pissed." American Dan punches the wall. "My jacket and pants were gone when we got in."

"I thought you were joking." I rub my forehead.

His late-night raving about a leather jacket didn't make sense to my drunk brain because who backpacks with a leather jacket?

"No, my jacket was the shit and they were the only pants I brought." He curses under his breath.

I blink. Who brings only one pair of pants on a backpacking trip?

"Hang on. We went to the bar last night to console Jan for her stolen stuff and forgot to lock the window?" Dejah asks, her voice riddled with amusement.

Baz laughs. American Spencer, Dejah, and I join in.

"Assholes," American Dan seethes.

I bite my lip. I forgot the Americans we've met in Prague have no sense of humor. But I would be grumpy too if my stuff was stolen. I roll over, grab my daypack, and pull out a piece of paper and markers to craft a sign.

WARNING
Thief enters through the window!
Lock the window if you're the last person to leave the room.

I hop out of bed and tape the sign over the window.

"That should help us remember. Sorry about your stuff, Dan." He ignores me as I climb back into bed.

"I'm going to London tomorrow," Baz from New Zealand sighs. "I'm not ready to go back to the rain."

"London?" I whip my head to him.

"Yeah, I live there. Unlike you guys, this is only a week's holiday for me."

"Would you mind bringing a small bag of my used film to my friend Dani? It would be great not risking it getting lost in the mail." Dani's my Canadian friend who lives in London. If Baz can bring her my film, she can drop it at my dad's in

Montreal on her next trip home, saving me worry and cash on postage.

"Is your friend hot?" Baz asks.

"Of course," I say.

"Then I would love to do that for you." Baz chuckles.

"Thanks." I one hundred percent trust Baz'll deliver my precious cargo now that I've piqued his curiosity to meet my friend.

I lace my fingers behind my head and scan the names and colorful words scrawled on the wooden slats of the overhead bunk, wondering if my bed's prior occupants had as much fun here as I'm having.

CROSBY'S behind the bar allocating spots to weary new arrivals when Khadejah, Baz, and I enter the room. We join the handful of others scattered at tables to wait for American Dan and Spencer. Molson Dry Evan and Eyebrows Aaron opted to sleep instead of joining us for sightseeing, but Dejah and I made plans to meet them here tonight to hang out.

"Spencer and I found Dan's jacket outside the hostel last night." Baz tips his head to the side and lights a cigarette.

"What?" My brow furrows. "Where were we?"

"Already inside. Spencer spotted it in the bushes when he was taking a piss," Baz says.

"Ok-*ay*." Weird, why didn't he wait to pee inside? "Why didn't you return it when he was going on about it this morning?"

"Because." Baz arches a brow. "We paid a Czech guy a tenner to wear it into the hostel this morning."

"Oh dear." I swipe my hand across my mouth.

This is such a bad idea. American Dan has zero funny bone, and he's not going to find an ounce of humor in this gag.

"The Czech guy'll be here any minute." Baz's eyes twinkle. "This is gonna be mint."

It's totally not.

"Can't wait." Dejah unwraps a new pack of cigarettes and hands me one.

Of course, she can't wait. This is going to be a train wreck.

American Dan trudges in and pouts as he takes a seat facing the front door.

American Spencer pokes his head through the entrance by the bar and gives me a wink. He slowly walks over, then hovers beside our table.

The door swings open, flooding daylight into the dark room. A white guy with shaggy black hair struts inside wearing an oversized brown leather bomber jacket. He throws his arms out and spins in the entryway with a cheeky crooked grin.

American Dan jerks at the sight of Czech Guy wearing his jacket.

My body tenses.

Baz giggles.

Spencer vibrates with excitement.

Dejah's on the edge of her seat, smoke swirling off the cigarette between her fingers.

"Motherfucker." American Dan's out of his chair, sprinting full tilt at Czech Guy.

American Dan's shoulder connects with Czech Guy's stomach. A loud crack sounds as the two of them land in a heap on the sticky cement floor. American Dan straddles Czech Guy, bunching the jacket in his left fist, and winds up his right. Baz and American Spencer race across the room as Czech Guy screams and shouts in Czech. They catch American Dan's arm before he can strike and drag him off Czech Guy.

"It's a joke, man," American Spencer yells. "He didn't steal it. We found it and paid him ten bucks to wear it."

American Dan's chest heaves as he shoves the guys off.

"Boys are stupid." I frown as Czech Guy unzips the jacket, tosses it, and rushes out.

"Bet that Czech guy wished he never took the cash." Dejah ashes her cigarette.

"I hope he's okay. He hit his head on the floor pretty hard," I say as the door slams.

"Candace or Khadejah, phone," Crosby shouts from behind the check-in desk.

"I'll go." Dejah races toward the bar with no fight from me.

The only person who knows we're staying here is Dude Davo because we shared our Prague accommodation plans with him over dinner in Kraków. *And* we've missed two rendezvous—the first night we were on a train and last night we didn't go meet him because we were here at the bar.

Phone to her ear, Dejah's frantically waving and mouthing, *"It's Dude Davo."*

I snicker as she hands the phone to Crosby and stomps over.

"We have plans to meet Dude Davo tonight at eight-thirty. I also lied and told him we only arrived this morning," she says.

"Seriously?" I huff. "I predict that'll end as well as the jacket-joke did."

WINDOW LOCKED with the jacket safely tucked away in our room, the five of us visit the Jewish Museum and cemetery. As we're entering a sacred place, the guys are asked to wear kippahs and don their paper skullcaps before entering the museum.

My heart aches as I wander past wall after wall of names and dates beautifully scripted in black and red. Nazi victims. Nausea spins in my gut. If Hitler had his way, this would have been the museum of an extinct people. Baz rights his kippah as we enter a breathtaking synagogue with gold and blue barreled ceilings so exquisite goosebumps sprinkle my skin.

Baz's kippah slips again as we enter the oldest Jewish cemetery in Prague. There are more than 12,000 tombstones tipped at all angles, but way more remains. The space was too small, and layers of new earth were brought in to accommodate the demand, and some graves are twelve layers deep.

"Dan's and Spencer's are fine. What's going on with your kippah?" I jab Baz in the bicep as we take in the tightly packed weather-beaten gravestones.

"I grabbed a kid one by accident," he says as he holds it in place.

Dejah cracks a smile, and I do as well, Baz's mistake offering some much-needed levity from the heaviness of this place.

The guys head back to the hostel while Khadejah and I continue to tour around town.

We visit the imposing baroque St. Nicholas Church. I cross the black and white tiled floor to a glowing table of candles behind the pews. Under the whimsical frescos, I choose one for my mom in the center of the flickering crowd. Coins clink as I drop them in the box, then pick up a long matchstick.

"You would love it here," I whisper as I light hers. "I miss you." The candles heat my face as I extinguish the stick in a small cup of sand for the next person to use.

We poke around the touristy shops near the Old Town Square, debating on which T-shirts, handmade beaded jewelry, and colorful postcards to buy. I resist blowing the daily budget and spend twelve dollars on a fist full of cards and three delicate beaded necklaces.

"We don't have enough time to go back to the hostel to change before we need to meet Dude Davo. Want to check email?" Dejah asks.

"Is that even a question?"

Nerves bloom in the pit of my stomach. This is it. I finally get to see if Josh is coming.

The sun is low in the sky, casting a warm red and orange

glow over uneven roofs as we enter the Internet café around seven-thirty. Classroom-style desks, forty computers, and a coffee bar. This place is another point in the pro column for Prague.

I type in my Hotmail password and clasp my fingers behind my neck as my email loads. My screen lights up with sixteen unread messages, and three of them are from Josh.

I click on his oldest email.

I'm in the Arctic Circle; I want to meet you soon. I'm really looking forward to seeing you and I hope you feel the same,

Josh xo

That's nothing new other than him sharing where he is. My heart thumps as I open the second note.

I know you said you would be in Prague soon. I'm thinking about coming to see you there about August 6th. Let me know if you'll be there,

Josh xo

My stomach contracts and pitches. Oh my God. August 6th is today. Is he here? Did I miss him? Or did he not come since I never wrote back? What was I thinking? I should have checked email as soon as we got here. I can't believe I might have missed him. My lip quivers as the last message whirs to life.

I'm coming. I couldn't wait to hear back from you, so I'm taking a chance. I'll be in Prague Thursday, August 6th arriving at 9:30p.m. on a train from Hamburg arriving at Hlavní Nádraží. I hope you'll be at the station,

Josh xo

My head spins.

Holy shit. He's coming.

I press my hand to the middle of my chest, and my heart booms against my palm.

In two hours. Josh will be here in *two hours*.

My chest ignites with happiness then tips and shrivels as my emotions dive and spin.

Hours and hours of my and Dejah's conversations over the last month and a half have revolved around what-ifs and *dreams are free* scenarios about Josh. But actually showing up? He was never supposed to do that. He was supposed to let me down like he usually does. I can deal with disappointment. I would have been sad for a while. Then I would have gotten drunk and picked someone to move on with.

"Khadejah!" I scream and dash to her computer.

"What's wrong?" She stops typing.

"Josh is coming to Prague in two hours." I take five quick breaths as I pace behind her chair. I stop and press the heels of my hands into my eyes. "I barely survived him leaving me in London. How will I deal with the fallout this time?"

He was only ever supposed to live in my dreams.

"It'll be all right." She grips my arm. "We'll figure it out. Go close your email. We have to meet Dude Davo. We can't stand him up again. No matter how tempting it is."

"Right." I retake my seat and tap out an email to Josh telling him I'm staying at the Twilight hostel in case I miss him at the station.

I shut down my computer and dizzily trail Dejah into the dark night.

"I know you're off with the fairies, but I need you to focus, mate. What are we going to say to Dude Davo?" she asks as we make our way to the rendezvous location.

"It needs to line up with your stupid lie." I tut.

"Okay, so we tell him we arrived this morning and that's why we missed meeting him for two nights," she says.

I nod as my feet somehow carry me across the cobblestones because nothing feels connected right now.

"How are you?" Dejah tilts her head.

"Numb." I swipe my hand down my damp face. "I don't know what to make of him coming here. It literally makes me want to hurl."

"Go see him. That's all you can do. But now I need you to pull your shit together because we're a block from the restaurant." She folds then tucks the map in her bag.

"Hey, girls! Girls!" Two Australian girls with big boobs who were on Lukáš's walking tour yesterday are waving at us.

My eyes bulge as they jog down the sidewalk, their gazongas swinging from side to side ready to bust out of their tank tops.

"Hey, you two," I say because I can't remember their names.

I've just referred to them as the Boob Twins in my head.

"We met your friend Dude Davo today," Boob Twin One says.

"Pardon?" Khadejah stops in her tracks, and my eyes bulge.

"You know Dude Davo? The dentist from Sydney?" Boob Twin Two says, popping out a hip. At least it wasn't a boob; those suckers are close to escaping.

"He said he might be a bit late," Boob Twin One says.

"I'm sorry?" I twist my head.

What the hell are the Boob Twins talking about? How could these two chicks, who we *barely* know, know Dude Davo? Better yet, how do *they* know that *we* know him?

"We met Dude Davo and his mate on a boat tour today, and we got to chatting. Dude Davo said he was meeting two girls tonight. A tall blond Canadian and a short brunette Australian. We put two and two together." Boob Twin One shrugs.

I puff out a breath. Are you kidding me? Meeting people who go to the same school as my brother is one thing. But this? How in the hell did the world become this small?

"Oh, yeah, well, we better get going to meet him." Khadejah grabs my arm and drags me away from the Boob Twins.

"Are we the only two people in Prague to fit that description?" I huff. "Shit, shit! He knows we were here yesterday." I press my fingertips to my temples. "We're freaking lucky we ran into them when we did. We would've looked like super assholes if we lied to his face."

What a mess. Dejah's lie was a terrible idea. But it's not the time for I told you so's.

"Calm your beans. We've got this." Dejah flicks her ponytail over her shoulder. "We just need to figure out what we tell him—"

"I've got it." I snap my fingers. "In the spirit of Josh's visit, let's *do a Josh*." I rapidly nod, and her forehead wrinkles. "*Doing a Josh* is admitting you made a mistake then throwing the ball in their court. We admit we lied, then Dude Davo can choose to forgive us or not."

During our time in London, Josh would take great pains to tell me how he didn't love me. Then he would say, '*If you don't want to be with me, I understand. It's up to you.*' Leaving him guilt-free and me with the choice to stay around or leave him.

My breath stalls as an ugly realization settles on my skin. I'm not bothered if Dude Davo doesn't forgive us and we end up leaving. But I would never carelessly *do a Josh* to someone I truly cared about. I would never risk them leaving or hurt them like that. My eyes glisten. Going to meet Josh tonight is such a terrible idea. He doesn't care for me the way I care for him.

Why couldn't he just stay away like I thought he would?

"Okay, *doing a Josh* it is," Dejah says as we shuffle down the steps to the basement-level Hogo Fogo restaurant.

Smooth jazz, laughter, pepper, and smoke fill the air. Soft lighting illuminates the bright modern art on the walls, and the cherry wood tables filling the room are occupied with people enjoying generous plates of colorful food.

"There he is." I flick my chin to Dude Davo, whose hands are flying around his face as he talks to his bulky friend. "Your penance for lying this morning is you're doing the talking."

I shove her ahead of me.

"We're so sorry," Dejah says as we stand beside his four-top table. "We were tired last night and feel terrible you came here and we didn't make it."

I clasp my hands in front of me and slap on a soft smile. The key to *doing a Josh* well is to stop talking after the delivery and wait.

"No problem." Dude Davo waves his wrist. "I'm just glad we could finally meet up."

He jumps out of his chair to give us each a hug. It worked. *Doing a Josh* worked. But I'm conflicted. I don't think less of Dude Davo for forgiving us, but it was way too easy to do *and* get away with. Is this how Josh feels when I accept his ultimatums? Like I'm a nice, desperate pushover?

"This is my mate, Karl," Dude Davo introduces the bulky white guy with a buzz cut and sloped forehead.

"Nice to meet you." I take a seat and shift out of kicking distance from Dejah. "I can't stay long. A friend of mine is arriving in town tonight, and I need to meet him at the train station. But Dejah's excited to have dinner with you."

"That's rad." Dude Davo pours us a beer from the pitcher of amber ale on the table, which I have no intention of drinking.

I sit across from Karl and dig my fingernails into my thighs below my shorts as our *doing a Josh* success claws at my insides. I shouldn't go tonight, but I can't shake the teeny, tiny bit of crippling hope that maybe he cares and misses me like he claims. And that he doesn't feel as indifferent toward me as I am to Dude Davo.

My throat constricts. This is such a disaster—

"Tapity, tap, whoever sits in my seat will get a slap," Karl says as he gets up to go to the bathroom.

My face scrunches. We all have our own chairs. So who would take his seat? And who talks like that? God, Dejah's going to kill me for leaving her here.

I spin my glass on the table, glancing at my watch a thousand times while contributing zero to the conversation Dejah's working hard at with Dude Davo.

"It's time." I chug my beer then slam the empty glass on the table. "I have to go."

I need the liquid courage, and one drink should be fine on antibiotics.

"Have fun." Dejah forces a pinched smile.

My gut twists as I stand. I feel like a big jerk for abandoning her. Because eating *the sandwich* would be less painful than staying alone with these two. For sure sleeping with Austin or Keith would be better.

I owe you, I mouth before I bolt out.

Please don't let this end with me begging to eat *the sandwich* for a re-do.

TWENTY-FOUR HOURS - PRAGUE, CZECH REPUBLIC

My foot thumps on the metro floor as I rehearse what I'll say to Josh. Because I need to understand why the heck he's here after he dumped me. If his explanation sucks, I'm leaving him, going to the Twilight hostel, and making every imaginable bad decision with a stranger.

Bells chime, and the doors whoosh open. I dash off and wait on the platform for a different train. The yellow light flickers overhead as I paw my frizzy hair. I sniff my armpit and cringe. In all my Josh reunion scenarios, I looked fabulous. Not reeking of dirty sweat, wearing an unwashed T-shirt, rumpled shorts, and stinky sandals.

A thunder of foreign words coming from a man an arm's length away jolts me from my thoughts. His greasy dark ponytail sways as he stumbles through the crowded platform shouting and waving his arms. I leap away as Drunk Guy shoves a gray-haired dad holding his pre-teen daughter's hand.

Angry Czech words fly between them. The Dad's mouth presses into a firm line. His eyes narrow on Drunk Guy as he lunges. I clutch my throat as the two of them land in a heap on the dirty tile. Elbows fly as they roll toward the platform. The daughter's shrill screeches bounce off the station wall as her blond pigtails swing.

I still. People on the platform give the fight a wide berth and look the other way. I bite my lip. I want to comfort the girl, but how can I when she won't understand me?

The grappling rolls precariously close to the tracks. Drunk Guy's on top of The Dad. The young girl leaps on Drunk Guy's back and yanks his mangy ponytail. I step forward to help, but a clean-cut guy wearing a GAP sweatshirt beats me to it. He peels the young girl off, places her behind him, then reaches for Drunk Guy's shoulder to yank him off The Dad.

The Dad's fists fly. The daughter cheers, and Drunk Guy grunts as each punch lands while GAP Guy holds him. I shake my head. I can't believe this is the second fight I'm witnessing today.

"They're picking on him because he's drunk, and that's a crime," a pasty, thin guy slurs in an English accent. He shoves his equally pale friend toward the fray, and they jump in to help Drunk Guy.

It's all elbows, arms, fists, and screams in Czech and English.

A rush of dusty warm air blasts my face. The platform vibrates as the left side of the tunnel ignites with light. The train rumbles into the station and the doors swish open in front of the melee of bodies. The fight stops—like the Coyote and Sheep Dog from *Looney Tunes* when the whistle blares at the end of the day. Shoulders roll, and torn shirts are adjusted. The Dad wipes blood from his cheek and grabs his daughter's hand, and everyone but Drunk Guy boards the train.

I enter through the other door of the compartment and sit as far as I can from *Fight Club*. I lean my head against the window as the train pulls out. I clutch my daypack to my chest as my stomach churns with nerves.

The metro arrives at Praha Hlavní Nádraží station at nine-fifteen. I race up the stairs, and cramps stab my gut as I rush into the closest bathroom. I rip the toilet door open and get my shorts down just in time for the beer and everything I've eaten today to slide straight out. The beer was a bad idea. I fist my fingers in my hair. This long-ass day started with plastic bags, lies, a fight over a jacket, a sorrowful museum, shopping, email, more lies, Dude Davo, another fight, an upset stomach, and now I need to track Josh down in this packed station.

I exit the bathroom at nine-twenty-seven. My shoulders slump. The arrivals board is hanging from the ceiling on the other side of the station. My sandals clap as I duck, spin, and shoulder-check through the mob who all seem to be going in the opposite direction. The loudspeaker bongs and buzzes as I search the names of trains and platforms on the large blackboard. Nothing from Hamburg. I groan. His train could have started anywhere.

My throat dries. It's nine-thirty. There are too many people. How am I going to find him? Panic screeches in my gut as I tear down the steps and wait by the main door, praying he doesn't head to the metro. I twist my clammy hands, shifting my weight from one foot to the other as I study the crowd.

My brain is mush. I'm beyond tired. And I have to poop again.

On my tiptoes, I scan face after face.

Air rushes from my lungs.

It's him.

His steps are slow and measured, his broad shoulders effortlessly carrying his heavy backpack. His head rotates as he searches the crowd, looking for me. But I stay quiet. I need a moment to get myself in check so I don't shout out his name like a lovesick schoolgirl. My knees wobble, and my heart swells with longing for the carefree times we spent in Greece and London. God, I hate that I've missed his face. Twinkling eyes, broad nose, and stupidly perfect symmetrical features.

His gaze lands on mine, and I freeze.

The hum of the station melts away, and everything blurs—but him.

His eyes pop and his white teeth twinkle as he grins. He sprints toward me as my feet stay glued to the dirty floor. Arms set at my sides; he lifts me into his chest. My nose presses into his collarbone, and the fresh, clean scent of his skin spirals me back to when he was mine. I press my lips together so I don't sob. It takes everything inside me not to hug him back, but I can't until I know why he's here.

"God, it's good to see you baby," he whispers in my ear.

My body locks. He lost the right to call me that. I step away.

"Why are you here?" I cross my arms.

"Candace, I just wanted to see you." He combs his hand through his short brown hair.

My back tenses at the insufficient words. I wanted more than that. I dig my fingertips in my triceps as he drags his gaze up and down my body. His blue eyes lock on to mine, and he bites his pink bottom lip. I look dire, but I don't think he cares; his eyes are heated and his nostrils flare.

My cheeks burn as goosebumps explode across my skin.

I take another step back as my stomach twists. I'm so confused. I want to punch his smug face, kiss his pouty lips, and bawl my eyes out all at the same time. I rush toward him, clenched fist leading the way.

I shiver as he catches my wrist and tugs me into him.

"I've missed you." His soft words are the balm I've longed for.

I peek up, and his mouth is hovering a whisper away—waiting. I close the gap and softly brush my lips over his. I gasp as electricity ripples across my scalp and down my spine.

This is such a bad idea because I'm not over him. Not one little bit.

My chest heaves with ugly sobs. I bury my face in my hands as hot tears stream down my cheeks. It's not fair he's here breaking my heart all over again.

"Let's find a place to talk." He hustles me to the door.

I suck in gulps of air as he guides me outside into the night to a nearby bench. I sit on one end, my hands gripping my knees. He unclips his backpack and sits with our thighs touching.

"I've been traveling for fifty-four hours." There's a soft glow around him, cast from the lamppost outside the train station. I hate that it makes him look like an angel with a halo because he's not.

"H-h-amburg isn't that far," I stutter, my face burning.

"I traveled from the Arctic Circle via Hamburg to see you." His pinky brushes mine.

My lips pinch. What was he doing all the way up there?

His cheeks puff as he blows out a breath.

Whatever he's not saying isn't going to be good, and he's waiting for me to ask. "What is it?"

"I have to leave tomorrow at midnight."

"W-w-hat?" My breath catches as my chest tightens.

"My friend Jason's in the military." Deep creases line his brow. I don't know Jason because he never shared anything about friends with me. "He leaves the Netherlands in three days for Pakistan, and I need to see him before he goes."

I study my feet and cling to the seat. I was never going to ditch Dejah to saunter off into the sunset with him, but I figured after his email we would have more time than twenty-four hours.

"Please say you understand," he pleads.

"I get it." My throat burns. "Why did you even come here?"

Dealing with him is like swimming in salt water with a thousand papercuts.

"Was it wrong to come?" His voice lifts at the end.

I blink as a sharp pain pierces my chest.

"I think you know it was, or else you wouldn't have asked." Such a stupid idea meeting him here. Nothing has changed.

"I just wanted to see you," he whispers.

I understand his desire to visit a friend before he goes into a war zone, but I want to be worth more than a day of his time. Dejah and I are flexible. Maybe we can have one day now and meet up for a few days later.

"What are your plans after seeing your friend?" I ask.

"After the Netherlands", he grins, "I'm going to Russia, Estonia, Latvia, Lithuania, and Poland."

"I was just there." Air rushes from my lungs. "You never planned or mentioned anything about going to those countries when we were in London."

They were all I talked about, though. When we were together and in the stupid group emails I've copied him on for the last six weeks.

"I couldn't travel with you. You get close to someone when you travel with them," he says. "It was easier for me to leave you in London knowing you were mad at me."

I ball my fists and stare up at the shadowy slate clouds blocking the stars. We've been down this road before. And his new offering of information still doesn't make any sense. Is he petrified to feel more than *like* for me? Or is he only capable of *liking* me? Or is this the most epic of all international booty calls?

"I just don't understand any of this." I shake my head.

"I'm so sorry, Candace." He sits quietly and says nothing more.

My insides shatter. He's *doing a Josh*. Leaving it for me to decide. Do I walk away, or stay with him for the next twenty-four hours? There goes my heart. Crushed. Because an hour ago I wasn't bothered by the outcome when I was *doing a Josh* to Dude Davo.

He doesn't care about me like I do him.

This is an international booty call. Nothing more. It's never more with him.

A group of people saunter past, backpacks draped over their shoulders, laughing and joking in English with different accents. My chest pangs. I wish I was with them. Or still with Dejah drinking beer with Dude Davo and weird Karl. Anywhere but here having to make this decision.

I bite the side of my thumb as Josh wrings his hands. I deserve more. I should tell him to shove his booty call and meager offer of time, then leave him here on this bench. But I'm leaving with a broken heart if I spend time with him or not. And we're in *Prague*. Romantic Prague that begs you to be wrapped around a lover as you get lost in the cobblestone streets. And I need to get laid. He's horrible at a lot of things, but not that. My heart isn't safe, but he makes me feel physically safe. And after all that's happened on the road, I need this.

And I know if I walk away now, I'll always regret it. Singing along to Dolly Parton's "Here You Come Again" in my mom's Vega as we drive to hunt kindling on Saturday mornings reels through my head. Because just like Dolly—here I go.

"Expect me to be moody." Like psycho level, but I'll keep that to myself.

"Yes!" He leaps up, plucks me off the bench, and his lips are on mine.

I do what I always do when we're together: I melt into him and hold on tight.

At a nearby phone booth, he calls three hostels and finds a double room tonight way up north. We stop at Twilight because I need to give my film to Baz to bring to Dani. I grab clean clothes for tomorrow, my last dose of antibiotics, and leave a note for Khadejah telling her I'll see her in twenty-four hours. My heart dips as we leave the hostel. It's the first time I've been apart from Dejah for more than a few hours since we left London. And I already miss her.

We find the new hostel and check in minutes before midnight. After his long trip and my sweaty day, we both need a shower. The ladies' toilets are empty, and we sneak down the dim hallway to the last stall. I peel my shirt off and toss it on the bench. The heat of his chest singes my back. The rest of my clothes join my shirt, and his hands circle my waist. Hot water hits my body, washing away the last of my doubts, and I nosedive into the electric comfort of his skin. What the hell, in for a penny, in for a pound as they say in England.

An hour later, we race to our room with cheeky grins and wrinkled fingers.

He throws me on the bed, and I giggle when he pounces.

"What are you doing?" I ask, wiping sleep from my eyes hours later.

"I can sleep tomorrow." He shrugs after getting caught watching me sleep. "I don't want to waste one minute with you."

A twisty ache flares in my chest. Oh hell, it's going to be excruciating when he leaves me again. He plunges his hands in my hair and smashes his lips to mine. My body ignites as his fingers sink into my skin. Everything else fades away as I straddle his hips and shove those worries into a deal-with-later compartment. I'm out here on an adventure. I'll pick up these pieces, along with all the others—later.

AFTER ANOTHER SLEEPLESS NIGHT, we leave his backpack in a locker at the train station then head for lunch at Joe's Garage near Charles Bridge. His hand presses the base of my spine as we pass ten dudes wearing orange vests occupying stools at the bar.

"I'm starving, baby," he says as he pats my ass.

I preen at the word that irked me last night as he directs us to a booth at the back of the bustling room. I slide into a seat opposite him and examine the one-page laminate menu.

"You'll love the food here." He stretches his arms across the back bench.

"You've been here before?" The menu slips my grasp.

I didn't know that. But then again, we didn't do a lot of talking last night.

"I swung by Prague after I ran with the bulls in Spain last month." He leans forward and clasps my hand. "How about nachos?"

My gut churns. I'm desperate to ask who he was with and what he did, but that's not what this is. Despite the possessive touches and hand-holding, there's no future here. This lunch is about refueling after our all-night sex marathon. So I swallow my questions. "Who doesn't love nachos?"

The server drops a mountain of chips drowning in gooey cheese on the table. My mouth waters, but my stomach's not on board because despite my bravado, deep down, I want this to be more than a booty call.

I pick at the overflowing platter while Josh dives in.

"Tell me about your trip so far. Is it all you wanted it to be?" Josh mounds a helping on his plate.

I crack a chip and share Khadejah and my adventures through Russia and the Baltics, sharing only the funny parts like the trip to Hel and *the sandwich*.

"Ah baby, I'm glad you've had fun." He grins. "After Spain, I went to Germany to see the castle in Füssen. Then I spent days in the mountains. They made me homesick for Colorado. I ran every path, and people thought I was mental, but it felt so good."

I sip my Diet Coke as he raves about visiting Lakselv in northern Norway because it seemed like a good idea.

It's easy and strange to be with him. Easy because when we're naked it's natural. But it's also strange because we're talking about our separate trips—that we were supposed to do together—like it's no big deal. I also find it odd how he zigzagged all over Europe by the seat of his pants. That would have driven me up the wall. Dejah and I have had a logical route and stuck to it with the occasional diversion here and there. And we've never fought, we never run out of things to talk about, and I don't have to guard my words. Being with her is even easier than being with Josh—

"You okay?" he asks as the server takes the empty platter.

"Yeah." I wonder what Dejah's up to right now. And how it went with Dude Davo and weird Karl. I smile because I'll see her soon enough.

"Ready to go?" He intertwines our fingers, and I luxuriate in the feeling of his skin next to mine for the time I have it.

My insides glow as we stroll across Charles Bridge in the bright sunshine, snap photos wrapped around each other alongside the statues, and laugh as we lean over the side and talk about nothing. This is what I wanted, to be immersed in the romance of this place, and it's nice. More than nice.

"Let's go there." Josh lifts his chin to the island in the middle of the river with gravel trails winding through pink flowers and green trees.

"Yeah, I haven't been there yet." I pout at my rumpled shorts, T-shirt, and plastic sandals. "If only I had a poofy blue dress … and maybe a carriage with shiny white horses at the reins."

"What are you talking about, baby?" He chuckles as we stroll to the island.

"This place." I shrug. "It deserves a fancy dress."

Okay, so romantic ideals are blurring the lines of this hook-up, but either way, I'll be scraping my broken heart off the floor when he leaves. So until his train rolls out of Prague, I'm going to pretend he feels more for me than he does and embrace my fairytale day.

My head on his shoulder, we stretch out on a grassy spot under a leafy tree on the Střelecký Ostrov island facing the arching silhouette of Charles Bridge. There's not a cloud in the brilliant blue sky. A warm breeze carries the rich honey-vanilla perfume of hydrangeas. Glorious white swans trumpet as they lazily glide past in the water. He strokes my hair, and I curl into him. It's a beautiful day. But our time is slipping away.

"I wish I could stop the clock and live in this moment a little longer." I swallow past the lump in my throat.

He scoops me off the grass and drapes me over him.

"I miss being friends with you," I whisper as a tear escapes.

"I've missed that too." His voice cracks.

His chest rocks under my cheek as he chokes on a sob. I cling to him as we weep on the quiet island in the middle of Prague. Me because he's leaving soon, because he came here at all, and because we can never be. And him because his crushing loneliness is palpable. I have Dejah, but he's been on his own—by choice—and I know it can get unbearably lonely on the road. I grip him tighter. It's going to cost me, but I don't begrudge him searching me out to connect with someone familiar.

He sucks in a breath and swipes his face with the back of his hand.

"Before I go to Nepal and you go to Africa—" I flinch at his words. Originally, we were both going to Nepal. But after he broke up with me, I booked a ticket to Africa to avoid any possibility of crossing paths in Nepal. "I want to meet up with you again."

I shove my face in the crook of his neck. What is he doing to me? This is my rosy glasses day. Day, singular. I've been psyching myself up for a forever goodbye in a few hours.

"We can make it work." He tightens his grip around my chest.

I nod, too afraid I'll blab how much I long to be with him. I need to keep that inside. Because despite what he says, I'm not sure if his loneliness, penis, or missing *me* brought him here. And holding out hope for another reunion is going to dominate my thoughts instead of enjoying my trip and dealing with my grief.

Josh's watch alarm chimes and my heart weeps with despair. Our time is almost up.

My steps are heavy as we enter the buzzing station. Backpackers hunched under the weight of their packs and harried families climb on the long blue train heading to Amsterdam. My lips tremble as I glare at the clock at the end of the platform. We have twenty minutes before it departs. Josh pulls me over to a bench opposite the open carriage door and arranges me on his lap.

"This is the third time you've left me behind," I whisper in his ear. "Crete, London, and now Prague."

"Next time, I promise you can leave me." He grips my hair and kisses the side of my face as he rocks me in his arms.

I breathe in the fresh smell of his skin and commit the sage and sea salt to memory because even though I want it, there won't be a next time. Because I know he won't make the effort to see me again.

"I have to go." He drags his thumb over the exposed skin above my shorts.

I crawl off his lap and stare at my dusty toes peeking out of my sandals. My knees are shaking, and a tired chill clings to my skin. He cups my face and consumes me with one last kiss.

"It will happen." He drops his forehead to mine. "I will see you soon, baby."

I bite my tongue so I don't beg him to stay.

He turns and boards the train, leaving me on the platform alone. The window of his compartment thumps as it drops open. He reaches his hand out. I race over and place my palm in his, desperate for one more touch. Our watery eyes connect, saying a thousand things and nothing at all. Because neither one of us knows what the future holds.

A whistle blows. The train hisses as it starts to roll.

He releases my hand, and my body sways at the loss. Wind swirls my hair as the carriages pass. A bubble of silence envelopes me as the last car leaves the station. It's nine-thirty, and our twenty-four hours are up. I double over as the deep ache I had when he left me in London floods my chest. My lips tremble as I straighten my spine. Then I do what I always do. Swallow the pain, put one foot in front of the other, and walk away.

HELL WITH TWO L(S) - PRAGUE, CZECH REPUBLIC

Vibrant orange light stretches over the eastern side of the city, and shadows dance on the placid river as Dejah and I lean against the waist-high stone wall in the middle of Charles Bridge. It's like we're the only two here presiding over sleepy Prague.

"This was a good idea," I say.

When I returned to the Twilight hostel last night, Dejah was out. The Green Room turned over, and four frat boys from UCLA now occupy the other bunks. I can't tell them apart. Blond hair, straight teeth, and two of them are named Chad. I declined their party invitation and cried myself to sleep the moment they left. Dejah woke me when she rolled in at six, reeking of booze and good times. She insisted I get up, and it took me exactly two minutes to brush my teeth, pee, put on a bra, and follow her here.

"I ditched Dude Davo and weird Karl after we ate. I couldn't get away from them fast enough." Last night's makeup is smudged under her twinkling golden eyes, and she's wearing her go-to party outfit, a black top and pants.

"Oh, thank gosh." I place my hand on my chest. "I thought you were going to hold that against me forever."

"I might have." She shrugs with a cheeky grin. "But I ran into Evan and Aaron at the Twilight bar after I left the restaurant. And I've been hanging out with them ever since. Both nights we danced till dawn, and I slept all day yesterday."

"After Dark Spice strikes again," I chuckle.

She tips her face to the sun, perfectly relaxed and implicitly happy. I, on the other hand, am puffy-faced, wearing the tank top and shorts I slept in, and am dragging my heart behind me.

But I do have a bra on, unlike my early morning in Narva with the border police.

"I missed you," I say.

"I didn't miss you." Her lips twitch as she fights a smile.

I scoff and set my hands on my hips.

"Aw, mate, of course I did." She throws her arms around me and gives me a big squeeze.

"You're mean." I tsk, then light two cigarettes and pass her one as we stare at the dark river. "Anything happen with Evan or Aaron?"

"They were heaps of fun; we just danced and drank both nights. But Aaron surprise-snogged me before they left for Budapest this morning." She smirks.

"Nice." I knew we met those two for a reason. Turns out it wasn't just for me to have a connection to home but also a safe place for Dejah to land while I was with Josh.

"How are you?" A wrinkle forms between her brows.

"Sad." I clench my fists. "And hungry."

She places her small hand over mine.

"I'll allow McDonald's today." She gives me a side grin.

"I'll gladly take you up on a pity burger." I know she saves junk food as a treat for dire occasions.

I blubber through the story of Josh and his mention of another meeting over a cheeseburger and chocolate shake. I slump in my plastic seat, drained but lighter after sharing with her. I dab my swollen eyes with a scratchy white napkin. I have no regrets. But as predicted, I'm in pieces. I don't know if I'll see him again, but I do know Dejah and I have plans. So I'll wallow for a few days, then get on with our trip.

Dejah teeters as we toss our wrappers and cups in the trash. I'm emotionally, not physically tired, so I return to the Internet café as Dejah stumbles back to the hostel to sleep off last night.

I click through messages from my dad, brothers Kev and Pete, Steph and Kelly, my two best friends from home, and each one is a salve for my fractured heart. I take time to reply with individual responses, a total indulgence I don't usually have time for.

One note left, from Chino Garth who we met in Kraków, titled *Gotcha*.

The other hit song is called "Don't Talk Just Kiss!"

The peppy tune explodes in my head and I chuckle. The Right Said Fred mystery that's trailed us from Pärnu is finally solved. My fingers click on the keyboard as I hum the cheesy song and tap out a group email. I don't mention Josh because my friends who I commiserated with over our breakup would be pissed at me for seeing him. So he'll remain my dirty little secret.

From: Candace

To: My Friends

Date: August 8, 1998

Subject: Prague the best so far

When we left Kraków we headed 100km south to Zakopane, a major Polish vacation spot in the Tatra Mountains near the Slovakian border. The temperatures were a scorching 35°C, and the hottest part of the day is 4:00 p.m., so we knocked out our hikes in the morning. Totally recommend visiting and the wooden boat cruise through the Dunajec Gorge is a must-do.

The night train to Prague was a gong show with annoying Italian schoolkids yammering all night long but it was worth it. Prague is magical and breathtaking; all the buildings are so bold and beautiful. Dejah and I have walked around the city, taken great pictures, and enjoyed the sunny summer days.

At the hostel, we met two Canadian guys who go to Bishop's and know my brother Pete, how's that for a small world? Tonight, we're going to see Don Giovanni at the Mozart Concert Hall where Mozart, himself, first conducted this opera. It should be epic.

Candace xoxo

DEJAH SHAKES me awake for the opera's big finish where Don Giovanni goes to hell. We only know about the hell thing because we borrowed a program from the old couple beside us and found out Donny G is a bad dude. I swipe my damp brow as the string orchestra lean into their instruments and Donny G's singing is laced with panic as the skeletons and ghouls haul him off into the darkness.

Dejah and I leap to our feet and clap as the red velvet curtain drops over the stage.

Thank God it's over. We're in the nosebleeds at the very top of the concert hall. Cattle class compared to the red velvet seats on the floor and the three tiers of arched private balconies around the perimeter of the gold-trimmed theater. The body heat from the folks below in tuxedos and sequined gowns has risen, and a thousand different perfumes stifle the clammy air.

"Mate, that was not casual," Dejah shouts over the whistling and cheering crowd for the performers lined up on stage taking their bows. "You slept, head back, with your mouth wide open."

"It was the heat." I shrug, and she laughs.

Or it could be because I walked around town for six hours after emailing this afternoon to clear my head. Either way, I missed half the show. But I'm not too bothered. The opera was good to try once, but I won't be rushing back.

Crystals on the chandelier in the concert hall vestibule cast twinkling rainbows over the patrons as we circle down the million steps of the grand staircase. Well-to-do opera aficionados linger, noses in the air, chattering in different languages. Totally not my scene. I rush to the door and sigh as the night air cools my skin. I pull my cardi over my short summer dress I bought for this trip when I was in Scotland with my dad.

"How about you come over here and sit on my face," one of three guys leaning against a brown stone building shouts as we pass.

I press my lips together, and my heels click over the cobblestones as I walk faster.

"Nice tits," a different group around the corner yells.

"Assholes," Dejah says as she scans the street for a safe restaurant.

"How can they even see our boobs? They're covered by sweaters." I resist the urge to flip them off.

"This is not on. Should we just go to Hogo Fogo?" Dejah asks. "They do fried camembert."

"You had me at fried and cheese. And I finished my antibiotics, so we're drinking tonight. A lot."

"I can do that." Dejah leads us to Hogo Fogo.

Despite the drugs, my belly button ring looks like shit. It's still swollen and hurts like hell. But it's staying. I'm as stubborn about it as I am about this trip. Josh, catcalls, being exhausted or sad, none of it will get me down because I have fried cheese and a good friend to share my worries with.

I RUB my sternum as I wake. Damn Josh; a few more days of moping, then I'm moving on.

The frat boys snore from their stinky half of the room as I search through Barney. They sleep through the rustle of plastic bags as I gather my Russian dolls, extra postcards, ticket stubs, shells, and the wooden plate I bought in Kraków. No affordable souvenir gets left behind because who knows if I'm ever going to get here again. I would throw in my film too, but Baz and Dani have that handled. I gently place my treasures in my daypack. Dejah clutches hers as we skip to the post office and happily mail everything home.

"Hogo Fogo?" Dejah asks after we post our boxes and step out into the glorious sunshine.

"Yeah." I lick my lips. "That fried cheese last night hit the spot."

Hogo Fogo has become our Prague equivalent to the panini café in Kraków. It's safe, and the food's tasty and affordable.

"It's amazing you're able to shit with the cheese you consume," she says as we descend the stairs and sit at our usual table—the one we sat at last night and the first night with Dude Davo—because consistency, when your life is variable, is a precious gift.

"Don't you worry about that." My gut is still a bundle of nerves over Josh, and pooing isn't a problem.

Prague sights ticked off our list, we indulge in an aimless stroll after we eat. A welcome treat as we usually have an agenda and destination. Laughter and the hum of voices draw us to the Old Town Square. Children giggle as they race between the rows of weekend market stalls. Locals carry baskets filled with carrots, peppers, lettuce, and fresh fruit. Tourists mingle among the tables laden with crafts under white tents.

"We're just looking," I say as I stop at a table with decorative eggshells hanging from an artificial Christmas tree.

"Sure." Dejah plucks a purple one with symmetrical triangles.

I reach for a bright yellow egg painted with a swirl of white circles that remind me of a field of twisting hay on a windy day.

"Damn," I say as it swings between my fingertips. It's as light as a whisper and more delicate than crystal. "We're going to need to go back to the post office." I can't carry these in Barney. I'll be lucky if they make it home in one piece, but they're two dollars each so worth the chance.

"Yes, we are." Dejah chooses three.

I add a red sparkly and teal blue starburst egg to my yellow one, hoping at least one makes it. We diligently file past every stall, blowing the budget on art posters, necklaces for friends, and T-shirts. We even buy a box and packaging.

On our way back to Hogo Fogo, we pass a bar with purple and yellow pansies dangling from window boxes and "Tainted Love" by Soft Cell blaring through the open doors. Dejah stops and tips her head to the entrance.

I shrug and step inside. Dark lighting, dark wood walls, and dark tables span the large room. Dejah orders beers and fries from the bar, and I set up at a table to the side, away from the handful of customers.

We sip our pale ales and spread our purchases across the wide wooden tabletop.

"So no more shortcuts," I say as I bubble wrap my eggs and shove them into the rectangular box between posters of Charles Bridge.

After we left the bar last night, we took a winding path through a deserted park to the hostel. Darkness clung between the trees, making it creepy as hell, and we ran the whole way in heels.

"I'm still catching my breath." Dejah opens her box and places a T-shirt inside.

"That would have been a good opening scene to a horror film," I say as I toss a fry in my mouth.

The tape hisses and slurps as I circle the box. It's a beauty, two feet long, and the width of my palm, a prize to open one day whenever I go home. As I reach for a pen, my eyes connect with a scowling white guy with brown hair sitting alone at a corner booth. I shiver, then scratch out my dad's address on the parcel.

"Have you noticed the guy staring at us?" I whisper over the '80s music.

Dejah's head swivels, and the guy's dull brown eyes narrow.

"No. Don't look at him." I frown. "Crap."

He reaches for his pint with a smug sneer and shuffles over.

"You mailin' boxes home?" he asks in an Australian accent.

He's about my height with absolutely nothing else exciting to say about him.

"Yeah." *Duh.* I refrain from rolling my eyes. He watched us poke around with our stuff and pack boxes for the last hour.

"My mate ditched me and hooked up with a local girl." He snaps his pink gum. "I've gotta fend for myself. It's a great town, but it's nice to talk to other people."

There's not one dip, twist, or emotion in his voice. If he spoke

Lithuanian, he could totally do those voiceovers of English movies.

"Don't mind if I sit, do yah? I wouldn't mind the company." He pulls out a chair and slouches into it.

My shoulders slant, and my parcel joy slides away as he invades our space.

"We got here three days ago ..." One long line of monotone words marches past his thin lips. He pauses to take a breath.

"Wh—" I try to ask a question about his friend.

"As I was saying ..." He speaks over me.

Sshhh, the man is talking.

I tap the table and Dejah chain smokes as he talks. On and on.

"What are you two doing tonight?" he asks at the end of his dull soliloquy.

"Uh, uh." I scratch my chest; I've got no excuse ready. "Going out or something."

"Great," he says with zero enthusiasm, because he can only speak in monotone. "I'll join you."

That's it. We're only going to Hogo Fogo from here on out; everyone there minds their own business. And we wouldn't be in this situation.

"We don't have any plans. We'll probably do nothing," Dejah says.

"It's okay, I'll meet you at your hostel." He shrugs.

I want to slam my head against the table. For a boring guy, he's persistent. I'm always the first person to invite people along, no matter what or where, because I know how hard it is and detest being on my own. But I would normally never choose to spend time with someone who bothers me like he does. I could lie and tell him we're staying at a different hostel, but lies haven't worked out so well for us. And maybe he won't be so bad in a busier place.

"We're at The Twilight. Meet us there at eight." I force a smile and grab my stuff.

Dejah drags me down the sidewalk to the post office with my long box tucked under my arm.

"What is that guy about?" I ask when he's out of earshot.

"The Drip. That's what we're calling him," she says as we join the short line to mail.

"That's perfect." I giggle.

The frat boys are lounging on their bunks when we return from mailing. We tell the Chads the story of The Drip. They scoff and look skeptical.

I shower late, leaving Khadejah to meet The Drip alone.

She's back before I'm dressed.

"Mate, move it along. I can't handle a conversation with The Drip alone." She glares.

"He must have rolled through his chat this afternoon." I pull on my shoes.

My mind blanks as I sit across from The Drip in the noisy hostel bar. Backpackers are crowded around tables, laughing and drinking, while the three of us stew in silence.

I don't want to ask him questions because then I'll have to hear his voice, and he won't listen if I tell a story.

"It's busy." I clasp my hands.

More silence.

"Girls." One of the Chads smirks as he drops on the bench beside me.

I breathe out a sigh of relief as the other frat boys pack around our table with two new frat-dude-bro clones. One of them tries to talk to The Drip, but he scowls with no response.

"I thought you were exaggerating," frat boy stage-whispers. "Dude is *lame*."

The six frat boys monopolize the conversation, comparing frat parties, keg stand records, hot chicks, and boobs—like I'm in an '80s spring break movie. But it's better than talking to The Drip.

We move the party to the Corona bar overlooking the Charles Bridge. Everyone ignores The Drip on the walk to the bar, and he drops off somewhere around the town square. It's mean, but he didn't do himself any favors. He contributes nothing, and his negative vibe puts us all on edge.

"I've not seen Charles Bridge yet," one frat boy says as we walk across it to the bar.

I roll my eyes. They've been in Prague for three days.

We dance under the patio awning overlooking the bridge.

"The Drip is standing at the bar." Dejah grabs my arm.

"Oh man, of all the bars in this town." I sneak a glance. "Uh, I just made eye contact."

I turn my back, but it doesn't deter The Drip. He joins our dancing gang. His shoulders shift roughly from side to side out of beat. Even his dancing is boring.

One of the Chads leans down and says into my ear, "You know, I think there is a hole in the patio awning, cuz I can feel a Drip."

I cross my legs so I don't pee my pants.

The Drip *finally* gives up and leaves. At least we won't have to see him again.

"HEY, Candace and Khadejah, you've been here a while," Crosby yells from behind reception when we roll into the hostel bar late one afternoon, days after our night at the Corona bar.

"Oh man, he knows our names, and they have a dorm room with sixty beds." I scratch my temple as we head to Hogo Fogo for lunch. "We should look into leaving Prague."

I have no idea what day it is. I've been a blur of drunk and hungover since the opera. The frat boys left yesterday, and we have four German girls in our room who aren't friendly but smell better than the Chads.

"We have five weeks before we have to meet Stella and Gwen in Istanbul. If we go to Vienna tomorrow, that'll leave us heaps of time in Croatia before we meet them," Dejah says as she swings the door open to our regular haunt.

"One more fried cheese and beer for the road," I say as we sit at our usual table and I order my usual lunch.

"You're such a dag." Dejah rolls her eyes as she orders a salad.

Dag is an Aussie insult or a description of a quirky, likable person. I'm going with the latter.

"But I'm *your* dag." I chuckle as a starburst of warmth spreads in my chest.

Unbeknownst to Josh, by refusing to travel with me, he has given me the greatest gift. Because Dejah is the right person for me to be having this adventure with. Not him. I whisper my fingers over my lips and sigh. I would like to see him before I go to Africa, but with our diverse plans, I have no idea how we can make it work.

"Cheers to Prague." I lift my frothy glass and clink it with hers. "It overdelivered on the fun."

"It sure did. Cheers, mate." Her eyes shine with happiness.

I take a big swig and swipe away my beer mustache with my tongue. Prague has run its course, and so has my drunken pining over Josh. I'm ready to get back to it: new food, palaces, museums, and fancy buildings. It's time for us to shake things up in Vienna.

CHAPTER 6
A VACATION FROM BACKPACKING

TUESDAY, August 11, 1998

THE DRIP – ON A TRAIN, PRAGUE, CZECH REPUBLIC TO VIENNA, AUSTRIA

Warm morning air rushes through our compartment window as the train chugs to Vienna. I sink my teeth into a peach, summer sweetness bursts on my tongue, and sticky juice slides down my forearm. I wipe it on my shorts, rest my head on the bench, and sway to the clickety-clack of the wheels rolling down the track.

Dejah's head is against the window, mouth open wide—reenacting my opera nap.

I toss the peach pit in the trash as fresh-faced, smartly dressed locals pass by in the hallway. I can do without the knock to my confidence from judging myself against the put-together locals and coming up short. I shift my back to the door to hide my sticky frumpiness until they're out of sight.

I snap *The Crash* alternative rock mixtape my brother Pete made into my Walkman and crack open my journal. The rhythmic beat of "1979" by The Smashing Pumpkins fills my ears as I glide my pen across the page. My printing is small and concise as I cram in every detail. I don't know if this six-hour trip will be enough time to recap Prague, but I'll make a good dent at catching up.

Dejah's eyes lazily open. She stretches her arms out, then wordlessly stumbles down the hall to the toilet.

I drop my pen and shake out the cramp in my hand.

A shadow clouds the compartment window as someone mopes past.

I sputter. Dark hair. Sulky walk. Miserable face. This time it's not a smartly dressed local. It's The Drip.

He doesn't see me, but he's heading toward the toilet Khadejah's in. I wish I could send her a telepathic message saying, *Stay in the toilet—stay, in, the, toilet.* But I'm not gifted that way. I snicker as I dash to the door and peek down the hallway.

The Drip is steps from the bathroom. Hopefully she's doing a number two because if not, she's been in there the right amount of time for a pee and should be done—

The *WC Occupied* light goes off, the door flies open, and Khadejah bursts out—right into The Drip. She steps back, sneers, then schools her expression to a forced toothy smile.

I choke down my giggles as I leap into my seat.

"You'll never believe it. I just ran into The Drip." She slams the door.

"Really?" I suck in my cheeks. It's all I can do to keep a straight face. I never thought someone so boring could make me laugh this much.

"Yeah, and he's going to Vienna. But not staying in town, as he has relatives somewhere in the mountains he's visiting. So that should be the last of him."

Famous last words.

HOT PROPOSITION - VIENNA, AUSTRIA

My clothes cling to my skin with sweat by the time we stagger into the bright hostel courtyard in Vienna. Golden late afternoon sun glimmers off the ivy creeping up the walls, and plant pots bursting with red, yellow, and pink roses circle the perimeter of the cozy space. I breathe in the sweet air as I dump Barney next to one of the handful of picnic tables. I rub my sore shoulders; I'm out of carrying practice since he's been under my bunk for a week. Dejah drops Hulk, waves her hand to the reception door, then shuffles off to sort out beds. I nod because we stopped talking an hour ago. It's over 40°C, and in this heat, neither one of us has anything nice to say.

After a luxurious high water-pressure shower, my stomach growls as we venture out to find a place for dinner. Tall white stone buildings tower over the formal and organized streets. I sharpen my spine. This city is all business, lacking the warmth and quirkiness of Prague. Sharply dressed hostesses hovering in restaurant doorways next to plastic-encased menus peer down their noses at us. We're turned away from four places, claiming they're busy, but not all of them are. The prim ladies didn't like the look of us, which is a shame since I'm not slouching and I'm wearing my cleanest shorts—the ones without the peach stains.

The restaurants we're not turned away from we veto because of the leering men clustered on the front patios. Dejah marches past the shouts we can't understand because they're in German, but the seething and derogatory tone is always the same.

I lift my chin as I follow.

Languages, currency, and buildings change as we move from place to place, but it breaks my heart that harassment remains the one constant of our travels.

We ditch the main road and happen upon a quaint venue on a quiet side street. A wall of open windows spills whimsical Italian music around the ten bistro tables draped in red and white checkered tablecloths in front of the restaurant. Four gray-haired men are hunched over a dice game on the corner of the patio. They cheer as one makes a good play and fill their glasses with red wine.

Not one sneer or any looks at all for that matter from the dozen other patrons.

"We're so staying here," I say.

"I'll order us a large jug of red and grab some menus." Dejah saunters to the bar inside as I slump at a table overlooking the quiet cobblestone street.

I stare at the starless sky and enjoy the latest song's graceful violin solo.

Achy panic flared under my skin when I closed my journal on the train this afternoon after recapping my time with Josh. Because if I don't come up with a reunion idea, I might never see him again. Guilt churns in my gut at the thought of breaking the promise I made to Dejah about not leaving her for him while we were hiking in Zakopane. She gave up traveling with Gwen and Stella to backpack with me so I wouldn't be alone. And I won't leave her alone either. The only way a Josh meeting can happen is if it's on a timeline that works for Dejah and me.

"Rather than faff about with a menu we can't read, I ordered two spaghettis," Dejah says as she pours our wine and places the glass pitcher between us.

"Perfect." I gulp three mouthfuls and shudder at the salty aftertaste. "So … I kind of want to see Josh again."

She drops her eyes and runs her fingers through her long black ponytail.

"Do you still want to go to Croatia and Hungary with me?"

"Absolutely." I reach out and squeeze her hand. "I'm not giving that up. I don't want to give up any of our time together. Can you help me figure out how I can travel with you *and* spend time with him?"

I pull my Eastern Europe travel guide from my daypack for inspiration.

"You've visited Turkey before, right?" she asks as I thumb through the pages.

"Yes, right after my mom died." At that time, I did a short backpacking trip to England and Italy and planned to visit the

Greek Islands. But it was too late in the season and the ferries were closed, so I toured Northern Greece and Turkey instead.

"I could meet Stella and Gwen in Istanbul in mid-September, and you could meet Josh then," she says as she tops up our drinks.

"That could work." My throat chafes as I glide my thumb across the smooth tablecloth.

Once upon a time, I couldn't get to the Greek Islands, so I went to Turkey. Years later, I went to the Greek Islands because I missed it the first time, subsequently meeting Josh in Santorini and kicking off this adventure. And here I sit, comfortable skipping Turkey because of those two trips.

"Where would I meet you guys?" My stomach twists as I slide my book on the table.

I can skip Turkey, but no matter how much I yearn to see Josh, I'm not missing Egypt.

"The plan is to overland straight through Turkey for Syria, then Lebanon," she says.

"It won't be easy to meet in those places." The pitcher of wine glugs as I refill our glasses. "Which leaves the next country on the list: Jordan."

"Probably easiest to meet in Amman. Then the four of us continue south through Jordan, over to Israel and Egypt. You'll still catch all the best bits." She shrugs.

My stomach pitches. It's a bummer to miss two countries I haven't seen, but something has to give. This way I get all my time with Khadejah and won't be leaving her in the lurch on her own. I get time with Josh, and it coincides with Oktoberfest—somewhere he's going and I would like to experience.

"I'll email him," I say.

I busy myself returning my book to my bag so she won't see the longing for this to work written all over my face. Because if Josh doesn't agree, then I'll have to close the door on him for good.

MY BRA and underwear are soaked. I have sweat dripping down my back, chest, and bum after our morning traipsing around Vienna. This city is modern compared to most places we've visited. Gothic buildings and endless fountains aside, it's like being at home from a convenience standpoint, like grabbing a sandwich with identifiable ingredients and buying hair conditioner at The Body Shop. But it's also twice as expensive as anywhere else we've been, making it impossible to stick to the budget like in Prague. So we're only staying one day and are leaving for cheaper Croatia tomorrow.

I sigh as we enter St. Stephen's Cathedral in the center of town. The cool air inside the tallest church in Austria is a welcome break from the sweltering heat. The vestibule is crawling with tourists, heads tipped back gawking at the domed ceiling, carved pillars, and shiny pipe organ that would make Keith weep. I veer to a table on the side flickering with candles and light one for my mom.

"I can't wait to hit the beach in Croatia," I say as I collapse on a pew next to Dejah in the center of the sightseer chaos.

"Same, mate." Dejah fluffs her ponytail to air the back of her neck.

"I hope the sea is as clear as Keith said." I unscrew the cap on my Nalgene bottle and chug my hot water. "I could go for a swim right now. Imagine the feel of cool water—"

"It's The Drip." Khadejah slouches in the pew.

"Ha, ha. You're hilarious." I roll my eyes.

"There." She jabs her index finger across the church to a solo man among the groups of visitors. His dark hair's swooped over one eye, and his face is scrunched in a miserable frown as he hunches over a painting of baby Jesus.

"You've got to be kidding me." I duck. "What's he doing in Vienna?"

"No idea. He should be in the countryside with his von Trapp relatives." She chuckles.

"Why can't we run into fun people over and over like Simon or Evan and Aaron." *And Josh.* My heart pinches. "Rather than the most boring guy on the planet."

"We've got to get out of here." Dejah scans the area for an exit.

Heads down, we slide down the pew and slink out a side door under the cover of a tour group.

We're a sloppy mess by the time we lope down the long paved pathway to the sprawling white Belvedere Palace. The surrounding gardens have no big trees, just boring grass cut in swirly patterns we're unable to walk on. But I'm not here for the garden; I'm here because inside the symmetrical building with a green copper roof is the largest and most important collection of Gustav Klimt's paintings in the world.

Dejah's not interested, so she sits outside in the shade journaling while I beeline to the Klimt section. I step inside the enormous room with twenty-foot ceilings and freeze.

Massive canvases in gold frames adorn the white walls, but my eyes zero in on the one in dorm rooms around the world —*The Kiss*. The cozy pair of lovers are pressed together and the gold leaf quilt encircling them shimmers under the lights. The man's face is buried in the woman's neck, his hands locking her in place. The woman's face is euphoric, her arms wrapped around his neck as she lists into him. My heart sighs as I get lost in the passion, tenderness, and love radiating off the canvas, wishing I had someone who wanted to hold me like that for longer than a day.

In the gift shop, I blow my already blown daily budget on a new navy journal with blank white pages and *The Kiss* on the cover. I do need a new journal as I've almost filled my current one, but more than anything, it will be a daily reminder of what love looks like.

I clutch my new journal to my chest as I step outside. Dejah pops up from her spot and gushes over my purchase.

"*Let's Go!* says there is a free Internet place. Interested?" Dejah asks as we leave the palace grounds.

"Yes." Because I need to send Josh my Oktoberfest proposal.

We share the passion of the couple in the painting but not the love. And as much as I want to see him again, I'm not compromising. If he doesn't jump on my offer, I'll be going to Turkey with Khadejah.

WE TRUDGE into the hostel courtyard after dark, every sight in Vienna ticked off the list, and an email sent to Josh. I'm ready to leave the heat of the city for the beaches in Croatia.

"Girls" is yelled out in an Australian accent. "Candace, Khadejah."

I tense. Ugh. Not The Drip. Again.

I turn to the voice and soften at a waving Dude Davo. He's at a picnic table, pen in hand, journal with colorful tickets poking out between the pages open on his right, and a half-eaten pizza in a brown cardboard box on his left.

Dejah rushes over, he jumps up to hug her and then gives me one as well.

He's lame, but it's nice to see a familiar face that's not The Drip.

"You must have been here a while. You left Prague ages ago," I say as we sit on the bench opposite him.

"Vienna's kept me busy, there's so much to see." He flips his leather-bound journal closed.

I flick my eyes to Dejah, and her lips twitch. She marched us past and through every major site in twelve hours. We would never spend days here. Besides, we couldn't afford it. But he's a dentist on holiday whose budget is probably more than fifty dollars a day.

"Want some?" He nudges the pizza box.

"Thanks." I peel off a slice and Dejah declines.

"I'm off to Sydney in the morning. Next time I see you will be in Oz," he says.

He and Dejah share stories about Vienna as I hoover a second piece.

"I have to go to the bathroom. Can you watch my gear?" He points to his bag and journal.

"Sure thing," Dejah says because my mouth's full of pizza.

As soon as he's out of sight, Dejah pounces on his journal, flipping to the date we met him at the salt mine in Kraków.

"We're in here." She holds the journal in front of her as she reads. "'*I met two girls today; they were nice and fun but the blond Canadian one was particularly crazy.*'"

I choke on my pizza.

"Me?" I cough. "Why me? You're the one who deep-throated a pint glass."

Dejah smacks the table and laughs.

I scoff as I shove in the last bit of crust. A year ago, before this adventure, crazy was the last word someone would have used to describe me. I grin as I chew. Crazy *is* better than sad and lonely. I'm taking Dude Davo's words as a testament to how far I've come. And as long as no one is calling me a kurwa, I'm happy.

RESURRECTION OF JESUS - ON A TRAIN, AUSTRIA TO CROATIA

We have the compartment to ourselves as the train labors through green mountains dotted with little houses. We're stamped out of Austria and into Slovenia, out of Slovenia and into Croatia—easy peasy.

The cabin door glides open after the first train stop in Croatia. Two men and one woman dressed in terracotta-colored linen crisscross wraparound robes, matching MC Hammer parachute pants, and floppy leather sandals enter. They settle on the opposite bench, the woman with clear skin, long blond dreads, and a woven crossbody bag sitting in the middle. The men flanking her have dark hair, tangled long beards, and no luggage. The one closest to the door with his foot resting on his opposite knee strongly resembles Jesus. I bite back a smile as I glance out the window. If this is what Croatia has to offer, I can guarantee it will be ten times more interesting than buttoned-up Austria.

"Where are you from?" Clear Skin asks in perfect English as she clasps her fingers on her lap.

"Canada and Australia," Dejah says.

She translates to the two men. The guy who looks like Jesus nods and replies in jagged Croatian. His deep brown eyes narrow on mine as he brushes his thumb across his full bottom lip. My cheeks flush. Phew. Is it hot in here? What is it with this guy? I'm not usually one to go for a beard, but he's dripping in naughty intentions.

"You are safe." Clear Skin snaps my attention back to her.

I scrunch my nose.

"Safe?" I ask. What is she on about?

"Yes, safe because Australia and Canada are not going to slip into the sea." Clear Skin scoffs.

I blink. Dejah snorts.

"Our leader"—she gestures to the hot Jesus-looking guy—"is the Meditator Yoga Guru who works directly for Jesus. There is a major event that's going to happen soon when Jesus is completely resurrected. And when it happens, the UK, the west coast of America, and Japan are going to go underwater. Jesus has already been resurrected in other parts of the world, and we're working on his resurrection in Croatia."

"Uh ..." My mouth opens. Then closes. Then opens.

"You should take our brochure in case you run into any trouble." Clear Skin reaches into her hippie bag and thrusts me a leaflet.

"Uh ... thanks?" A smoldering photo of hot Jesus-looking guy stares back at me from the page.

"Call us anytime." She smiles and nods. "We can cure all ailments right over the phone via intergalactic healing in a pristine universal language that goes right to your soul."

I'll bet—with hot Jesus-looking guy at the helm.

I press my lips together and glance at Khadejah, whose eyes are twinkling.

Oh, this country's going to be fun.

EIGHT DAYS WITHOUT LUGGING BARNEY – ZAGREB, CROATIA

The sky's a wash of gold and navy as we stroll Ivana Racica Street in Old Town Zagreb searching for a place to eat dinner. Two-story buildings in cream, yellow, and dusty pink line either side of the pedestrian thoroughfare. Occupied tables fill the sidewalks in front of trendy bars and cafés, and a mix of soft music and lively foreign chatter drifts on the humid summer air.

"Italian?" Dejah asks as we stop at a restaurant with an empty two-top on the tightly packed patio.

"Might as well." I shrug.

We take a seat elbow to elbow with the other diners. I scan the menu as the server in a micro mini skirt and sleek black hair hovers. I close it. Another language we can't read.

"I miss the fried cheese in Prague." I sigh.

"You would. The usual?"

I nod, and Dejah orders our safe choice of beer and spaghetti so we don't end up with mystery meat playing menu roulette.

"We have four places left to check in the morning," I say as I glide my palm across the city map.

Our books said traveling within Croatia is expensive, so we decided we'd look into renting a car for our journey from Zagreb to Dubrovnik. After checking into our hostel, we went straight to the tourist office, and the lady marked nine car rental places on the map. We marched from one end of Zagreb to the other to investigate our options. We found one for fifty-eight dollars a day, then ninety at the second place, and the other shops were out of cars as tomorrow's a holiday. We couldn't visit the last four shops as the hour grew late and they were closed.

"We should have taken the first car," Dejah says as she lights a cigarette.

"But we didn't know it was going to be the best price."

"I'm gutted. I really want to rent a car and get a break from our packs." Her shoulders hunch.

"Me too," I say as Sleek Hair drops two beers between us. "We'll find one tomorrow."

"You're speaking English. Where are you from?" one of the two guys at the table next to us asks in a smooth French accent.

He and his friend are both built with sharp short dark hair. They're in between hot and not—kind of just like that.

"Canada and Australia." I point to myself then to Khadejah.

"I'm Florian from France, and this is Marko from Northern Macedonia; we both work for NATO. Would you like to join us to eat dinner?" Florian asks.

My shoulders tighten. Our tables are inches apart, making it awkward to say no. I'm having flashbacks of Scotland when a dude asked me the same question. That ended in stranger danger vibes and me racing out of a dingy Holiday Inn bar. Dejah tips her head, signaling she's okay with it. It should be all right because we are together and they work for NATO, so they can't be *all bad*.

"Sure." I share our names as Florian slides his table flush to ours.

"How long are you in town?" Marko asks in a rumbly accent.

"One day. We're planning on renting a car and leaving in the morning," I say.

"As you're only here one night, can we give you a tour of Zagreb after we eat?" Marko asks. "We've been stationed here for six months and know the area well."

I quirk a brow at Dejah—my signal for her to make the decision. I'm a yes because it would be a good way to see the city we had no plans in other than finding a car.

"We'd love that," Dejah says.

Sleek Hair places two heaping mounds of spaghetti smothered in rich red tomato sauce in front of us, returning a couple of minutes later with two bowls of mystery meat in orange sauce for the guys. I gag as they dig in then focus on my plate of simple garlicky goodness. We entertain them with stories of border crossings in Russia and night train trips through Poland because they can't share details of their work.

Florian and Marko lead us up hundreds of wide stone steps, and I'm heaving by the time we reach Gornji Grad—Upper Town. The sweeping city view is a blur of twinkling lights around the focal point of the spiky tips of the Cathedral of Zagreb. We descend to Lower Town via a pathway and circular stairways, then amble along the cobblestones to St. Mark's Church. The colorful mosaic roof is lit up, proudly displaying the medieval coat of arms for Croatia and the emblem of Zagreb. We twist through a maze of streets past the parliament buildings and a big clock tower to an area packed with bars and stop for a drink.

The tour was great, but my feet ache. The guys are decent but not *that* interesting. After one drink we leave them to it—walking not running away because they don't set off our internal stranger danger alarm. So far so good, Croatia. Now we just need to find a car.

THE DOOR SLAMS as we exit the hostel early the next morning.

"They have a phone at the train station; we can ring the last four places on our list from there," Dejah says.

We buy a phone card and flip through the phone book. I read out the numbers as Dejah presses the keypad. We can't reach them all, and the ones who answer don't have cars available. We check the price of a train ticket to Pula, and it's double the cost of one day of a rental car.

"We're not giving up on the car dream. Let's go to the one place that didn't answer their phone." Dejah's face is severe as she bundles out of the train station, map in hand.

On the way, we spot a car rental shop not on our list and rush inside.

"Do you have any cars?" she asks the man with a shiny plump face behind the desk with a hopeful smile.

"Yes." He leans an arm on the counter.

I hold my breath.

"I have one car left for two hundred and sixty-nine kunas a day."

I do a quick mental calculation; that's roughly sixty-seven dollars. A bit above budget, but I'm sure we'll be able to round out the cost with cheaper accommodation.

"It's a compact five-door Opal Corsa hatchback with a tape deck," Shiny Face says.

I have no idea what car that is, and I don't care.

"We'll take it." Dejah slaps her credit card on the counter.

My chest ignites with happiness. This is it—our vacation from backpacking. No waiting for trains. No weird passenger interactions. No wasted time. Going exactly where we want. Checking out remote locations. The options are endless.

"Mate, you have to drive, it's on your side of the road," she says as she fills in the paperwork.

"Sure thing, as long as you chauffeur me when I get to Australia." I grin.

"I got your back," she says.

We sign the rental agreement for eight days.

Shiny Face parks the rounded hatchback in front of the building. It's unremarkable with a black antenna jutting up from the back like a bumper car. But to me, it's the prettiest vehicle I've ever seen. He passes me the keys, and they dig into my palm as I clutch them in my grip.

"Ready to go?" I ask as I climb behind the wheel.

"So ready." She beams as she drops into the passenger seat.

Backpackers milling about gape as I park in front of the hostel. I can't wipe the cocky smirk off my face as we toss Barney and Hulk in the trunk.

"This was the best idea." I giggle as the engine purrs to life.

"Freedom." Khadejah pushes a George Michael cassette into the tape deck.

"It is." I flip the visor and use the mirror to apply a coat of lip gloss.

"No, the name of our car—Freedom," she says as she flicks the map open.

"Oh, perfect." I shift the car into drive and hit the gas, ready for a whole new spin on our adventure.

WHO NEEDS BRAD PITT ANYWAY - ZAGREB TO PULA, CROATIA

Windows down, cigarette in hand, we sing along with George as our little car rolls west along the smooth, dark tarmac. The signs are clear and easy to follow for Pula, our destination tonight on the tip of the most western peninsula in Northern Croatia. The highway narrows to a two-lane curvy mountain road parallel to the Slovenian border.

"I'm getting major *Thelma and Louise* vibes, just with not as cool a car." I press the pedal to the floor and will Freedom upward as we motor past stone houses with terracotta tile roofs nestled in the green slopes.

"I'd like a better ending," Dejah says, bare feet on the dash.

"I promise not to drive off a cliff." Freedom squeals through a hairpin bend, and I clench the wheel. "On purpose anyway."

"And we need Brad Pitt." She sighs.

"Don't you mean Brados Pittos?" I snort at the memory of the dubbed movie we watched on the bus in Lithuania. "Maybe he'll be around the next corner."

"I wish." She ejects the cassette and flips it over to play the other side.

My stomach's happy for the twisty break as the car descends the mountains to our first coastal stop on our driving adventure, Rijeka. I tap the steering wheel as we cruise down the waterfront to the marina and park across the street from the brilliant yellow Adria Palace. We haven't seen the sea since Gdańsk in Northern Poland, and I've missed the infinite blue water.

I peel my sticky thighs off the seat and rest my forearm on the hot roof. My face scrunches at the limited bay view surrounded by green mountains. Moored sailboats bob in the glimmering sea next to fishing boats, and workers in orange vests unload container ships on the dock. Shouts to direct cargo, beeping trucks backing out with their loads, and people hurrying along the waterfront don't scream relaxing vacation.

"I reckon we can do better." Dejah gets back in the car, and I follow. "Best part about having Freedom: If we don't like it, we leave."

"Direct me out of here." She flaps the map as I fasten my seatbelt.

We stop at the next information center along the highway for a detailed map of the area, hoping to uncover a hidden gem we wouldn't normally see traveling by bus or train. The woman behind the desk doesn't speak English but unfolds the large map and taps her finger on a town along the coast called Opatija, which is now our next stop.

The afternoon sun singes my shoulders as we wander the maze of pristine pedestrian streets of Opatija, searching for the sea. The warm sandy-colored buildings lining the pathways flow seamlessly into the matching flagstones beneath our feet. Violet and white flowers dangling from boxes at the base of the sash windows add the only color to the symmetrical sandy city. It's quiet—no one's hanging out the open windows or on the street. The path ends at the top of a steep stone stairway. The clean smell of saltwater floods my senses—we're close. I glide my hand against the rough stone wall as I descend the shadowy trail because the center of each step is worn and concaved a couple of centimeters.

My eyes widen as I ease onto the smooth sandstone platform —the size of a tennis court—that edges the aquamarine sea. There's not a cloud in the endless azure sky, and the jagged rock walls arching around the platform make it a cozy not claustrophobic oasis. Children's laughter followed by splashes draws my eyes to the endless blue water I've been longing for. I grin as the local kids leap off tiny fishing boats anchored a few meters off the platform. This is where everyone is, and I don't blame them. The handful of locals sunning themselves on the warm stones greets us with enthusiastic waves as we encroach on their private cove paradise.

I blink.

"They're smiling." My mouth parts. "Outside of Zakopane, no one does that."

"It's bloody off-putting," Dejah says as we wave back and walk toward the water.

I take off my shoes, perch on the smooth stone edge, and sigh as my toes hit the cool lapping sea.

"I wish I had my swimsuit." I frown as Dejah plunks down beside me. "It looks so nice out there. Maybe we should have rented a boat instead."

"I don't think that's within the budget. But there would be lots to visit. I read in my book there's over a thousand islands in Croatia and only sixty-six are inhabited," she says.

"Seems a bit greedy for one country to have all those." I swish my feet and take a slug of my warm water.

"Yeah." She shoves her shoulder into mine and chuckles. "We'll get on the water after Dubrovnik on a budget-friendly ferry."

"I love ferries." I kick water at her. "Besides, who needs a boat when we have this place?" I spread my arms out and tip my head to the brilliant sky.

We spend hours talking about nothing and watching the boys —who probably have no idea they're growing up in paradise— play in the crystal-clear water. Not even twenty-four hours into our car adventure and we've found a hidden gem—is Brados Pittos next?

———————

AFTER LOTS of driving in circles, I park under a tall, leafy tree in front of a two-story yellow stucco house with an orange clay roof at twilight. The Pula Youth Hostel is smack in the middle of a residential neighborhood and it would have taken forever to get here on public transport—score one for the car. Breakfast is included, which they serve overlooking Soline Cove. I peek out the window behind the check-in desk and curl my nose. The water is the same magical color as in Opatija, but the simple gray pebble beach around the horseshoe cove is bland, and the rickety picnic tables look like they've been stolen from a sketchy campsite.

The temperature exponentially increases as we climb to the second floor where our four-bed dorm room is. Heat blasts my face when we enter our squishy room, but the heat is nothing compared to the death stares we get from the pinched-faced chicks lounging in the other two beds. They flip their long dark hair and hiss guttural words as they glare. I ignore them and head to the washroom to do a much-needed underwear hand wash while Dejah leaves to scout for food.

Panties drip between my fingers as my eyes dart around the room, puzzling out the best way to hang them without encroaching on the bitchy chicks'—who are thankfully absent— side of the room. Dejah waltzes in clutching two white plastic bags as I finish the final weave of my elastic clothesline around the slats on my chipped wooden bunk. She smiles at my underpants dangling from the looped line like Christmas decorations.

248

"Nice one. I reckon that's worth a new Spice Girl name: MacGyver Spice."

"Oooooh." My lips part. "I like that one. I totally accept."

"Let's eat." Dejah tips her head to the door.

I sigh as the cooler but still hot air hits my skin as we exit the hostel. Small clusters of people are grouped around the cove. Foreign music blares from a ghetto blaster. My sandals wobble over the uneven stones as we make our way to a sloped table under the one large tree shading the beach.

The picnic table groans as we sit. Dejah tears the plastic bag to cover the dirty wooden tabletop. Swiss Army knives flicked open, I slice tomatoes and cheese as she hacks into the white loaf, then we slap our sandwiches together as the brilliant orange sun dips into the sea, lighting up the sky in a blur of gold, fuchsia, and auburn.

"Not as nice as Opatija. But not bad either." I bite into the thick French bread, and my stomach rumbles as I chew. It was hot and we didn't eat much today, but now that the sun's gone, my appetite's back with a gusto. I shove more in my mouth.

"Mate, I don't know if anything can be bad here. What are we doing tomorr—"

"Hi girls, can I join you?" A white guy towers over our table. He's bald on top with a ring of shaggy dark hair around the sides.

Dejah and I stare at each other with full mouths and big eyes.

"I'm Anthony from California, and I'm a ballet dancer." The muscles twitch in his arms as he poses in his tank top and board shorts.

His posturing does zero to spark my interest. I swallow my bite, and Dejah gives me the slightest nod, but I know she's not into him either—he's friend-zoned after two sentences.

"Sure, have a seat." I tip my head.

He folds his tall body onto the bench, and brown paint chips fly as he drops a six-pack on the table.

"You should have started with that," Dejah says as he passes us each a tepid can of local beer. Nothing is ever cold here; it's just too darn hot all the time.

"I did ballet when I was five. It wasn't my thing," I say as I snap open the blue can. "It was too slow for me. Hold the bar, point, sweep, point. I got bored."

His chest shakes as he laughs, but his back remains perfectly straight.

"I was once The Beast in *Beauty and The Beast*, the stage production. That was far from boring," he says.

"I'll bet. I saw it once with my mom. I've always wondered how the big reveal at the end works on stage." I scratch my chin. "How can the actor transform from The Beast so quickly?"

"Ah, well." The corners of his eyes wrinkle as he smiles. "I'll let you in on my secret. For the scene right before it, someone else plays The Beast while I get prepared in the back as the prince. Then the magic happens."

"That makes so much sense." I take a dainty bite of my sandwich since it's not polite to jam it in my mouth around company.

"What are you ladies doing tomorrow?" He opens a second beer and passes us another.

"Touring around Pula—*in our car*," Dejah brags.

"I can join you." He swipes his fingers along his bare shoulder.

My spine sags. Drat. We fell straight into that one. And just like with The Drip, Florian, and Marko, we're stuck because it would be rude to say no. He *seems* more interesting than the others—but only time will tell.

THE THREE OF us tip our heads back and gape at the Pula Arena the next morning. The pristine stone open-air oval amphitheater is 2,000 years old and looks like a painting against the backdrop of the deep blue sky. White vans are being emptied by workers dressed in jeans and T-shirts, and through the three levels of arched windows, we watch the crew install large black spotlights on tall metal scaffolding around a dark stage.

"José Carreras is performing tonight." Anthony's eyes bulge as he points to a banner over the Arena entrance archway.

"Who's that?" Dejah asks as she adjusts her daypack on her shoulder.

"The third tenor." Anthony scoffs. "We need to go."

"We might as well." I wipe my brow, wishing I had brought my hat.

We buy three tickets for fifteen dollars.

My ankles swell as we wander the smooth stone streets. Anthony and Dejah climb a tower while I lean against the trunk of a tree that offers little shade and watch the bags. Next, we hike a hill to visit the Archaeological Museum of Istria. It's as hot inside as out. Sweat soaks my hairline as we stroll past priceless urns, earth-toned frescos, and crumbling stone walls. My head's pounding when we reach the Arch of the Sergii, an eight-meter-high Roman triumphal arch with Corinthian columns from the 1st century BC.

"Guys, I'm not feeling great." I dig my fingertips into my temples, attempting to dull the stabbing pain.

"Let's get lunch." Dejah marches us to an air-conditioned café across from the arch.

I rest my head on the table as she orders sandwiches and a pitcher of water.

"We need to get you hydrated," Anthony says.

Dejah shoves a glass of water in my hand. I drink it. Then another. And another.

"Thanks." I sigh as the pressure eases behind my eyes.

"It's what Louise would do for Thelma," Khadejah says.

"Who says you're Louise? I'm the one doing the driving." I wet my napkin and glide it across my forehead. "And you're the one looking for Brad, who Thelma falls for."

"Okay, you can be Louise." Her lips twitch as she lights a cigarette.

I always fancied myself more of an independent Louise, played by Susan Sarandon, than troubled Thelma, played by Geena Davis. But that was before my mom died. Maybe I'm a Thelma now—

"Well." Anthony presses his palms together and tips them against his red lips. "I can be your Brad Pitt."

"Ha, hhh …" My glass slips and lands upright on the table with a thud.

Whether I'm Thelma or Louise, Anthony is okay for a day, but he's not someone I want to spend a prolonged period with. How are we going to get out of him joining us? Because this is not the Brad Pitt we're looking for.

LUNCH ROLLS in my gut as the car bounces down a narrow rocky lane leading to a beach Anthony swears we must visit. I swerve to avoid a pothole and park in the tall yellow grass next to the other cars at the end of the laneway.

We gather our swim gear and the watermelon Dejah bought at a roadside stand on our drive here, then hike the dirt path through tall trees to the sea. Frothy waves lap against a dark brown rocky shoreline that melts into water so brilliantly blue it hurts my eyes. Small clusters of people are swimming or relaxing along the expanse of shore.

Anthony was right; this place is beautiful.

"Wait. Are they … *naked*?" I squint at the folks on the left side of the path, but my far vision is so bad that everyone languishing on the rocks is a creamy-brown blur.

Anthony taps a white sign with his knuckle, wearing a coy grin.

"Klaonica Beach has two sides. Care to join me in clothing-optional?" He quirks a brow.

"We'll be over there." Dejah points to the right side filled with clothed families.

"Your loss." He winks. "Come get me when you're ready to go."

Anthony swaggers through the fuzzy nudists like they should be happy to be in his presence. He might not be ours, but he sure is acting like Brad Pitt.

"Come on." Dejah tugs me to the clothing-required side.

We spread our sarongs over the pebbles, and I wiggle to make an indent for my butt.

"This watermelon is going to be perfect." She lays the green oval between us.

I flip my Swiss Army knife open and stab the watermelon as she holds it steady.

"We owe Keith," I say as I hack through the tough rind.

"Yeah, we would've never come here without his recommendation."

The watermelon quakes then pops open with a slurp, revealing the rich red inside.

"We have to send him a postcard." I pass her a jagged slice.

I moan as I bite into the warm, sweet fruit. I tangle the seeds in my tongue and spit them to the side beside a shiny golf ball-sized rock laced with crystals. After my second slice, I reach for the stone. I lie on my back, turning it over at arm's length, examining the sparkly veins from different angles.

The rock slips from my grasp.

My body locks as it hurls toward my face.

I bolt upright as pain shoots through my mouth.

"Are you okay?" Dejah asks.

I fly my hand across my teeth and exhale. No blood and they're all in place.

"Can you see if I chipped any?" I flash my straight smile from spending my teen years in metal braces.

Khadejah leans in. "No chips I can see. Are any wobbly?"

I bounce my finger from one to the next. "They're good." My

heart races. "What a dumbass thing to do. I could have lost a tooth."

My throat dries. I got lucky. It only takes one moment of doing something stupid to change everything. If I broke a tooth, would a dentist pull it? Then what? I walk around looking like a hockey goon with no front tooth. Or maybe they fix it. How long and how much money would it take to get right? I could blow all my cash because of one monumental lapse in judgment.

We've hit our stride in backpacking. This is my new normal, and I've become complacent. I stomp to the water's edge and toss the offending rock into the sea.

"I hear you, Mom," I whisper, then promise myself I'll be more vigilant because no way do I want to cut my adventure short and end up back at home because I was being an idiot.

"It's getting late. We should head back to get ready for the show tonight," Dejah says as she packs the uneaten watermelon in a plastic bag. "And since you dropped a rock on your face, I elect you to get Anthony."

"Haven't I suffered enough?" I stuff my sarong in my backpack and throw my clothes over my swimsuit. "That's not something I want to see."

"Bad luck. It's your punishment for being a galah." She crosses her arms.

"Fine." I don't even know what she called me, but I do know it's not worth the fight when her arms are crossed.

Dejah stands by the sign on the path leading to the cars.

I square my shoulders and weave between the naked bodies. I flit my eyes from one set of saggy boobs to the next, never lingering too long as I search for Anthony. I flinch as my gaze locks on a flaccid penis resting on a hairy thigh next to a saggy ball sack dangling in the breeze. I shake my head. I've seen way too many old man penises on this trip.

I hop across the uneven stones and continue my search. Did he have to go so far from the trail? I stop in my tracks and squint. Anthony's sinewy frame is mostly sheltered from view by a big rock. And thanks to my bad eyesight, he's a uniform golden hue. I can't see specific parts, but he's definitely naked.

"Anthony." I wave.

Nothing.

"Anthony," I scream, wave, and jump.

Chests jiggle as nudists' heads turn. Everyone's but Anthony's. I growl. Dejah so owes me for this. I inch closer, flapping my arms like I'm signaling a plane. Why can't he hear me? I train my eyes on his blurry face. Oh man, he's wearing headphones. He's getting more in focus with each step, and it's impossible *not* to look at his penis area. And … he has a long one.

"An-ttttthhhhon-yyyyy," I holler and focus on his face.

He sits, smiles, and waves. I sag with relief when he gives me the universal index finger one-minute signal, and I leg it back to Dejah.

"You could have come right over." He smirks as we walk to the car. "I wouldn't have minded."

But *I* would have.

It's a quiet ride back to the hostel. The heat's zapped us, and my headache's back. I take an icy shower to cool down. But it's all I can do to stop myself from pounding my head against the shower tiles to divert my attention from the excruciating pain blinding my vision. I swallow three Tylenol and crawl into bed.

"WAKE UP." Dejah places a hand on my shoulder.

My head's pounding and my sheets are soaked with sweat.

"You've been asleep for two hours. I got burgers and water from the food truck a block away. Come sit outside in the fresh air and eat."

Dejah helps me out of my bunk and outside to our table under the tree. The warm salty breeze chills my skin, and Dejah passes me a hoodie. I shrug it on and nod. She's thought of everything.

"Drink." She passes me a bottle of warm water, and I chug it.

"There'll be no third tenor for me. I'm sure I'll be disappointed later, but right now I don't care. My head feels like someone's drilling into it. You should go with Anthony."

I rest my cheek on the rough tabletop.

"I'm not leaving you." She circles her hand on my back.

Tears burn my eyes. It's been a decade since someone's taken care of me while I've been sick. My mom's intensive chemotherapy wiped out every bad *and* good cell. She couldn't afford to get sick and would ostracize us to our rooms if we had the slightest sniffle. My dad and brothers were zero help. So since my early teens, I've taken care of myself while I was sick.

Dejah unwraps a burger and places it in front of me.

I push upright and take a small bite. A hot tear rolls down my cheek as I chew but don't taste. I forgot what this type of kindness is like. How it warms you from the inside out. How it nurtures your heart knowing someone will give up seeing a once-in-a-lifetime performance so you're not alone.

I grip the burger as guilt tugs at my chest for leaving Dejah in Vilnius when she was sick. But it was too hard to stay. Years spent at my mother's bedside have made the act of caring for another more painful than this headache.

"Have a bit more, then we can chill in the hammocks I saw on the other side of the beach." She angles her chin at the burger.

"Really, you should go." I take another flavorless nibble. "I'll be good on my own."

"Not happening." She crumples her silver wrapper. "I'm staying with you."

"Like Thelma and Louise." My lip wobbles.

"Just like that." She collects the trash and dumps it on our walk around the cove to the rope hammocks.

My throat tightens, and warmth blooms in my chest as I swing under the stars between twisty pine tree trunks. The choice to stay was easy for Dejah but changes everything for me. It's a reminder I'm not alone. That it's safe to rely on another person. And that it sucked looking after myself for so many years. And because of her sincere compassion, my grief-stricken heart stitches together and heals that little bit more.

Dejah and I drive away alone the next morning. Anthony never outright asked to come with us but hinted a few times he was going in our direction. He's more interesting than The Drip but not someone we want to share over seven hundred kilometers of our special car time to Dubrovnik with. Dehydration and rocks aside, we're doing just fine on our own. Besides, Thelma and Louise would have been way better off without ever meeting Brad Pitt.

THE ADRIATIC SEA - PULA TO POREČ, CROATIA

We park under one of the dozen weeping willows circling the white colonial plantation house outside of Poreč. The house has a wide wraparound veranda on the ground and upper floor. Iron garden tables are dotted around the vast green lawns next to sprawling lavender and green stalks of proud iris bending on the morning breeze.

"The tourist office guy was an asshole, but this place rocks," Dejah says as we step out of the car.

The dude barely looked at us when we asked for help finding a place to stay. At our insistence, he made a call, marked it on the map, and here we are.

"It's like Tara from *Gone with the Wind*. Is that a bowling alley?" I lift my chin to the long green stretch of grass lined with benches on the right side of the sprawling house.

"Probably for bocce or lawn bowls," Dejah says.

Two black cats race through the ankle-length grass to a frail Granny rocking under the biggest weeping willow in the garden. They meow as she tosses treats. A hound dog with floppy ears barks and lumbers over to join the Granny crew. She grumbles in Croatian as she feeds her menagerie of pets.

"Can we stay here forever?" I inhale the rich smell of lavender and sigh.

Flowers, trees, pets, what's not to love?

"Two nights." Dejah grins as a woman my dad's age wearing a flowy green top and jeans leans over the second-floor balcony and greets us in Croatian.

We grab our packs from the trunk and march up the outside steps to the second floor. She leads us along the wide veranda to a bright room with a double bed, plenty of space for our bags on the floor, and a mini fridge. Ken pays her, and she leaves us to it.

Khadejah rips open the door on the tiny fridge.

"It has a freezer." She turns to me with wide eyes. "We need to hit the shops for supplies because a freezer means frozen juice boxes."

"I'll get the keys." I haven't had a cold drink in forever.

We buy fresh fruit, stuff for dinner, snacks, hair dye for me, postcards, and juice boxes. Back in our room, we stock the fridge and freezer, then drive to town to sightsee.

Poreč's Old Town peninsula juts into the sea. It's a maze of sandstone streets and buildings with vibrant orange terracotta roofs. The perimeter of the point is corralled by a smooth road that butts against the cobalt sea. Heat waves undulate off the street as we track down the most popular site in town, the Roman Catholic Eufrazijeva Bazilika. We enter the simple stone church, and Dejah points to the large *Silence Please* sign. I nod as we slink to the back pew and take a seat. I soak in the stone pillars, the wooden trellis overhead, and the delicate angels painted in the domed nave.

A dad and two kids march down the aisle and settle in a pew near the front. The mom glides down after and moves to the bench behind them. The sound of a loud fart ricochets through the silent church as the mom's backside hits the squeaky bench.

Dejah, the kids, and I giggle. The dad's chest is shaking. The mom goes beet red and hisses at the dad before she storms out of the church. I slouch as she passes. It was just a squeak that sounded like a fart—what a different moment if only she had giggled, too.

Sweat soaks my skin as we trudge out of the church.

"I need a swim," I say.

After our missed opportunity for a dip in Opatija, we carry a bikini and sarong in our daypacks because you never know when the heat or urge to swim will hit—and we prefer to do it with clothes on.

"Let's find a spot." She nods.

I drop my bag on the edge of the perimeter stone road next to an anchored boat in the marina. I wore a dress today to make on-the-spot changing easy. I slink out of my underwear and wiggle up my swimsuit bottoms, swap my bra for a bikini top, then drop my dress beside my bag.

I whoop with delight as I leap off the stone edge. My skin sighs as I hit the cool water. Dejah jumps in next to me. We float on our backs in the salty sea staring at the cloudless sky until our fingers wrinkle, then drive back to Croatian Tara.

Dressed in a tank top and shorts, I lounge in a comfy chair outside our room as Khadejah snaps on the gloves and applies my hair dye. My natural color is a dull, mousy blond. I used to hit the salon at home and get foils to brighten it up. But now that I'm on the road, it's a cost-friendly box dye on a veranda overlooking a garden at sunset. Not exactly a step down. Wet chemical hair cemented to my head, we smoke and write postcards—including one to Keith—until I rinse it out.

The plastic bag of cold cuts, cheese, fresh bread, fruit, and chocolate from the fridge rustles as Dejah sets up dinner. The black kitties race up the stairs, and their claws scratch the wood as they scurry under the table and rub against my leg.

"Dejah, we've found someone who likes the sound of rustling plastic bags." I chuckle as I drop them some ham.

"Granny must have gone to bed." She rolls her eyes.

"It's time," Dejah says after we eat, then rushes into our room.

She slaps a frozen juice box in my hand, and goosebumps ripple across my skin. I tear the top off, squish the bottom, and scrape my teeth across the icy block. I moan as I suck on the sweet, frosty grape juice. Every day is a new adventure, but the sites aren't always the shining moments. Warmth expands in my chest at my luck to be sitting right here, right now, with freshly dyed hair, a frozen treat, and a good friend—because more and more, the simple in-between times feel like the most important part of this trip.

I FIRE up the Opal and we drive down the coast to Rovinj, another Old Town peninsula jutting into the clear blue sea. Pristine tightly packed stone buildings spiral around the perimeter of the point, circling to the center, where a sleek church tower soars into the sky.

I'm beginning to think there are no ugly places here.

We park next to a line of clear pay phone booths overlooking the water. It's a perfect spot to call home. I walk to the booth on one end, and Dejah goes beside me.

"I can't get through," Dejah says as she hangs up the receiver before I've even dialed.

"That sucks. I'm sorry."

"I'll try again later." She shrugs. "Give me your bag. I'm going to wait in the shade."

She walks to a nearby bench with my stuff as I key in the numbers.

I bounce on the spot as it rings after my first try.

"Hi, Can. Where are you today?" Dad asks.

He's my steady, grounding link to home and the only other Canadian accent I've heard since Evan and Aaron in Prague. There's a warm comfort in hearing the same accent as your own

—just another reason why these calls home are so important to me.

I share snippets of our car adventures from driving along the coast.

"I spoke to Kevin this morning. He's running twenty-one miles today," Dad says.

"Ew." I wrinkle my nose.

"He's doing the Portland Marathon on October fourth—his thirty-second birthday."

My brother's a loser. I plan to spend my birthday drinking and dancing on top of a bar somewhere.

"Oh hey, before I forget, can you send Khadejah's parents an email, telling them you heard from us? We've not seen a place to email in a while, and she couldn't get through to them today." I twist the phone cord. "And, uh … can you also send one to Josh, saying I'm still keen to meet up later?" I cringe. It's lame to use my dad as a messenger, but I want Josh to know I haven't changed my mind about meeting.

"I'll send those later today. What body of water is Croatia on?" he asks.

I blink.

"I'm looking at it right now. It's sparkly—"

"What's it called?" he presses.

My mind blanks. I know this … crap. The jaunty final *Jeopardy* tune blares in my head. I have seconds to answer. And Khadejah has my bleeping bag, so I can't check my guidebook. Hurry, brain. I need to answer this correctly. I think he thinks I'm just having a boozy jolly over here. When actually I'm working hard sightseeing, learning stuff, and healing. Okay, maybe we're boozing a bit, but not last night. Last night was all about frozen juice boxes.

"Come on, Candace, you should know this." His voice is ripe with disappointment.

My heart sinks to my toes.

"We've visited loads of beautiful sites, Dad. Just yesterday we were at—"

"Yes, but you don't know what body of water you're on." He scoffs.

I lower my head in shame. I've failed his travel test.

Our conversation goes downhill quickly, and I end the awkward call.

Khadejah hands me my bag, and I yank out the dozen postcards I painstakingly wrote last night. I groan. There it is, labeled clearly on the front of every postcard—The Adriatic Sea.

Bugger.

I buy stamps and mail my stupid postcards, then we roam the circular Old Town flagstone pathways. There's a great photo opportunity at every turn: an ornate wooden door, stone staircases, and towering buildings with a blue-sky backdrop, but most shops are closed, and no one is around in this searing 40°C heat. My breathing's labored. Heat seeps off the stones and coils around my legs. I'm not interested in another dehydration headache, so we snap a final photo and trudge back to the car.

"Kev's running twenty-one miles today," I say as I crank down the window.

"God, why?" Khadejah frowns as she inserts the George Michael cassette.

"I know, right? Marathon training. I have no concept of how far it is. Let's clock it."

I check the odometer as she lights and passes me a cigarette. Then another.

"Is that it?" she asks.

"Nope." I stub out my second cigarette. "It's only been ten miles."

More driving.

"Still running?" Her fingers dangle out the passenger window.

"Yup."

We've smoked three cigarettes each and have listened to half a George Michael tape when we pull into Croatian Tara.

"That was just over twenty-one miles," I say as I turn off the engine. "Not even a full marathon."

"I'm going on the record. I'd rather root Austin and Keith on the boat while eating *the sandwich* than run that distance." She sparks one more cigarette for good measure.

"Totally agree." *The sandwich,* ew.

We curl up in the cozy seats on the veranda and write in our journals to the sound of the lawn bowls cracking, locals laughing, the neighborhood dogs having a bark-off, and Granny burping, farting, and ranting to her animals from under her weeping willow.

What a life. I totally want to be that granny one day.

I close my journal, throw my feet up on the veranda banister, and sigh. Despite my bad phone conversation with my dad, my mind is clear. Nothing is pressing on me, hanging over my head, or being puzzled out. My usual busy thoughts are blessedly silent. Dejah and I sit side by side and stare at the glistening stars in the sky as the crickets chirp. I haven't felt this at peace since my mom died, and I feel like a veiled part of me has been uncovered. I want to hang on to this feeling, but how do I keep my brain this quiet when we leave this paradise?

THE UGLY - POREČ TO ZADAR, CROATIA

Dejah's arms are crossed as we lean against the hood of the car opposite the concrete marina in Senj three hours after leaving Croatian Tara. I wrinkle my nose. The water is duller and smells swampy, and this place lacks the usual relaxed Croatian vibe. But we're here because it's two hours from Plitvice Lakes National Park—a guidebook must-see, boasting terraced lakes and waterfalls. The tourist office told us it's a budget-busting fifty dollar entrance fee—so we want to go for a full day if we visit—and there's no available low-cost accommodation around the park, so we would need to stay here in Senj.

"This place has bad vibes, and the water smells like shit." She curls her nose.

"Yeah, this place is awful." I blow out a breath.

"I'm not staying here for even one night. We need a new plan." Dejah flips through the pages of her guidebook. "I reckon we drive to Otočac near the lakes. We might find a cheap place to stay there." She taps a town on the map inland and to the west.

"And if we can't find a place, I think we should skip the lakes and spend the night in Zadar. I don't want to spend fifty bucks to see something for an hour." I hate to miss them, but we're already pushing the budget with the car, and there are so many pretty things to see here for free.

"Yeah, it's bloody expensive. Let's move on." She snaps the book closed, and we get back in the car.

The two-lane highway out of Senj is like driving on a roller coaster. White knuckles on the wheel, I maneuver through uphill curves and plunge down dramatic switchbacks with tall trees obstructing any views of the road ahead. After listening to the A and B side of Dejah's favorite '80s mixtape, I let out a breath as the road levels out to green farmland dotted with boxy cream houses with tipped orange roofs.

"We're close to Otočac," Dejah says as she folds the map.

"Sounds good." I shake out one hand then the other to get the blood flowing.

The small houses cluster together along the highway, and we pass one gas station with a fruit stand out front.

"That was Otočac. With zero places to stay." Dejah frowns as the houses thin out to flat farmland once again. "Keep driving east to the lakes?"

"It's worth a shot."

The Opal revs as we leave the flat roads, returning to twisty, craggy ones. We drive past countless isolated hamlets with handfuls of houses on platform breaks in the mountains until we drive down the last steep hill to flat land with tall yellow grass.

"We're not far from the Bosnia and Herzegovina border," Dejah says.

"What?" My mouth gapes. Being the driver, I haven't paid much attention to the map. "I don't know why it freaks me out, but that's a little creepy."

"After all the places we've been, this one scares you?" Her face scrunches.

"The Bosnian war only ended three years ago." The images of bombing and armed soldiers hiding behind city rubble shooting at each other was all over the media at home. It's a chilling prospect to be so close to something that until now was far removed from my life and was nothing more than a sad story on the nightly news.

Freedom thumps as we roll off the worn highway onto a newly paved smooth dark tarmac. Minutes later, we pass through a town with modern buildings butting up against the highway. Happy people are on the sidewalks, popping in and out of shops. The town ends, and so does the new pavement as we transition to cracked, bumpy roads.

A few kilometers away, we reach another town. Doors and windows are boarded up with sheets of plywood, and long jagged pieces of broken glass are scattered on the overgrown lawns. Prickles sweep up my arms as we creep through the ghost town. This is no small hamlet. It was once a thriving village with homes, shops, and schools. My heart lurches at the bullet holes along the side of the houses with *Hrvatska* spray painted on the crumbling brick walls.

"Why do you think no one came back here to rebuild?" My head swivels from side to side, to one deserted home after the other.

"Maybe it's easier to start fresh in a new place," she says.

What she doesn't say is that maybe there is nobody to come back.

Our mood is somber as I stop the car outside the gates to the National Park.

"We'll never get our money's worth if we go in now. It closes in a few hours. And I doubt we'll find a place to stay later. I reckon we skip the lakes," Dejah says.

"I'm not too bothered." My heart is still back in the abandoned village, and I have zero desire to visit the lakes now.

"Let's push on to Zadar."

"Maybe today wasn't about the lakes," I say as I pull back on the highway.

"No, I reckon it wasn't." She tugs at her bottom lip as she stares out the window at the tall yellow fields of grass.

I was wrong about there being no ugly places in Croatia. What happened here was ugly. I was detached when I heard about it on the news, but being here and seeing it with my own eyes, I can't look away or change the channel. It happened here, to these people who lost their homes and maybe their lives. My stomach flips, and I'm once again overwhelmed by just how freaking fortunate I am to have grown up where I did.

We follow the road south, parallel with the Bosnia and Herzegovina border, then we swing west up the steep rocky mountain two-lane highway toward Zadar on the coast.

I frown at the Pepsi truck ahead grinding up the incline and check the rearview mirror, cursing at the green convertible who's been riding my ass for ten minutes. I dip into the oncoming lane, and the coast is clear. I press the pedal to the floor, and the Opal whines as it struggles to pass with the green convertible hot on my tail.

"Come on." I grip the steering wheel and chant.

I intake a breath as I slide into the lane ahead of the truck just as an oncoming white van rushes toward us.

"More gray hairs to add to my collection," I say. "Damn."

A police officer standing in a lay-by points and waves an orange lollypop stick—no bigger than a pen—for us, the green convertible, and the Pepsi truck to pull over. I tuck the Opal next to the cliff near the cop's chrome motorcycle. Green convertible pulls in behind and the truck ahead. I dig under the waistband of my shorts to my money belt and retrieve my driver's license as the cop speaks to the truck, then waves them away.

His broad shoulders roll as he prowls toward us. He's wearing a white helmet, mirrored shades, a crisp, tight navy uniform, a gun and nightstick on his belt, and knee-length black leather boots. He looks like he's straight out of one of my favorite childhood TV shows *CHiPs*. God, I loved Erik Estrada.

"Holy hot cop." I sigh.

His spine is straight as he clips at me in Croatian through the open driver window.

"English?" I widen my eyes.

"Deutsche?" he asks.

I shake my head.

The muscles on his cheeks twitch as he barks in Croatian. *I know* he's asking me if I know what I did. And yes, I know I passed the truck on a solid line. But I have no intention of letting *him* know that I know. So I smile and continue with the dumb routine.

The cords in his neck tense as he yells. He grips the holstered gun at his waist and motions for me to get out of the car. My chest seizes as I fumble to remove my seatbelt and leap out onto the gravel shoulder. His anger has my knees trembling, but I'm not worried he's going to hurt me or haul me off to jail. First, we're in the middle of nowhere. Second, the green convertible is meters away. And third, all I did was overtake on a solid line.

Mirrored shades travel from my messy bun over my glowing makeup-free face, past my purple tank top and beige shorts, to my bare feet, toe to toe with his shiny boots. His shoulders tense, and he barks at me in Croatian. The only word I understand is *papers*, so I thrust out my Quebec driver's license.

He whips his glasses off—in that cool guy way—with one hand then snatches my plastic card. I stare at his face as he examines it. Long lashes, square jaw, red lips. Man, he's stunning. His nostrils flare as he talks and mimes through a dramatic replay of me passing the truck, his deep brown eyes on mine, ensuring I'm following.

"Oh." I nod with a straight face.

He's puce, and the lines on his forehead deepen as he starts miming again. He stops mid-rant, fists on his hips, and shakes his head. He tosses my license at my chest and flicks his hand for me to leave.

I bite back a smile. I've worn him down with my vapid routine.

"Nice job." Khadejah smirks as I twist the key and fire up the car.

"That poor green convertible. The cop is so pissed I'm sure he's going to let them have it." I not so speedily pull out. "Did you see how cute he is? Seriously, Croatian men are the hottest of all countries we've been to so far."

"Only you would be drooling over the cop who pulled us over and yelled at you." She shakes her head.

"He was intimidating, but I never felt like I was in danger." I shrug.

I chuckle when the green convertible passes us on a solid line a few minutes later. They don't give us the finger, so maybe he wasn't *too* hard on them.

My heart aches at the number of vacant bullet-ridden homes lining the highway as we approach Zadar. I don't know if there's more in this area or if I'm looking for them. But it's disturbing because we haven't seen any of this until today.

It's well past dark by the time I shut off the engine in front of the Zadar Youth Hostel. My eyes are bleary from ten hours of dusty driving, and I'm ready for a shower. We trudge to the glass door of the two-story rectangular building and stumble into reception. There's one lamp on the desk casting a soft glow and no one around.

"Maybe there's a bell." Dejah leans over the desk.

"Are you looking for reception?" A guy saunters in from a side door. "I'm it."

I blink when he steps into the light. He's my height, with metal-rimmed sunglasses resting on top of his smoothly shaved head. He's wearing a white silk vest with a loud pattern of bright yellow and black triangles over a canary yellow silk collar shirt, unbuttoned to his navel showcasing a carpet of black chest hair. He looks like a member of Right Said Fred.

"Dorm room?" Fred asks as he flips through a large book on the desk.

"Uh …" Words escape me because I haven't seen someone dressed like him since high school.

"Yeah." Dejah elbows my ribs.

"I've put you in a smaller dorm room, and I won't put anyone else in there if I can help it." He hands me a key and smiles kindly.

"Thanks. Where's a good place to eat?" Dejah asks as she pays for the room from Ken.

Fred grabs a map from his desk and circles a spot. "They do nice burgers here."

"Great, we're starving." I think we've had burgers every day since we left Zagreb, but I'm so hungry I don't care.

"Where have you been on your travels?" Fred asks with a flirty grin.

"We started in Russia two months ago," Dejah says. "Then we—"

"Russia?" Fred's face turns to stone, and his body vibrates with anger. "Why would you go there? It's unsafe. Terrible people live there."

I raise my eyebrows at Dejah because his reaction is the same as the Polish guys we met on the night train.

"You better get going. That place closes soon." He retreats to the side room.

"Sure, uh. Thanks." I nod, missing his warmth, but I get that there's a long history with Russia and pretty much everyone.

And I don't know enough about it, so I take no offense.

Note to self: don't talk about Russia anywhere outside of Russia.

Wind swirls my hair as we leave the McDonalds-esque burger joint Fred recommended—back when he liked us. The air is thick, and the gusts are so strong they force our walk into a jog. We sink on a bench opposite the hostel by the marina filled with three-story super yachts as lightning stabs the ominous sea and cracks of thunder reverberate in my chest.

"You know, I think burgers have become our new spaghetti. It seems to be the easiest thing to find here," I say as the storm churns offshore.

"They're good, though."

"They are." I jump as four bolts of lightning illuminate the sky followed by a boom of thunder. "Which is your favorite boat?"

"That's hard; there are some sweet ones here. That one." She points to a three-level floating palace bobbing in the rough sea with a hot tub and massive sundeck.

"Hey." Fred waves as he stalks toward us.

"Hi. Are you here to watch the light show?" I ask.

"No, to apologize. I'm sorry for slagging on Russia before." He tilts his head and offers us a small smile.

"It's fine. No one has had anything nice to say about Russia since we left there," I say, and Dejah shrugs.

"Croatia has had so many problems." He clears his throat and rests his hands on the back of our bench. "It's hard for me."

"We drove through abandoned villages today. And saw bullet holes," Dejah says softly.

The ugly beneath the beautiful.

"The war wasn't limited to the borders, and there are abandoned towns like that all over Croatia due to the Serbians. There was a lot of shelling and bombing just outside of Zadar." His eyes have lost their sparkle and are filled with sadness. "How was your dinner?"

"It was good, thanks," Dejah says.

Because what else can we say? We're just passing through; I have no idea of the horrors he's lived through. Pellets of rain fall from the sky, but we don't move. The three of us from different corners of the world watch the dazzling storm rage hoping it brings us sunshine tomorrow.

THE LEVELS OF SPLIT - ZADAR TO SPLIT, CROATIA

The highway from Zadar to Split makes our mountain drive feel like a jaunt in the park. Winding roads cling to the edge of the cliff with a jagged rock face on one side and a tiny guardrail beside the sheer drop into the lush blue *Adriatic* Sea. The water glimmers under the sun's rays around endless green and brown islands—not that I get to enjoy the view because my eyes are glued to the road.

"This would be a great place to film a movie with a dramatic chase scene." I pluck a juicy red grape from the bunch propped between our seats and pop it in my mouth.

There are loads of fruit stands on the side of the highway, and we bought these this morning outside of Zadar.

"How about you just focus on keeping us *on* the tarmac." She points to the upcoming hairpin turn.

"I'm on it." I lean into the turn as the rich sweet flavor bursts in my mouth, then crunch the grape seeds between my molars. The pits I manage not to swallow I spit at Dejah.

She chuckles and launches seeds in my direction that bounce off my knee and disappear on the floor beneath my feet.

"This car is going to be foul by the time we hand it back." She laughs.

"Oh well." I shrug with no intention of giving up our favorite driving pastime. "Plus what's a couple of seeds added to the dust and sand we've collected over the last few days?" The worst that can happen is a cleaning fee, but it will be worth it.

"Oh mate, no way." She points to the whole pig on a spit by

the side of the road. A gray-haired man is cranking a metal rod so it roasts evenly over the half-steel drum filled with smoldering coals. "A change from a burger?"

"I'm happy to pass on that." I press my palm into my budding Buddha belly.

The heat is bloating me, and *maybe* it's also all the burgers I'm eating. I have an angry swollen heat rash on the back of my legs that flared up after wandering the boiling stone streets of Old Town Zadar yesterday. They have more ancient sites and Roman ruins stuffed into their peninsula than all the other towns we've visited, and it took the whole day to see everything. I've taken an antihistamine, but it hasn't curbed the mad itching. On a positive note, our daily saltwater swimming is working its magic on my belly button. It's not healed, but it's not painful or seeping puss, so I'll take it.

"I wonder if we're going to meet anyone." Dejah flips through our meager tape collection. "Not that I'm bored of you; we always find crap to talk about."

"I get it. The car doesn't give us much chance to meet new people." And I'm behind in my journal. I'm not missing the packed trains and stinky buses, but they are a good way to keep up to date with my writing. "Not having to carry Barney is awesome," I say as she inserts Pete's *The Crash* mixtape.

The other drawback to the car I don't mention is that I've been thinking a lot about Josh as I drive. I want to see him again and have no idea if it will happen because of our email drought. I crack my neck. According to the guidebook, they have an Internet café in Split, so in a few hours, I'll know once and for all if I'll be in Germany or the Middle East in October.

———

SPLIT'S A TOWN OF LAYERS. The city center is built on top of, around, and intertwined with the 4th century Diocletian's Palace which was once the residence of a Roman emperor and their military garrison. Today, the palace ground floor is an underground ruin, and the original upper levels are walls in modern homes.

"How does a city get covered up and built over?" My voice echoes against the damp stone walls as we slink our way through the warren of narrow underground passageways of the palace. "What happened to the original city? Did a big storm come in, blow sand, dust, or water over everything, and hide it? Then everyone is like *Oh man, I thought there was a big city here, guess not, so I'll just put up something new*? And how does the modern city not collapse and cave down into the level below?"

"That's a lot of questions." She chuckles. "I have no idea."

We pop out of a long dark hallway into a large, barreled ceiling vestibule. After more tunnels, our underground tour ends in a bustling market selling fruit, vegetables, food, postcards, and snow globes. We buy a burger and climb the stairs out to modern-day street level. The heat steals my breath as we step into a smooth stone courtyard surrounded by towering columns that were once part of the original palace. Sweat drips from the fold of where my ass meets my legs as we wander Old Town Split. My stomach turns at the half-eaten burger between my fingertips.

"I'm so over burgers, pizza, spaghetti, and our homemade sandwiches," I say as I toss my unappealing lunch in the trash. "I love crappy food, especially pizza, but I need to eat better."

Khadejah stops in front of a housewares shop.

"They have plastic containers." She taps the window.

"Yeah. So?" I flap my shirt to get some air, and it does nothing to cool me down.

"We can buy a container, then stuff for a salad." She smiles.

My lips part. "You're a freaking genius." We haven't been able to make a salad because we have nothing to put it in. Until now. Hopefully, eating better will make me feel less bloated.

With two plastic boxes in our daypacks, my heart pounds as we traipse to the Internet café. Finally, I'm going to find out if I'll see him again. The tiny shop has a glass storefront and five computers. The air is heavy with humidity and smells like pepperoni oozing off two fat guys hunched over one computer. I breathe through my mouth as we each buy an hour for ten dollars. I sit at the far desk, away from the cured meat stinkers, and fidget my hands as the computer churns. Ten new messages line my inbox. I click on Josh's name in the center.

I need till about the middle of September before I can make plans.

Then if you want to see me, baby, we can work something out.

Josh xo

My lips twist into a snarl. *He* was the one who said we *need* to meet again. And this is his response to the proposal I sent him from Vienna about Oktoberfest. I vibrate as disappointment seeps through my pores. I thought I would know today. I'm so dumb to think this time would be any different and that he would actually commit to a plan with me.

I roll my shoulders. Screw that, I'm not waiting around. My fingers fly over the keys.

I want to see you, but I need to know before mid-September.

I'll be in Budapest on September 2nd.

If I've not heard from you with a firm plan to meet up by then, I'll be going to Istanbul with Khadejah instead of meeting you.

Let me know,

Candace xoxo

This time *he* can take it or leave it.

From: Candace

To: My Friends

Date: 8/20/98

Subject: Sun and blue water

After Prague, we went to posh Vienna, where we buzzed past the fancy buildings and museums in one day. I particularly loved the Gaudi-style residential block Hundertwasserhaus—a mosaic of odd angles and bright colors. It was designed by Austrian artist Friedensreich Hundertwasser in Dejah and I's favorite musical decade—the '80s. The heat has been our newest nemesis. It gets trapped in the cobblestones and each step is like walking on hot coals. We kept cool by dashing through park sprinklers and dipping our feet in hundred-year-old fountains alongside the locals.

Next, we caught a train down to Zagreb, where we had one mission—to rent a car. We managed to track one down and have been riding in style ever since. Croatia is our vacation from backpacking and we're lovin' it. There are Roman ruins for days and there's so much coastline, everyone swims everywhere. The heat has followed us here and I can confirm a dip in the clear blue Adriatic Sea is ten times better than a sprinkler.

Croatia wasn't originally on our countries to visit list. But now that we're here, I can't imagine not having experienced this magical place and totally recommend it for a holiday.

We're in Split, and leave for Dubrovnik tomorrow, where we'll drop off the car and revert to being backpackers. I'll be sad to lose the easy mode of travel, but it's been a bit isolated, so I'm ready to resume our casual lifestyle and meeting interesting people as we move from place to place.

Candace xoxo

THE END OF THE ROAD - SPLIT TO DUBROVNIK, CROATIA

THE WIPERS SWISH on high across the windshield but are futile against the deluge of rain. Fog hangs in the air, and water flies as the tires spin through newly formed puddles along the coastal highway. My heart thunders as we hydroplane inches from the cliff edge. I right the car and reduce my speed so we don't have a *Thelma & Louise* ending by toppling into the sea.

"We've got to drive through Bosnia and Herzegovina to get to Dubrovnik. In the peace treaty, they got a five-kilometer stretch of coastline, basically the town of Neum," Dejah reads from her book.

She holds our passports as we approach the border. Two soldiers clutching rifles are on the side of the road next to an open parking gate barrier. I crank down the window and slow to a crawl. Dejah flashes the cover of our passports, and they wave us through with the tips of their guns.

"Ok-*ay*." I glide past as they stop the next car. "I thought they would at least have a look at our passports."

"Anticlimactic." Dejah shrugs.

The terrain is steeper and rockier with not a tree or patch of grass to be seen, just tall, heavy square buildings stacked side by side from the edge of the sea far up the slope. My skin gets tight. It's the complete opposite of the villages with quaint stone houses between stretches of overgrown purple wildflowers we've experienced driving down the coast of Croatia. This is claustrophobic, hectic, and overwhelming. Like everyone was in a rush to stake their claim on a footprint of coastal space.

"It's like being in Warsaw." I frown as we cruise down the busy highway of tailgating cars and mobs of people along the side of the road.

"Yeah. We're almost out; the checkpoint is ahead." Dejah tips her chin to a small white hut in the middle of the road next to a lowered boom gate.

I stop beside two guys with dark hair, guns, and muscles for days.

"Hi." I smile as one of the dreamy duo glances around the interior.

"Have a nice holiday." His eyes twinkle as he waves us into Croatia.

"I will." I wave as we speed off.

The word *holiday* warms my heart because this time has been exactly the relaxing vacation from the logistical challenges of backpacking we were hoping for. We wouldn't have been able to get to Croatian Tara, visit the mountains, or take scenic breaks along the wild coast without the flexibility offered by the car.

I park Freedom at the dead-end of a long dirt road next to the one-story rental company the guy marked on the map before we left Zagreb. Small pebbles from the beach litter the floors. Dirt and dust from the mountains cling to the dash, and grape pits are everywhere. I needed this break, but after driving from the top to the bottom of the country, I'm tired and ready to let someone else take the wheel.

We hand over the keys and escape without paying a cleaning fee. I pop the hood on my yellow jacket to ward off the rain, and we hoof it back to town, ready for our next adventure.

I KICK back on my bunk the next morning, waiting for Dejah to finish her makeup. Our dorm room is simple and airy with eight beds, but there are only three of us in here. We haven't met our roommate, which is odd as it's the butt crack of dawn and there's no sign of them. We're up because we want to avoid the extreme heat while we sightsee. I flip through my guidebook to prioritize our touring as we have one day in Dubrovnik before we catch a ferry to Korčula tomorrow. Man, I can't wait to get out on the open water—

"Hi," a girl says in an Australian accent as she enters wearing a loose tank top and leggings toting a rolled-up yoga mat under her arm. "What a beautiful morning."

This must be our new roomie. Dew covers her pale, freckled

face and bare shoulders. I blink. God, was she exercising? I can't remember the last time I did that.

"Hey, mate." Dejah slides her mascara wand into the tube and screws it closed. "Where're you from?"

"I'm Nora from Sydney." She's taller than Dejah but shorter than me.

"Same." Dejah introduces us.

"Hi." I wave and smile, but Nora doesn't acknowledge me as she flounces her lithe body on her bunk. My smile fades as she natters exclusively with Dejah about Sydney, where she has been, and what Dejah is doing next—without a word in my direction.

"You should come with us today. Right, Candace?" Dejah includes me in the conversation for the first time in ten minutes. "We're going to walk the city walls first."

"Sure." I slam my book closed and jam it in my daypack.

I don't want her joining us, but I'll look like a total cow if I say no.

"Great. Let me pop on my shoes," she says—to Dejah.

My jaw clenches. She's not the new blood I was looking for. I was hoping we would meet someone or people who are keen to talk to both of us. This is going to be a long day if this chick treats me like I'm invisible.

I hide my dagger glares behind sunglasses while Nora monopolizes *my* friend as we trek the two kilometers of limestone walls surrounding Dubrovnik. We're twenty-five meters above the sprawling Old Town with unobstructed views of the neatly tipped roofs, stone towers, and church spires. And even Nora can't put a damper on the sparkling turquoise sea views.

This city is just more: more pedestrian walkways, more churches, more palaces, more grand. It's a showpiece that hasn't changed for centuries except for the sporadic shock of bright orange roof tiles mingled alongside faded brown ones. They are visible scars from the recent war and were painstakingly repaired by UNESCO but remain a jarring reminder of the devastating conflict.

I bite back a smile as Nora returns to the hostel after the wall walk. Dejah and I resume our easy alliance and get lost in the gleaming wide marble-paved squares, steep cobbled streets, bubbling fountains, and lush hanging gardens.

The hostel courtyard is sizzling with energy when we return at dusk. Large tan umbrellas shade the group of backpackers socializing like they're at a backyard party. I rock to the beat of Latin music and lively chatter. Now this is more like it: mixing with people we can *both* engage with. I chat with a couple from Brazil while Dejah catches up with Nora and a lanky Aussie dude.

Bottles clink in plastic bags as our boisterous group relocates to a nearby outdoor cinema. Paper cups are passed around as we line blankets on the lawn to watch *Phoenix,* a complex crime film about a gambler. I lose track of the characters after ten minutes because I'm here for the party, not the movie. Dejah bumps my shoulder and holds out a bottle of wine. I extend my cup, which she fills, then passes it along to the next person.

"Best referral ever. Keith's the man," I say.

"He is." She taps my cup. "Korčula in the morning."

It's hard to imagine how this country can deliver more magic, but the tour book's opening line for Korčula is: *if you don't plan to get off the ferry here, you'll regret it.*

"I've been longing to get out in the open water since I caught my first glimpse of it outside Zagreb." I sigh.

"Don't you mean—*The Adriatic Sea*?" She pokes fun at my conversation fail with my dad, and I flip her the bird.

I'm going to miss the ease of traveling by car, but I've missed the buzz of connecting with like-minded backpackers more. I bristle as Nora laughs at something Lanky Aussie says. My nose curls. Okay, maybe not *her*. I'll never have a shooting star friendship connection with Nora like we did with Keith. But it's not a big deal because we'll be leaving the mainland *and* her behind in the morning.

CHAPTER 7
THE SPLIT

SUNDAY, August 23, 1998

TAG ALONG - FERRY, DUBROVNIK TO KORČULA, CROATIA

Sweet, salty air fills my lungs as the ferry glides through the sapphire sea a few hours after sunrise. I stretch out on a plastic chair in my yellow bikini among the other smiling passengers lounging in the hot sun on the boat bow. Dejah's foot taps to the music blasting through her foamy headphones, and Nora's executing a warrior pose on her yoga mat.

Yup. Nora. She looked me straight in the eye at the end of the movie last night—in front of everyone—and asked if I minded if she tagged along. Talk about being put on the spot. I bit my tongue and told her it would be fun. We don't jive, but she's not as bad as The Drip and makes Dejah happy. So I have to suck it up for a few days. But if she wants to travel with us past Korčula, I won't be guarding my words if it's still strained between us.

I clasp my fingers on my lap and squeeze my eyes closed. Being on a ferry reminds me of being in Greece with Josh. Back when we were pure and new. Back when I thought he wanted to be with me as much as I wanted to be with him. My heart squeezes. God, I want to see him again, but I also want to go to Istanbul with Dejah and travel across Turkey.

Excited chatter fills the air as passengers congregate near the rail. I tug on my shorts and pad to the side of the boat. My breath catches at the turquoise water lapping the fortified stone walls circling the orange-roofed buildings of Korčula Old Town.

My hands throb as I grip the railing. Stupid Josh. I should be appreciating every moment of this postcard-come-to-life view, but instead, he's occupying space in my mind he doesn't deserve. My gut twists. I set the parameters of our rendezvous, yet *he* holds the power over where I'll spend a month of this holiday. How did I let this happen? Again?

PARADISE - KORČULA, CROATIA

I step out of the rusty car onto the packed dirt beside Dejah and Nora in front of a boxy two-story house. Beside the driveway, there's a short brown fence corralling a garden and white sheets flapping on clotheslines between craggy trees bursting with lemons, limes, and avocados.

"What do ya think?" the burly Australian asks as he slams the driver's door.

Burly was loitering outside the information office and offered us a cheap room in the house he shares with his Croatian wife. Despite his patchy beard and mustard stain on his T-shirt, he didn't trigger my—or the girls'—stranger danger alarm. So we took him up on his offer.

The outside is nice, and if there are enough beds and it's decently clean, we're staying because I have zero desire to hoof it back to town in this afternoon heat searching for a different place.

Burly unlocks a metal door on the side of the house and leads us up steep stairs into an airy room off the second-floor landing. Plain beige walls, green tiled floor, three single beds with crisp sheets, a tiny bathroom in the corner, and a balcony overlooking their garden oasis. Our gamble paid off—this place is perfect.

Dejah slides Burly the cash as I drop Barney next to the cot by the window. I shower, wash panties in the sink, and then for the first time in months of traveling, we take a siesta as a citrus breeze drifts through the open patio doors.

Crickets trill as we trek along the gravel shoulder toward Old Town. The sun dips behind the pine and cypress trees edging the two-lane road, and the sky morphs from shades of orange to deep blue. Unease knots between my shoulder blades. We haven't seen anything but vegetation in fifteen minutes, and I'm worried we'll run out of light before we reach civilization.

"Reckon we're going the right way?" Nora asks.

"No idea." Dejah scrunches her nose.

"Everything looks the same," I say.

Seems none of us were paying attention during the ten-minute drive from town with Burly.

The whir of engines stirs up the night, and three helmetless guys in shorts and T-shirts zoom past on scooters.

"Hey." Nora waves and jogs after them until their red taillights wink out of sight.

"They could have given us directions." I frown.

"A lift would have been—" Dejah's words stall as three headlights light up the dark road.

Three scooters screech to a stop in front of us. The dark-haired, light-skinned guys our age drop their feet on the pavement as their scooters idle.

#1 Scooter Guy rumbles something in guttural words I've not heard before.

"English?" I ask.

"Hun-g-*ary*." He shakes his head.

My eyes bounce over each face as the guys fire foreign words at each other. They're decent-looking, with sharp cheekbones, clean fingernails, and unscuffed sneakers, but we can't communicate because I don't speak Hungarian and they don't speak English.

"Now we'll never find out which way to go." I toss my hands in the air.

Their words stop, and they slide forward on their black leather seats.

#1 Scooter Guy smirks and tips his head to the space behind him.

"Lucky for us, *'Want a lift?'* is universal." Nora grins and throws her leg over the bike, parking her butt behind #1 Scooter Guy.

"Beats walking." Dejah jumps on the back of the second scooter.

I stare at the space of seat behind the third guy. Walking on this road is bad, but it's not as bad as road rash or ending up mangled in a ditch. He twists the throttle, and I huff as I hop on and grip his hips. This guy better know how to drive this thing. The bike shoots off. I quickly change position and circle my arms around his waist. I press against his back as he guns it up hills and whips around corners, praying this ends well.

My knees quake as I swing my leg off the bike onto the stone sidewalk outside Korčula Old Town walls. He drove fast but knew what he was doing. But it didn't make it any less nerve-wracking, and I won't be rushing onto the back of a stranger's bike again anytime soon.

"Thanks," Nora says to the trio idling on their Vespas.

#1 Scooter Guy speaks slowly. He points to his friends and then us, leaving airtime between each punctuated foreign word.

"Why is it people think if they talk slowly or louder that we'll understand them?" Dejah shakes her head.

#1 Scooter Guy's face twists into a frown.

Then we do what we always do when we can't communicate —we smile and nod.

Their shoulders slump. Not sure what they were expecting.

But nothing is happening here. They get the message, dip their chins, and drive away.

We climb the sweeping stone steps and pass under the stone entryway into Korčula Old Town in search of somewhere to eat. Golden streetlights illuminate clean stone walls with white mortar, shuttered windows, and arched doorways. The stone pathways are worn to a smooth shiny surface. I know it'll never happen here—but they would be killer covered in ice. Salty air from the sea lapping the fortress walls tickles my nose as we peruse the food offerings posted outside lively cafés, searching for recognizable dishes on the Croatian-only menus.

My lips part at the pink neon sign flashing *Internet*. I sprint three doors down and press my face to the window below the blinking sign. Two computers. One is occupied by a dude typing at Bionic Man speed, and the other is free.

"I just need like fifteen minutes. Please?" I bat my eyes at Dejah.

"Go on." Dejah waves her hand. "Be quick, we're hungry."

"I will." I dash inside.

I cringe as I pay the outrageous price of ten dollars for fifteen minutes and throw myself in front of the monitor. My pulse races as my inbox loads. I skip past notes from family and friends, zeroing in on Josh's name beside one message and a Hallmark Electric Greeting card.

Time to get my power back and determine my next steps.

I flex my fingers then click on his email.

I want to see you. I truly hope we can make that happen.

Josh xo

My jaw locks as I fight the urge to launch my keyboard across the room. There's no acknowledgement of my ultimatum, just more of his non-committal bullshit. *And* to balance the cost of this email time with my daily budget, I have to eat the cheapest thing on the menu tonight.

I move the mouse over the electronic card. It takes ages to load. The front of the card has a daisy on a blue background. It unfolds at a snail's pace, and the inside reads:

I miss you,

Josh xo

My stomach rolls as the card mocks me on the fuzzy monitor.

God, I hate him. I hate that he didn't give me a straight answer. I hate that he's left me hanging to suffer in limbo for another week until my deadline expires. And I hate that this stupid card gives me hope that he misses me as much as I miss him.

WE STEP inside an airy café in Korčula Old Town overlooking the sea after a lazy morning the next day.

"Of all the gin joints." Dejah tips her chin to the Hungarian Scooter Trio drinking icy cold pints of beer and eating crusty French bread sandwiches at a table by the open window.

I wave at the guys as we take a seat nearby. I hum along to the soft instrumental music as the sea twinkles out the window while #1 Scooter Guy stares longingly at Nora. He thumps his fingertips on the tabletop. He opens his mouth, then closes it. Opens it again, sags in his seat, sighs, and nods.

"Aww, Nora, you have a fan," Dejah teases.

"Yeah, I just need to learn Hungarian." Nora rolls her eyes.

Dejah orders three beers and vegetarian sandwiches from the busty server with perfectly round boobs in a tight tank top. Dejah and I rock a solid B cup, Nora an A. But those puppies she's got have to be at least a double D if not larger. Busty Server drops our beers on the table, then fawns over our Hungarian neighbors as they fumble through a few common words I can't understand.

"Looks like you have competition," I say, and Nora shrugs. I stare at their half-eaten sandwiches as the Hungarian Scooter Trio stares at Busty Server's cleavage. "I wonder if the sandwiches here are as good as her boobs."

"I hope so. I'm starving." Nora chuckles.

"I reckon I've got the perfect Spice Girl name for Nora." Dejah smiles as she takes a drink and then shares the concept of it. "Nature Spice."

"Good one." I bite back a cringe.

I find Nora's morning yoga off-putting as I'm usually smoking while she does sun salutations, but I respect she's a natural no-nonsense woman, so the name is fine. But she still bothers me. Dejah and I collaborate and share the burden of this trip. And we've met others who we brought into the fold and completely trusted and relied on to be part of our team, like Keith. But it's not the same with Nora. It feels like we're hosting her.

"Aww, thanks," Nora says as Busty Server drops our lunch on the table.

My Nora grievances scatter as I dig my fingers into the crusty bread. I moan as my teeth cut past the bun to the fresh tomatoes, lettuce, and tart cheese.

"I don't want to leave tomorrow," I say before I take another bite.

"We don't have to; we can stay another day. Are you coming with us to Hvar, Nora?" Dejah asks.

I clear my throat. Just because she has a Spice name doesn't mean she should join us in Hvar. This is not on. I'm going to talk with Dejah—

"I'm going to see how I feel." Nora rubs her cheek. "My

wisdom tooth is bothering me; I might have to go back to Dubrovnik to look for a dentist."

I frown. I don't want her to join us, but not because of that. Teeth issues in a foreign country aren't something I would wish on anyone; I wince thinking back to that stupid rock I dropped on my face and how lucky I was to avoid a trip-altering accident.

After sandwiches, we wave goodbye to the Hungarian Scooter Trio—who've transferred their affections to Busty Server —to scope out a place to swim. Ninety-nine times out of a hundred we'll find an amazing place to swim in Croatia, and today is no different. Around the corner from the ferry dock along the rock wall is a wooden plank diving board. No one is around. Just us and the cerulean sea. We strip down to our bathing suits and take turns leaping off the plank into the clear, cool water. We climb up on the sea wall, dangle our feet over the edge, and eat red grapes we bought from a street vendor while the sun dries the salty water on our skin.

"Having a car was a vacation from backpacking, but this, this is just a vacation." Dejah sighs.

"I wonder if a grapevine will grow up out of the sea?" Nora asks as she spits a pit into the water.

"You never know." I snatch another plump grape from the bunch. "With a place this magical, anything can happen."

We have a nice place to stay, we've met nice people, they have great food, and we have a whole extra day here to experience it. What could go wrong?

ANTHONY WAS RIGHT - KORČULA, CROATIA

Dejah steps up to the counter in the tourist office to ask how to get to a remote cove she read about in her book.

"You need to catch the bus," the lady says, passing us each a leaflet with a horseshoe shoreline around brilliant blue water.

It looks perfect—as usual.

"Follow the stone wall for three kilometers to the beach. The bus is just about to leave." She points to the idling short bus out the window.

"Can you stop at the cove please?" Dejah shoves the brochure in the driver's face as we board, and he nods.

I slouch into a single seat, and my thighs stick to the pleather seat. It's not even noon and it's already 40°C. I pull my Nalgene bottle from my bag and frown. I drained half of it on the thirty-minute walk from our room to the tourist office.

"I'm low on water," I say as the bus exits town, rolling along the two-lane tree-lined roads.

"There'll be a 'non-stop' in the village near the cove." Nora shrugs.

'Non-stop' is the name for a corner shop that doesn't close for siesta. My stomach rumbles. Hopefully she's right. We ate our leftover fruit for breakfast, and I'm already hungry.

The bus driver stops at the side of the road next to a handful of buildings. He opens the door and flicks his hand toward a winding road surrounded by tall yellow grass.

"Must be the road to the cove," I say as I step off the bus onto the hard shoulder.

The door slams and the wheels kick up dust as he peels away.

"Oh," Nora groans. "The general store's closed."

Shutters block the windows of the store and the three other structures in the hamlet.

I cross my arms. No scout badges for us today. We're in the middle of nowhere with half a liter of water each, no food, and no idea when the next bus is or when the shop opens.

"We might as well go." Dejah has her heart set on seeing the cove. "They have a brochure. I'm sure we'll find something along the way."

"Why not." I tug on my baseball cap, and we start down the road.

The stone wall the tourist lady mentioned runs parallel to the road. Long grass and violet wildflowers shoot up between the crumbling stone houses that dot the hillside. There's not a breath of wind, a tree, or a cloud in the sky to offer relief from the blazing sun. My feet burn as the heat rises from the pavement up my legs. I sparingly sip my hot water as the paved road turns to gravel, then packed dirt. We walk and walk and *walk*. Up and down little rises, back and forth around corners. It's like walking on a roller coaster. As the road rises, the cove is visible in the distance, but like in the desert, it never seems to get any closer.

"Three kilometers my ass. I reckon this has to be at least five." Dejah wipes her brow.

I don't reply because my throat's scratchy.

We trudge down a long, steep slope, and the open fields give way to tall trees. I sigh as the shade cools my tight skin.

A dirt path perpendicular to the main road leads to an A-frame cottage with red ceramic gnomes playfully mingling in a healthy flower garden.

My dry lips part.

"They have to have a hose. Hello. Hello?" I holler as I trot down the driveway and snoop in the garden looking for a spout.

"Hello?" Nora shouts as she passes, jogging toward the cottage. "No cars. I'll check around the house for an outside tap."

Dejah searches one side of the waist-high garden, and I search the other.

"I would take a pail of water at this point," I say.

"I found an outdoor shower," Nora yells.

We take off in her direction.

A white plastic shower stall is nestled between two pine trees across from the front door of the cottage. Nora spins the tap as I study the showerhead.

My shoulders slump when nothing comes out.

"They turned the water off." My throat stings with disappointment.

"At least we have shade amongst the trees," Dejah says as we continue our trek.

"And no one's around, so we'll have the place to ourselves," Nora says.

I watch my feet as I descend the steep incline so I don't slip.

"That's it," Dejah says.

I look up and intake a breath. Two small fishing boats are anchored and bobbing in water so clear I can see fish swimming over round stones on the seafloor. Three ergonomic houses blend into the wild olive and prickly juniper trees hugging the perimeter of the cove. And one empty pebble beach is waiting for us.

We race over. I drop my bag, whip off my clothes, and sprint into the sea. I whimper as the cool water hits my clammy skin. I float on my back, admiring the bright blue sky as the girls splash nearby.

"I'm ditching my cossie." Nora treads water and peels off her black one-piece.

She slaps her suit on the deck of the fishing boat, then Dejah and I toss ours on the wet pile. We giggle and joke like schoolgirls as we swim naked in the clear blue sea.

Pure heaven.

"Anthony was right." I sigh as the cool water caresses my skin. "Naked is the way to go."

EACH STEP UP the dirt road is a battle, and we have more walk ahead than behind us. My skin is stiff, and I'm hardly sweating anymore. I swish my last sip of stewed backwash from my Nalgene bottle in my mouth. Man, we better find some water soon because I don't know how much more dehydrated I can get and still function. And it's so freaking hot I left my modesty back at the cove. I'm hiking in my bra and G-string. Nora's down to her yoga bra and panties. Dejah's sporting her tank top and bathing suit bottoms.

"Mate." Dejah snickers. "With your daypack on, it looks like you're naked from the waist down. All I see is ass."

I whip off the G-string, replacing it with my wet bathing suit bottoms that chafe my sore skin with each step up the gravel road.

A dude whizzes past on a dirt bike.

A small car honks as it bounces by with a pine tree strapped to the roof.

When the gravel road switches to pavement, we pass an older man shuffling in the opposite direction. His eyes widen, and he flashes us a gap-toothed grin—three half-naked girls are probably not what he usually sees on his walks.

"Siesta must be over. We should get dressed," Dejah says, and we pull on our clothes.

Each step sends pain shooting up my legs, and my throat is swollen.

After an excruciating ninety minutes, we're back at the hamlet on the main road.

"Look!" Khadejah races toward a waterspout on the side of the general store we missed earlier.

She spins the tap, clear water blasts out, and I whimper at the sight of it. Dejah fills her bottle, then Nora, then me. I hope this water doesn't cause me gut problems later, but right now, I don't care. I down four liters until I'm too full to drink another drop. Water sloshes in my stomach, but it hasn't quenched my thirst.

Dejah stomps to the bus stop—a paper schedule behind plastic laminate strapped to a metal pole in the dirt beside the road.

"We've missed the last one." She drops her head.

"We'll hitchhike." Nora stands with her thumb out by the side of the road.

We don't wait long. A guy driving a sporty red convertible picks us up. He's beautiful like all Croatian men: tall, dark, and handsome, and knows enough English to understand where we're staying. He drops us close to our place. We shower, then march on the dark roads for thirty minutes to our usual café in Korčula Old Town with Busty Server. I eat every bite of my crunchy sandwich, then stare longingly at my empty plate.

"Ice cream?" I ask the girls as we pay the bill.

"Yeah." Dejah leads us outside, and the amber streetlamps illuminate our path to the shop a block away.

"I'm totally getting a double scoop." I rub my belly.

"We deserve it after today," Nora says.

"Remember me?" A lanky American guy with big ears steps into my space. "We met at the email café two days ago."

I glance up at his angular stern face.

"Uh, yeah." He was the bionic typer at the other computer. We exchanged zero words, so I wouldn't classify us as meeting.

His wide brown eyes stare over my head as he clenches and unclenches his fists.

"Well, we're going to get ice cream." I swerve around him because I need my double scoop. "Bye—"

"I'll join you." Bionic Typer nods.

"Sure." *Oh, joy.*

"It's good to see you. I was worried we wouldn't cross paths. Although the probability was high of us reuniting due to the size of the island," he says, matching my stride.

"Ok-*ay*." Whatever. Should I get chocolate? What am I saying? Of course, I will.

"You look nice. I like your hair," Bionic Typer says as we wait in the short line outside the shop to place our order at the open window.

"Thanks." I wrinkle my brow. What's with this guy? My face is tomato red from the grueling hike in the sun, and my hair's wet in a messy bun.

Dejah orders, then passes me my towering cone. I take a huge unladylike bite and shiver as the rich creamy chocolate glides down my throat. The four of us sit at a round metal table outside the shop on the quiet pedestrian street.

"I'm from San Francisco, I'm a programmer, and I'm thirty-nine ..." Bionic Typer rigidly holds his single scoop of vanilla, speaking directly to me and blanking Khadejah and Nora as he strings together one continuous sentence running me through his life statistics.

Nora ignored me the first time we met, but at least Dejah was keen to talk to her. I could totally do without this guy's monolog because I have ice cream to eat. I zone out and lick the side of my creamy chocolate cone.

He stops talking, and his ice cream drips on the table.

"We're from *Austr-al-ia*." Dejah points to herself and Nora.

Bionic Typer blinks. Then shakes his head.

"Where was I?" He focuses on me like Dejah never spoke. "Oh yes, my car, it's the latest model ..."

Dejah rolls her eyes. Nora and I giggle.

"Did I say something amusing?" Bionic Typer flushes, and the corners of his eyes crease. "My house is by the ocean." He stands. "I need to leave and get dinner." He marches away, clutching his untouched drippy ice cream.

"What was that?" I shove the bottom of the pointy cone in my mouth.

"He wanted in your knickers." Nora smirks.

"I don't think that dude has sex." I scoff. "He's worse than The Drip. Why do all the boring guys talk to us?"

"Mate, he wasn't talking to *us*. He only had *eyes* for you." Dejah chuckles as she wipes her hands on a napkin.

"Oh, man. That was *flirting*?" I twist my lips. "Ugh. Not fair. At least Nora caught the eye of the Hungarian guy. He couldn't communicate but was way more interesting."

"Yeah, but they ended up crushing on the server." Nora shrugs as she crunches her cone.

"I would kill for her boobs." Dejah sighs.

"Totally," I say as Nora nods.

My skin's sticky with sweat, and I could use another double scoop by the time we enter our room. I tug off my shoes as the lopsided ceiling fan struggles to turn. I whip off my shirt and sniff my pit. Whiffy but not terrible—

"We need to talk money," Burly rumbles, his Australian accent heavier than usual as he barges into our room.

I gasp, and Dejah tosses me her damp sarong. I plaster it to my naked chest as Burly's glassy eyes bounce between me and the girls, who are also half-dressed.

"Now?" Dejah growls as she tugs on her shorts she was taking off.

Burly licks his lips. The stench of whiskey oozes off him. He was okay to start with, but his creepy meter has risen since we've been here. He ogles us from afar when his wife's back is turned. We've managed to avoid him as she's been here when we have. But we saw her working the night shift at the bus station a few hours ago, so he must be trying his luck.

"You need to pay more tourist tax." He slurs an amount.

"We'll bring it to you when we get it together," Nora says, shoving him out the door.

"Tourist tax is such a rip-off," Dejah seethes as she counts the cash in Ken.

It's been a constant add-on during our Croatian travels with no rhyme or reason to how it's calculated.

"He probably needs money to pay for the alcohol he drank tonight." Nora passes Dejah her portion of the tax as I throw on sleep clothes.

I sit by my pillow and brush my damp hair.

The door swings open, and Burly stumbles in. Dejah passes him the cash. He counts it as she sits on her bed. He shoves it in his shorts pocket, then drops his big ass on the end of my bed with his back to me, facing Dejah.

"Where are you from in Australia again?" he asks her boobs.

Nora and I stare on as Burly has a deep and meaningful conversation with Dejah's chest. A car door slams. Burly pales. The wife's home, and I bet he'll be in trouble if she catches him in here. I giggle as he scurries out.

I flip the lock and press my back against the door.

"Dude, your boobs are epic. Who knew they could have a twenty-minute conversation?" I slow clap.

"Impressive, right?" She shimmies her chest.

"Bet the server couldn't do that," Nora says.

Korčula has gifted us this relaxing beach vacation, but I'm ready to move on to something new in the morning. Hvar promises a wild nightlife, and the timing is perfect because it's my twenty-seventh birthday tomorrow.

I have lots to celebrate. I was in Greece this time last year where I met Josh, and months later, I left my life in Canada and moved to London. And now I'm on my dream travel adventure. But my greatest achievement this year is I'm chipping away at my grief—getting stronger with each passing day. Unlike my marathon-running brother, I'll be honoring my year by ringing in this birthday as I shake my ass on a bar top. Hvar better get ready because I intend to live up to my Dude Davo crazy.

GOOD TIMES WITH THE WARRIOR - HVAR, CROATIA

Barney digs into my rotator cuffs as we step off the ferry in Hvar at dusk. Wrinkly ladies are vying for our attention like they're working the trading floor at the New York Stock Exchange. Arms are waving. People are shoving. And my ears ring from the layers of shouts in Croatian demanding we stay at their house.

I reach for Dejah, and she reassuringly squeezes my hand.

We're back to our dynamic duo, and I'm glad. This morning we said goodbye to Nora, who returned to Dubrovnik in search of a dentist. We didn't go with her, and she didn't expect us to. We have three weeks until we meet the girls in Istanbul or I divert to meet Josh. We don't have the time to backtrack with Nora, see everything on our list, *and* travel over a thousand kilometers to Old Constantinople. We parted ways with a hug and new details in my address book I'll never use.

"Back. Off." I shrink back as three screaming women crowd me.

They move away.

"Great." I place my palm on my throat. "We need a room, and I've chased everyone off."

"It's okay. We'll figure it out." Dejah studies the heaving mob.

I pout as she contemplates our next move. This hasn't been the super fun birthday I envisioned. We schlepped from our room to Korčula Old Town laden with our packs. I filled and drained my water bottle six times on the windy ferry, but I still have a lingering dehydration hangover from the hike yesterday. Bionic Typer was on the same boat, but thankfully he's lost in the chaos, hopefully forever. And now because of my short temper, we have no hope of finding accommodation.

"Hey." A white guy with an Australian accent wearing a backpack strides over with an older woman in a flowered dress. He tips his dark head to the woman, who barely reaches the middle of his broad chest. "She says that she has a room for seventy kunas a night if you want it."

Numbers swirl in my foggy brain; that's about seventeen dollars for both of us.

"What about the dodgy tourist tax?" Dejah plants her fists on her hips.

The Aussie backpacker asks the older woman in Croatian.

My lips part. He speaks the language. We've been lucky as people at our accommodations—apart from Croatian Tara—have spoken English. But I figure we'll have as much luck communicating with this local crowd as we did the Hungarian Scooter Trio. So this Australian guy could be saving the day.

"That's with the tax," he translates.

"We're in." Dejah nods, also knowing we couldn't do better on our own.

The old woman's sandals clap against the smooth stone streets as she marches us away from the ferry dock up a maze of steep pedestrian pathways. I've walked Old Towns around

Croatia and been so curious about what lies behind the stone walls and arched doorways. I grin because today I'm going to find out.

"I'm Owen." The Australian guy's words are clipped, and he doesn't smile. I get the feeling he doesn't smile a lot.

"How do you know Croatian?" Dejah asks after she introduces us.

"My Croatian grandfather taught me." He shrugs.

Owen's steps are sure. His hair's clipped short, functional rather than fashionable. He's not attractive but not unattractive either. It would be difficult to ascertain where he's from; he would blend in with any setting and be a perfect spy.

The older woman—Grandma—speaks to Owen in Croatian.

"This is her house." Owen tips his chin to the one-level bungalow with small windows on either side of a metal screen door.

"He's going to be helpful." I smile, excited to go inside.

"Oh yeah." Dejah's eyes are shining with mischief.

Owen doesn't know what he's in for; since he can translate, he's stuck with us. I'm not into him in a sexy way, but it's going to be fun to get him to loosen up—if he doesn't ditch us at the first opportunity.

The door squeaks as Grandma pulls it open. Packs on our backs, we traipse through a narrow front hall to a screened-in gazebo. Leafy potted plants sit in each corner, and the room is lit by the single desk lamp on a buffet table near the entrance. A fragile old man with wispy hair and suspenders over his sleeveless undershirt is sitting at the head of a ten-seat table. His gnarly fingers stroke a black and white Portuguese water dog curled on his lap as his astute brown eyes assess us.

Grandma flicks her wrist at Grandpa and says something.

"Bella." She points to the dog, and the pup yips.

I nod and wave as Owen greets him in Croatian.

Frowning, Grandma grumbles and motions for us to follow. She directs us to three doors adjacent to Grandpa's sitting area.

The doors lead to one bathroom and two simple bedrooms with double beds. Owen takes the smaller room so Dejah and I have more space. We pass her the cash for three nights, and she disappears. I'm not disappointed by the clean and basic room, but I was hoping the mystery behind the stone walls would be grander, maybe have a fresco or something.

Grandpa's hunched in Owen's doorway as I dump Barney on the floor next to Dejah's and my bed.

Owen pops his head into our room. "He's asking us to join him."

"Sure," Dejah says as I grab my water and cigarettes and follow to the long table.

A light breeze blows through the screens, cooling my skin. I sip my water as Owen chats with grinning Grandpa. Grandma must be the scout and Grandpa the social committee.

"Ken is going to be extra generous with no budget tonight. What do you want to eat?" she asks.

"Seafood." My favorite and not something we eat often as it's expensive.

"Done." She nods. "Hey, Owen, it's Candace's birthday. Do you want to come out with us? Seafood dinner and dancing."

"Yeah, I'll join." Owen nods and shares with Grandpa in Croatian.

A big smile takes over Grandpa's face. He claps his hands and babbles.

"He's happy because it's his oldest son's birthday today too," Owen translates.

"Happy birthday to your son," I say.

Grandpa leaps out of his chair and shuffles out of the room.

"Is everything okay?" I glance at the other two, who shrug.

Grandpa's leather slippers drag across the tile floor when he returns holding a wooden tray. Dishes clatter as he places the tray with three generous slices of cake on the table.

The fork rattles against the white crockery as he shakily places a plate in front of me.

"What's this for?" I gape at the spongy vanilla square topped with a bright red cherry in the center of a caramelized pineapple slice.

Grandpa firmly shakes my hand as he speaks.

"He says happy birthday and to enjoy a slice of his son's favorite cake." Owen's monotone translation lacks all the enthusiasm in Grandpa's voice, just like the Lithuanian movie translator.

Grandpa passes the other two plates to Dejah and Owen.

"Thank you." I shove my chair back and throw my arms around Grandpa's frail frame. "I never thought I would have cake today; this is a special gift."

Owen translates, and the corners of Grandpa's eyes crease as he nods.

Tears well in my eyes as I bring the fork to my mouth. The last time I had a piece of homemade cake on my birthday was before my mom died. I savor the spongy sweet base that contrasts with the tart pineapple. This is the first time I've ever had this kind of cake. And I know for the rest of my days if I ever have another slice, it'll bring me back to this perfect moment, sitting in a cool gazebo on an island in paradise with two new acquaintances and the best friend a girl could ask for. Grandpa's kind gesture has rocketed this birthday out of the gutter. And I have a feeling this night will wrap it in a bow.

I SHOWER, shave, slink into a tight white tank top, and fashion my colorful sarong into a short-fitted mini skirt, securing it by wrapping it around twice and knotting it at the waist. I apply makeup and even brush my hair before I slide my feet into my rarely-worn black heels.

Feeling brighter and more put together than I have in weeks, Dejah—in a blue skirt and white top, Owen—freshly shaven in a green button-up, and I, say goodnight to Grandpa then step out into the humid night. We descend a flight of stone stairs into the rectangular piazza the size of a football field. Warm sea air blows in from the million-dollar ships docked at one end of the open space to the adjacent cathedral spire on the opposite side. I sigh as I glide along the smooth stones, past cafés blaring lively music. Beautiful people from the palatial yachts dripping in designer finery drink cocktails side by side on packed patios with locals dressed in cut-off shorts and no-name open-collar shirts.

No one stares. No one judges. Everyone is welcome and included in the heart of Hvar. And it's the best gift to be part of the crowd rather than singled out like we usually are for either our clothes, speaking English, or just looking different.

We agree on a restaurant with a side patio filled with potted orange trees and grapevines clinging to the six-foot-high crumbling stone walls just off the piazza. Our round table is beside the largest tree, and the smell of citrus wraps around the salty breeze. We order a bottle of Luviji, a local white wine, and a sharing platter of seafood risotto.

Owen pours the icy golden wine, and I shiver as I swipe the cool condensation on the side of my glass with my fingertips.

"Cheers." Dejah raises her wine. "Happy birthday, darlin'."

Owen and I join her, and our glasses tinkle as they meet.

I tip the glass to my glossy lips. Rich, sweet, and tart liquid tangles my taste buds—reminiscent of the pineapple-upside-down cake.

"Thanks for making it special." My heart pinches as I think of home. All the great birthdays I've celebrated with my family and friends. But it's not the same without my mom—just one more reason why it's easier to be away from home.

"It's what you deserve, mate." Dejah nods. "Owen, what's your story besides being an Aussie with a Croatian grandad?"

"I live in Japan teaching English." He tops up our glasses. "Hvar is my last stop on my ten-day backpacking holiday around Croatia."

"What's been your favorite place?" I ask.

"Dubrovnik, I have relatives there. But I think Hvar's going to be fun." He rolls his bottom lip.

"It is." Dejah chuckles. "And you're stuck with us for the rest of your trip."

"Glad for it." Owen smirks, the closest thing I've seen to a smile on his serious face.

Having a translator, we don't have to work as hard to figure out our day. We can diversify our food choices as he can read the menu, he can bargain, ask for the time … anything. And so far, he's fun to hang out with. Fingers crossed it continues.

Heat rolls off the oval platter loaded with fish fillets, calamari, clams, and shrimp mixed with rice in a rich, creamy sauce. Dejah grabs two spoons and piles our plates high. The smell of garlic floods my senses, and I sigh as the delicate fish melts in my mouth.

"Best food we've eaten in forever." I moan as the others hum in agreement.

Dejah and Owen exchange stories about home and his love for martial arts as I get lost in my meal. He never smiles, but the smirks are plentiful as they exchange fun quips. Gruff and serious dudes like Owen aren't her type; she likes them pretty and lighthearted. But she loves a dry humor battle, and Owen's delivering that in spades. Yeah, I think we'll all get along just fine for the next few days.

I slurp my strong wine, go in for seconds on the risotto, and happily listen to their banter until the platter is scraped clean, the wine is empty, and the bill is paid.

Techno music is pumping from the open door as I skip up the steps into the dimly lit club across from the marina. A dizzying array of bottles line the shelves on the mirrored wall behind the long bar. Small groups of pretty people are gathered around high-top tables, and the dance floor in the center of the room is packed with raging partygoers.

I love sightseeing. I love chocolate. I love meeting fun people like Owen. But what I love more than anything else is dancing.

I squeal as I throw my arms in the air and skip to the dance floor. I close my eyes, flip my hair, and shake my ass to the pulsing beat. Dejah bumps my shoulder, Owen appears on my other side, and the three of us bounce around without a care in the world.

Unlike Nora, he's an addition to our team we both like.

My makeup has melted off, and my once-organized hair is a frizzy mess.

"I'm going to get some air," I scream in Dejah's ear.

"All good?" she asks.

I give her a thumbs-up, then stumble through the rowdy crowd out the door and wobble down the stairs. I slouch on the last step and lean against the wall so I don't fall over. The boats bobbing in the marina are a drunken blur of twinkly white. So pretty—

"Hey." Three guys with their shirts unbuttoned to the navel and dark chest hair on full display tower over me. "You … swim?" They pinch their fingertips together and shake, pointing to themselves and then to me with big grins. "Swim … marina… molto bene."

I blink. Are these Italian dudes for real? I can barely sit up and they want me to swim?

"No molto bene." I shake my head as Dejah rushes by toward the boats. "I gotta go." I dash past the Italians toward her. "Are you okay?"

"I'm going to be sick." Dejah pales and throws her hands over her mouth.

"Hang on." I hook my arm around her waist and drag her away from the noisy bar to a quiet part of the marina.

She drops on the smooth stone between two huge yachts. I gather her dark hair in my fist as she grips the edge, leans forward, and projectile pukes. The water splashes as our delicious meal returns to the sea. I peel the hair tie off my wrist and wrap it around her hair as she continues to blow.

I kick off my shoes and light a cigarette. The stones are worn and soft like velvet under my bare feet, the moon glistens on the sea, stars twinkle in the sky, and low-level techno from the disco muzzles the sound of her heaves.

I purse my lips and nod—man, I picked a great spot for her to puke.

"There you are. I've been looking everywhere," Owen says as he storms down the gangway.

"Owen." I throw my arms out to the side. "Welcome to our spot."

"She okay?" he asks as Dejah vomits again.

"There's been loads of puke with no end in sight." I offer Owen my last cigarette.

"Keep it." He waves it off. "I'll go buy more."

"Sounds good." I sway to the music as Dejah feeds the fish and Owen marches off on his errand.

"Hello." Five different guys circle me with dark hair and big smiles.

Dejah retches.

"You should come to the disco with us," one says in an Italian accent.

I blink. My friend's passed out at the water's edge. In what world would I leave her?

"I'm good. I was just at the disco." I slant my chin to the stairs leading to the techno bar.

"No, *the disco* is up there." Italian guy points to the hilltop.

Beams of colorful lights cut through the night sky from the stone fortress overlooking the city. I twist my lips. I hate that we missed that place; I just know it would be the perfect venue to dance on the bar top. But we'll have to go another night because this one is over as soon as Owen's back. The guys throw words at each other that sound like a heated argument—but since it's Italian, it's probably just regular chat.

"Ciao bella." They smile and wave as they leave.

I squat beside Dejah and swipe the hair off her cheek that's come loose from the hair tie. She bats my hand and lunges her chest over the edge. I swear as I race to her feet, grab her ankles, and tug her back so she doesn't tumble into the water as she vomits. It's a good thing the stones are smooth—

"Candace?" I drop her legs at the sound of Bionic Typer's voice. "What are you doing out here?"

I bite back a groan. Of all the times for *this* guy to show up.

"I'm surprised to see you. You look uh, nice. Would you like to join me for a drink?" Bionic Typer asks.

My mouth opens then closes as my eyes flick to Dejah flopped on the ground.

Is he blind?

"I can't—"

"There's a nice place close by." Bionic Typer tips his head.

Dejah heaves, and it splashes into the water.

And deaf?

"I found some smokes." Owen's jaw ticks as he strides toward us.

Relief pours through me he's back. Owen's a protector. And an intimidating presence for someone who hasn't been joking and dancing with him all night. For sure, he'll stop the crazy train of people stopping by for a chat.

"Are you okay, Candace?" His legs are planted apart and his arms steady at his sides as he glares at Bionic Typer.

Bionic Typer's spine straightens, and his eyes widen. Owen told us over dinner he chose to work in Japan to further his karate practice. No way would you catch him painting Mr. Miyagi's fence; based on the hard lines on his face, he would totally hang at the Cobra Kai dojo.

"Yeah, I'm good." I blow a stray strand of hair out of my face. "But it's been busy with all the puking, Italians, him, and now them ..." I wave my hand to the two stern-faced cops in crisp navy uniforms marching our way.

"Maybe another time." Bionic Typer scurries past the cops barking in Croatian at Owen.

"We need to go." Owen narrows his eyes on Dejah and tips his chin to the angry cops.

"I guess my strategic puking spot is not isolated—like at all." I huff as I grab our purses and prop Dejah's limp body under my arm.

I cart her through the square, up the steps to Grandma and Grandpa's, and dump her on our double bed.

"Here." Owen passes me a bucket lined with a plastic bag.

"You're the man, thanks." I adjust Dejah on her side, head over the bucket, and throw a blanket over her.

I grin with my hands on my hips. What a night. Despite the busy spot, I'm on fire with taking care of my friend, unlike when she was sick in Lithuania. My heart softens at how far I've come. My empathy's still alive inside me; it just needed time to recover—

The heat of Owen's body presses into my back. He pulls my hair to one side and his lips whisper across my neck.

"Why don't you sleep in my room?" he murmurs in my ear.

I elbow him in the gut, and he chuckles. It's the first laugh I've heard. It's gritty but does zero for my libido. "Hard pass. Go to bed."

"Can't blame a guy for trying." He steps back and shrugs.

"You're the worst." I roll my eyes.

I send him next door, then pass out in bed next to Khadejah with a smile on my face.

Best birthday in ages.

And I can't wait for our next few days in Hvar.

———

MY EYES FLUTTER open the next morning to Dejah's scowling face.

"I was awake all night. Either I was spewing or shoving your drunk, cuddling ass off me. No matter how many times I pushed you away, you kept coming back for more, and you never woke up."

"I *am* a proficient drunk cuddler." I giggle.

"I hate you so much right now." She punches her pillow and rolls over.

I stretch my arms over my head, feeling surprisingly good despite all I drank last night.

"Knock, knock," Owen shouts through the door.

"Come in." I sit crisscrossed in a tank top and shorts as Dejah flops an arm across her eyes.

"Grandpa said there's a food market in the piazza, want to come with?" Owen leans against our doorframe in a fresh T-shirt and shorts.

"I'll come, but grumpy probably won't because she didn't like my cuddling." I hook my thumb at Dejah.

"I would've happily put up with it." He shrugs.

"Of course you would have." I chuckle.

"Don't feel special. I knocked him back after he tried it on with me on the dance floor." Dejah doesn't move but cracks a smile.

"Second string." I splay my hand on my chest and mock horror.

"Can you blame me? I'm an equal opportunity guy." His lips twitch as he stares at us together in bed. "How about the three of us try again now?"

"Still no." I chuckle.

"You wish." Dejah waves him off.

His chest rattles with low laughter as he shuts the door.

The three of us clicked last night over dinner with our similar humor and backgrounds. And his hitting on us isn't threatening or uncomfortable or awkward. I admire his straightforwardness; it's a refreshing change from cagey Josh. He tried his luck; if one or both of us were in, he would go for it, but our *nos* don't change our easy friendship.

I step out into the hot morning with Owen, leaving Dejah to sleep. Covered stalls are set up at the church end of the square opposite the marina selling produce, lace doilies, pottery, and jewelry. We buy crisp grapes, lush strawberries, and warm French bread, then eat our fill on the way back to Grandma and Grandpa's.

Owen joins Grandpa for a smoke while I rouse Dejah. I drop the plastic bag with water and food on the end of the bed and cover my nose to block the waft of vomit and booze clinging to the air in our dark room.

"Get up, it's a lovely day," I say as I slip into my bikini. "We're going to the beach. You'll feel better after a swim."

"I would rather do Austin and Keith then eat *the sandwich* than get out of this bed." She ignores the bag.

"Sounds like more work than getting up." I snicker as I pull a dress over my swimsuit. "And you forgot about the boat trip to Hel."

She throws a pillow at me as I dash out.

Owen and I traipse past the marina to a small cove Grandpa recommended.

A pier juts out into the clear blue sea, and ten people are lounging on the beige stone beach. It's pretty, but nothing beats the spot we hiked to in Korčula.

I arrange my sarong, sun lotion, water, and book as Owen drops his shorts.

My mouth falls open.

He's completely naked from the waist down. His long, thick penis is there—right in front of my face. I snort. Objectively, it's a nice one and better than Anthony's or the flaccid old man ones I've been flashed along the way. But like the others, it does nothing for me.

"You couldn't have changed before we got here?" I ask as he reaches for his swim trunks.

"Where's the fun in that?" He drags the suit up his legs and bounces as he adjusts himself into place.

I tip my head back and laugh. I was so wrong when I initially pegged Owen as serious and in need of loosening up. Turns out his dry humor and easy manner is just what *I* need. Waiting for Josh's answer has me in knots, and I know Dejah feels my stress. So Owen is the perfect person to join our duo and bring the fun. But just not in a sexy way.

I'M DRAGGING through our Hvar sightseeing tour because Owen and I danced on the bar till dawn last night at the hilltop disco. I fulfilled my birthday wish, just a day late. Dejah opted out, so she's fresh as a daisy and has been nominated as our tour guide.

Owen and I lean on a cannon as we take in the sweeping views of the yachts anchored alongside small fishing boats in the sunny harbor from Tvrdava Fortica. Dejah explains that this defensive fort at the top of the city was built in the 6th century, but I miss the rest of the details because I only slept for two hours, and I'm more drunk than sober.

In the sprawling piazza, we duck into a touristy shop along the perimeter. I'm spinning the postcard rack when my daypack knocks a Hvar tourist plate off the wall. I wince as it crashes to the floor. I pile the white shards in my palm as Owen explains my accident to the woman behind the cash desk. She waves us off, and we leg it out of the shop.

We try our luck at the outside market in the square Owen and I bought food at yesterday. Dejah and I are trying on silver bangles at a jewelry stall when Owen picks up a pair of oval ceramic earrings. They slip from his grasp and shatter on the ground. He casually picks them up and slides them back on the counter unnoticed. Dejah rolls her eyes as we replace the bangles and move along to the next stall with piles of sarongs and blankets—way safer for our clumsiness.

"I should call home," I say as Dejah and Owen flip through a pile of sarongs. "I'm sure my dad wants to wish me a happy birthday."

I'm not *sure* he'll remember. But it's worth a shot, and we need to make up for our bad conversation when I couldn't name the Adriatic Sea.

"I'm going to wait till next week," Dejah says as she holds out a green sarong covered in white fish.

Dejah and I usually call home at the same time, but it's her birthday next week, so she's saving her call till then. And I'm positive her parents will make a big fuss when she does.

"Maybe we should shop later," Dejah says, replacing the sarong on the pile.

"I was hoping for your help to buy my girlfriend a present," Owen says.

I choke on saliva, and Dejah whacks my back until my coughing turns to laughter.

Owen smirks and shrugs.

I'm surprised he has a girlfriend based on his double-wooing attempts on my birthday. But I don't know anything about their relationship. Maybe he got a hall pass. Or maybe he's just an opportunist, like he said. But he's an adult, and I'm not judging either way.

"How about a sarong?" Dejah suggests.

"What color does she like?" I ask.

"Red," he says.

We help him choose delicate dangly earrings and a ruby scarf for the mystery woman. He places them in his daypack as a damp breeze swirls through the piazza, making the canvas covers on the stalls flap. The boats are bobbing in the marina, and the skies behind them are an ominous gray.

"There's a storm coming in. And it's moving fast," I say as my hair blows in front of my eyes.

"Let's get coffee." Dejah points to an indoor café across the square.

"I'll meet you there after I call home."

I march into the wind swirling off the foamy sea to the post office beside the marina. From the tiled entryway, I glance past people waiting in line for help from one of the two older ladies behind the counter. I zero in on two pay phones attached to the wall between the front windows with a view of the storm rolling into the harbor.

Sweet. They're both available.

I yank the handset off the black phone and dial the magic code. Dad answers as lightning flashes over the boats followed by a boom of thunder.

"Hi, Da—" The call cuts off, and the phone drones in my ear as the lights flicker, then wink out.

The air in the post office whirs, and the lights flip on.

I dial again, and he answers on the first ring.

The sky's black, palm trees are bent over from the wind, and rain thrashes against the window as my dad tells me about my brother Pete's university football camp and Kev's upcoming holiday to the Cayman Islands. The sound of my dad's voice makes me long for home more than usual. So I indulge in the moment, close my eyes, and imagine myself having this conversation over a cup of coffee at his kitchen table surrounded by red poppy wallpaper. The storm rages, and I twirl the phone cord as he updates me on the Bill Clinton and Monica Lewinski scandal—convinced Bill had sex with Monica.

"I got an email from Khadejah's parents. They were happy to hear all is well and send their love. And I got a note from Josh telling me what a special daughter I have," he says.

"That's cheesy." I scrunch my nose, and we both laugh. But it *is* cool Josh took the time to respond to my dad. "I'll pass on the news to Dejah from her parents."

"Well, happy birthday, Can. Mom cried when you were born and said, *'I got my girl.'* She loved you very much."

I gulp past the lump in my throat at my dad's uncharacteristically heartfelt comment and that he remembered my birthday.

"I'll talk to you soon. Love you," I say as I place the phone on the receiver, both happy and sad my escape to home is over.

I dash across the slick stones to the coffee shop. The thunder and lightning have blown over, but the rain remains. My dress clings to my body, and rivets of water roll down my bare arms from the short jaunt across the piazza. I tip my face to the dark sky as I stand outside the café delighting in the rain gliding down my skin.

I'm already soaked; I might as well enjoy it.

"What are yah doing?" Dejah yells from the doorway.

Living. Finally.

"Join me. It's glorious," I say, standing ankle-deep in a puddle.

Owen and Dejah step outside.

"It's warm." Rainwater pools in her outstretched palms.

"Right—" I hiss as water splashes up my leg.

Owen's lips tip up as he stomps in the puddle under my feet —again.

"Oh, it's on." I chase after him.

The three of us shriek as we zigzag through the piazza. Deep, honest laughter—that makes you feel good down to your soul— rings through the square as we leap into puddle after puddle, soaking each other.

I double over to catch my breath. Dejah and Owen join me, and we face off in the center of the piazza with big grins, chests heaving and steam rising from our sopping clothes.

"Owen needs a Spice Girl name," Dejah says, then tells Owen how it works.

"I vote for Splash Spice." I swish my toe in a nearby puddle. "Oh, no wait. I have a better one. How about: Hit On You When You're Drunk Spice."

Dejah and Owen snicker.

"That could work, but it's a bit long." She swipes away the hair plastered to her cheeks. "How about Warrior Spice because he loves martial arts and Japan."

"That works," I say.

"Thank you." Owen slaps his palm across his soaked T-shirt and bows at the waist.

"And now we need beer."

"Yeah, we do." Dejah races across the square into the closest bar.

"You first." I lift my chin to Owen because I don't trust he won't splash me again.

He saunters ahead, and I remain a few steps behind. He pauses at the door. Then kicks his leg back—like a horse—swiping it through a puddle.

Water soaks my thighs.

"Totally should have gone with Splash Spice." I laugh, so very glad to be exactly where I am.

———

OWEN'S GONE before we wake the next day. He left us his details and a sweet poem. Dejah and I howl with laughter as we read the clever rhyming page describing how much fun he had with us after he got over the letdown of us denying him a threesome under Grandma and Grandpa's roof.

Yesterday's storm signaled the end of the summer in Hvar. It's blustery, and for the first time since I arrived in Croatia, I need a sweater. I tug the long sleeves over my cold hands as we wander through the beautiful piazza. But it's lackluster, just like a shooting star slipping out of sight, Owen took the light and fun with him when he left. We head back to Grandma and Grandpa's to hunker down, plan our time in Budapest, and workshop what happens if I do and don't meet with Josh.

We sit cross-legged on the bed and crack open our guidebooks.

"If we both go to Istanbul, that would be a train through Romania and Bulgaria, or Serbia and Bulgaria from Budapest," she says, studying the map.

"I don't know if I need visas for those places. And I don't want to get pulled off a train again." My time spent with Stern Man to get an entry visa for Estonia is something I never want to repeat.

"We fly then. Either together or just me." She shrugs. "I emailed Stella and Gwen when we initially came up with this plan in Vienna, and they promised to get to Istanbul before me so I'm not on my own."

"That's great." My shoulders dip.

Guilt about leaving her—even though it would only happen once she can reunite with the girls—has been hanging over my head, and it's a relief to know she won't be alone other than on the flight.

"Logistically, if I do meet Josh, we'll be going to Germany. After we part ways, I'd like to visit my old Toronto flatmate, Irma. She lives in Utrecht, and it's super close to Amsterdam, so I can fly from there to Jordan."

"That works. Anything else?"

"Do you have any idea how much time you guys will spend in Turkey, Lebanon, and Syria?" I ask.

"We talked about that as well over email, and we reckon you should meet us in Amman at the end of September."

"Okay, that covers it. I'll email and ask if I can stay with Irma. Then I'll need to find a KLM office in Budapest to add a flight to my around-the-world ticket."

I can change existing flights for free or add one for a fee to the ticket I bought before I left London. I used it to fly to Russia, and my next scheduled flight is from Cairo to Nairobi at the end of November. Hopefully, it won't cost much to add in a leg.

"Sorted. Cards?" She closes her book.

My stomach tilts. It's all so simple. Too bad the choice isn't.

"Yeah." I reach for my daypack. "We haven't played Crazy Eights in a while."

I swap my book for the deck in my bag and shuffle. Budapest

is where I'll decide if I go forward with Khadejah or back to meet Josh. I frown as I deal the cards. Dejah and I've made a point of not going backward, and here I am contemplating doing just that. Oh, please, please, let me make the right choice when the time comes.

TURNING POINT - BUDAPEST, HUNGARY

Whistles blow and bells chime as we trudge down the crowded train platform at Déli station in Budapest. Fatigue weighs heavily in my bones. Yesterday started with a gusty ferry ride from Hvar to Split. Then we spent ten hours sweating our asses off in a sketchy park with our big packs waiting for our night train to Budapest. We bungeed the train compartment door closed but had three break-in attempts during the night from shady-looking dudes looking to join our cozy campout. We slammed the door in their faces, but I barely slept out of fear they might come back.

We stop near a bench on the busy platform as Dejah studies the map from her book to figure out the fastest way to get to the hostel. My teeth are fuzzy, my hair's greasy, and I've been wearing the same underpants for over thirty hours. I need a shower and a toothbrush, pronto.

"Hi girls, are you looking for a place to stay?" A blond guy with a goatee and an easy smile joins our reading circle.

"You're wasting your time. We're going to stay at The Pad," I say.

Like Burly outside the tourist office in Korčula or the old ladies at the ferry in Hvar, this guy's here to scour the train station for weary backpackers and convince them to choose the hostel he scouts for.

"You don't want to stay there." Smiley waves his hand. "Our hostel is way better, man. Tell me, where're you from?"

"I'm Canadian, and she's from Australia."

"Canada. Oh, *wow*." He places his hand over his heart with a dreamy look in his eye. "The place where the goddess Pamela Anderson's from."

He rapidly blinks his bright blue eyes with a cheeky smirk on his baby face.

Dejah's picked The Pad because we'll be celebrating her birthday here in Budapest and she liked the sound of it from what she read in her book. But I doubt we'll be going there because this guy is totally her type: he's fair, on the corny side of funny, and mischievous.

"Do you have laundry?" I ask because my clothes are past due for a wash and I don't want to trek all over Budapest to do it like we did in Kraków.

"I know a place." He tilts his head and shirks his shoulders. "It's close to the hostel."

"Your choice," I say to Dejah, even though I already know her answer.

"We should go with him." She sighs.

"We're in," I say.

"I'm Vladimir, but you can call me Vlad. The hostel's not far." He guides us off the platform and out of the train station.

"Where are you from? Your English is so good," Dejah asks.

"I'm from Budapest. I taught myself English," Vlad says as he smooths his hands down his shirt.

Dejah hangs on his every word as I quietly plod alongside them. The sky's a dull gray. The air tastes like dust and petrol. Boxy cars speed past, stirring up food wrappers littering the sidewalk. The buildings lining the streets remind me of Vienna, but these white stone walls are tarnished from years of grime and pollution. I frown because the severity of this place matches the decision I have to make.

At the check-in desk to the left of the hostel entrance, Vlad slides me a map with the laundry location and says he'll catch us later. Beyond the desk, there's a large common area with worn green sofas, mismatched tables, and chairs. And a free-standing bar with one beer tap on the right flanked by dartboards.

My stomach clenches at the steep price of twenty dollars a night for a dorm bed. Double what we paid in Croatia and more expensive than Vienna. Either our room will be spectacular or Vlad's recruiting cut is significant. But we came in under budget in Croatia, so we have some flex to balance it out.

Our room is clean and spacious with a sturdy lock. The one big window along the back wall fills the space with light. And there's no handmade two-by-four bunks here. We have four unoccupied bouncy single beds with fluffy white duvets and pillows. A treat from the scratchy bedding we've grown used to. And there's an attached bathroom. I strip off my clothes and race to the shower. As the spray beats on my back, I don't care how much this place costs because this is the best water pressure I've experienced since I left Canada.

I pull on pants—without underwear as I have no clean ones —and my yellow jacket for the first time since the Baltics. My head spins as we walk to the Internet café two blocks away because today is the day I'll know my future.

The hum of the dozen computers set up around the room, tapping of keys, and cigarette smoke hanging in the air amps my nerves. We each buy an hour and sit side by side at the last two unoccupied desks. My heart lodges in my throat as I jiggle the mouse and dial up my email account.

If I haven't heard from Josh or he doesn't want to meet, I'm going to Istanbul.

If Josh does want to meet, then I have to choose—go back to him or forward with Dejah.

The café blurs as I click on Josh's note in my inbox.

Baby, I want to meet and go to Oktoberfest with you. I'll meet you in Prague on September 12th, can't wait.

Josh xo

I grip the edge of the desk as joy and disappointment collide in my chest.

He wants to meet—in thirteen days.

A tiny part of me was hoping he would turn me down so I didn't have to make this decision. My knee bounces as I study his words on the screen and consider my options. Taking the people out of the equation, I've been to Turkey, but not to Lebanon or Syria. It irks me to miss those places, but they've never held the same appeal as Jordan, Israel, and Egypt, which I won't miss with either choice. I've never been to Oktoberfest and am keen to go, and I'll get to see Irma. But I'll have to go backward to do it. And I hate going backward. It's a waste of time and money to see things twice.

I drop my head in my hands. What do I do?

I glance at Dejah; she throws me an encouraging smile and resumes typing.

My cheeks puff as I blow out a breath. I compose an email to Irma asking if she'll be around at the end of September and I get an immediate reply. She's free and has invited me to stay with her for as long as I'd like.

I square my shoulders. That seals it. I open a new note, type my reply to Josh, and hit send.

I'm going back to Prague.

I click on other notes in my inbox, but it's difficult to focus on anything because my nerves are shot. I need food, and I need to talk to Dejah.

We exit the café and walk straight to the hole-in-the-wall pizza restaurant next door. We order two calzones and Diet Cokes and sit at a table overlooking the street.

"I'm going to meet him." My face flushes as I twist my paper napkin.

"I figured." Her golden eyes lack their usual sparkle.

"I can't believe this is our last stop." A wave of sadness makes my heart dip.

"It'll be fine. I'll see you again in less than a month." She places her warm hand over my fidgeting one and squeezes.

"But what will I do without you until then?"

"Oh, mate." The usual mischievous twinkle returns to her eyes. "If you need me to tell you, then you shouldn't be meeting him."

The knots in my chest unravel as we tuck into our calzones.

It's only four weeks.

I STARE down the wooden stairs descending into a black abyss the next morning. We're at Vlad's 'place' for laundry. The door to the building was unlocked. In the vestibule, stairs are going up, and at the end of the ground floor, there's a tiny sign above this door leading *down* that reads *Laundry*.

"This can't be it." I step back and cling to my plastic bag filled with every gross article of clothing I have other than the clothes on my back.

"Vlad said it's fine, just go." Dejah shoves me toward the steps.

"Why do I have to go first?" I hiss.

"You're taller." She lifts a shoulder.

"That's a terrible reason," I say as I creep down the uneven stairs.

My nose twinges at the smell of must and mold as I step onto the concrete floor. A trickle of light eeks through one tiny window covered with newspaper. I reach up and pull the cord on the naked bulb dangling between the exposed floor joists. Stark white light casts over the only things in the damp space: one washer, one dryer, and two dented metal fold-out chairs. This place would be a perfect secret spy interrogation cell. But there's no hooks or blood on the cement walls, just decades of dirt and grime.

"Told you Vlad wouldn't lead us astray." Dejah raises her chin.

She's crushing hard. He could tell us anything, and she would believe him.

"The faster we get them in, the faster we can get out of here," she says as she dumps her bag on top of the dryer and I do the same.

We sort them into a light and dark pile, insert the coins in the slot, and start the first load. I drag my metal torture chair so it's facing hers. It's cold on my bum but better than the floor.

"I'm totally quitting smoking when you leave. When we see each other again, I'll be smoke-free," I say as I take a long drag on my cigarette.

"Oh, same," she says, lighting another.

We vow to quit every morning and never do because smoking has become part of our adventure.

WE SKIP into the common room with our precious cargo of clean clothes four hours later.

"How did it go?" Vlad leaps off the eyesore sofa as we approach.

"Good. Now we just need to find the KLM office and a place to buy a cheap airline ticket," Dejah says.

"I know a place." He smirks.

Of course he does.

"I can take you there now," he says.

"We just need to drop our stuff." Dejah sighs as we walk to our room. "Best decision ever to stay here."

We catch a tram from outside the hostel to the east side of the Danube River called Pest. And the Buda Castle stretches across the riverfront on the opposite bank in Buda.

"Vlad, it's Dejah's birthday tomorrow. Any suggestions on good bars?" I ask as I cling to the overhead rail on the tram.

"I'd love if there was '80s music for dancing," Dejah says.

"I know the perfect spot. And my friend Eli has an apartment downtown. We can go there for drinks before we go to the bar I have planned."

I hide my grin in the crook of my arm. Guess he's coming with us. But by the smile on Dejah's face, she couldn't be happier. It's her party; if she wants him there, I'm cool with it. Plus, it saves us from having to figure out where to go.

At the KLM office, I add a flight on my around-the-world ticket from Amsterdam to Amman for a reasonable $225. The lady says she needs to work on the ticket, and I can pick it up tomorrow. Our next stop is Vista Travel, where Dejah scores a cheap flight from Budapest to Istanbul for $115.

Leaving in *three* days.

My body locks as the consequences of my choice sink in. Except for the twenty-four hours I was with Josh in Prague, I've spent every day of the last ten weeks with Dejah. We've had the best time. We've never fought. And I'm completely at ease and comfortable in my skin when I'm with her.

But … the one day I was with Josh I was on edge and guarding my words.

My gut rolls as we exit the travel agency.

Have I made a terrible mistake by choosing to meet him?

"They're showing *Lethal Weapon 4* not far from here. Interested?" Vlad asks. "It's in English with Hungarian subtitles."

"That sounds fab." Dejah nods.

It sure does. I could use some Mel Gibson and Danny Glover action to distract me from the fact that I've quite possibly made the worst decision ever.

We buy a big bucket of popcorn and Diet Cokes, then find three seats in the busy theater. My doubts are forgotten as Mel and Danny argue on screen about how to deal with a bad guy wielding a blow torch. This is just what I need, to get lost in the action—

"Did you see that?" Vlad yells as Blow Torch Guy shoots at Mel and Danny. "Oh man, what do you think of that?"

My cheeks flush, and I slouch in my seat.

As Blow Torch Guy lights up the big screen with bullets and fire, the patrons in the theater shout and yell comments in Hungarian.

"That guy is so dead," Vlad hollers before he shoves popcorn in his mouth.

I blink. Totally not like home, where you're shushed for a mere whisper.

Vlad and the rest of the moviegoers shout comments throughout the film. Not the distraction I was anticipating, but it's one all the same. I reach for the popcorn and shrug. I'll enjoy the escape and figure out the rest later.

I'M EMOTIONALLY and physically exhausted by the time we return to our room after laundry in the torture chamber, ticket doubts, Hungarians yelling at Mel and Danny, and then finishing off the day playing darts with Vlad and a weak-chinned strawberry-blond American veterinarian dude in the common room.

A girl with pale golden skin and shoulder-length brown hair waves from one of the previously empty beds as we step inside.

"Hi. I'm Lyndsay from Allentown, Pennsylvania." She flashes her perfect white teeth.

"Just like the song?" I ask as I drop my daypack beside my bed.

"Yup." The skin at the corner of her warm brown eyes crinkles.

Dejah belts out the first line of the Billy Joel song named after her hometown.

Lyndsay and I join in. We end the drawn-out 'stay' in fits of giggles.

"You must hate that," I say as I flop on my downy duvet.

"Nah, I'm used to it." She shakes her head.

Dejah introduces us.

"Hey, we're going out tomorrow night for Khadejah's birthday if you want to join us," I ask, not bothering to confer with Dejah because after our impromptu serenade, I know Lyndsay's a kindred spirit and welcome in our friend group.

"I'd love to." A broad smile lights up Lyndsay's face.

And just like that, we have a new friend I didn't realize we needed.

FACE FACTS - BUDAPEST, HUNGARY

Dejah's twenty-sixth birthday starts with a tram ride to the KLM office. My clammy fingers stain with red from the transfer backing as I hold my new airline ticket. I thought I would feel confident with it in my possession, but my gut swirls with uncertainty as I zip the ticket in my money belt under my clean green cargos.

At Vista Travel, Dejah collects her airline ticket. I ask about the price of train tickets to Prague and pale when she quotes me a price higher than Khadejah's flight to Istanbul.

"How can that be?" I knew I would have to shell out cash to fly to Amman, but after penny-pinching for ten weeks, it's a hard pill to swallow that getting back to Prague will cost me more than going forward to Istanbul.

My chest tightens. I've made the wrong choice.

"You can think about it," Dejah says. "Let's get some food."

She leads me to a bagel shop a few doors down. The menus above the cashier's head thankfully have pictures and a condiment station with chopped tomatoes, peppers, and sauces we can point to. We order the meal deal and settle at a table overlooking the quiet street.

"You can always come to Istanbul," she says as she cuts into her tuna melt.

"It would make so much sense if I did." I stare at my untouched food.

"What does your gut say?" she asks.

"Istanbul," I blurt.

Her body jolts.

"Logically it's the best choice." I grimace. "No backtracking. It's cheaper. It's with you and the girls, and I'll get to visit Syria and Lebanon. I've been telling myself it's not a big deal to miss Turkey, but I loved it there and have been dreaming of having a massage at a Turkish bath since we left London."

We're also a week ahead of our planned rendezvous. And since I need a visa for every country in the immediate vicinity, I'll have to loiter in Prague while I wait for Josh, a city where we spent the most time and have seen everything.

"Oh." Her eyes pop.

"But my gut's also screaming that I'll always regret it if I don't meet him. And my heart? Well, my ridiculous, romantic heart is one hundred percent behind going to Prague." I jab my fork in my tuna bagel, cut off a huge chunk, and shove it in my mouth. "It's a double whammy."

"Everyone deserves a second chance." She gives me a warm smile.

"I *know*." I drop my plastic cutlery on the tray. "But I'm desperately sad to leave you."

"If it makes ya feel any better, I'll miss you too."

"It does." I rub my temples.

"Prague, then?" She tilts her head.

No more flip-flop doubts. A gut/heart combo defeats gut logic.

"Yes." The decision settles in my chest as I say it out loud.

After we eat, we troop back to Vista Travel. I purchase my costly train ticket departing the morning after Dejah leaves, then we head out to visit a nearby church.

St. Stephen's Basilica is the largest church in Budapest and is visible from the travel agent, so it's an easy walk. The massive dome is almost one hundred meters high and inlaid with gold, but it's not our main draw. Dejah's keen to see the mummified right hand of the church's patron, King St. Stephen, and I want to light a candle for my mom. While she searches for the hand, I choose the perfect candle. As the wick ignites, I ask Mom to watch over us as we head in opposite directions.

We hop back on the tram to the Internet café near the hostel. Dejah wants to check for birthday emails and send Stella and Gwen her flight details. I email Josh asking if he could get to Prague sooner, send the girls my arrival details in Amman, and write to my dad, outlining my new travel plans.

We're quiet as we drag our feet to the hostel, like at the end of a favorite movie or book where you need a moment to reflect.

"Hi, girls!" Lyndsay waves with a beaming smile from the green sofa as we enter the common room. "I can't wait for tonight. Should we get ready?"

My chest ignites with warmth as Lindsay's infectious enthusiasm chases away my melancholy.

We head to our room to start the process. Showers are taken in turn. Tops are tossed back and forth, and outfits are evaluated. I borrow a blue scoop neck from Lyndsay, she wears the white one I wore on my birthday, and Dejah sticks with her favorite boat neck black tank that accentuates her tanned arms.

A knock at the door interrupts our primping.

"Hi girls, looking hot," Vlad says as he struts in. "I can't make dinner."

Dejah picked Fatal, a local favorite to dine at tonight.

"Are you sure?" Dejah asks as she slips a cardigan over her top.

"Yeah, I got something to do, but I'll drop by the restaurant to pick you up at eight and bring you to Eli's apartment." He salutes as he leaves.

I'm not disappointed. It'll be nice for the three of us to have girl chats over dinner.

Caraway and marjoram tickle my taste buds as we enter the

cozy ten-table restaurant. Green walls with splashes of color from the folk art embroidery of loud flowers and delicate birds warm the space. Jaunty violin and accordion music are the backdrop of the diner's boisterous chatter.

We order a jug of red wine and soak in the charming chaos from our table in the center of the room. Lyndsay shares that she's an emergency room nurse from Seattle, halfway through a three-week vacation as we tuck into rich chicken goulash on a bed of wild rice. Dejah hits the highlights of our weeks on the road, the food woes, remote locations, and our upcoming separation in two days.

"I'm off to Turkey, and Candace is going to meet a guy," Dejah says as she drains her wine.

"One I can't seem to say no to." I top up our glasses, then share how Josh and I met in Greece to our tumultuous breakup in London.

"Oh man, I have one of those." Lyndsay sighs. "He and I are passion and destruction all rolled into one. I needed to clear my head, which is why I'm out here."

"How's that going for you?" I ask as I fill my fork with flaky rice.

"Not great. But I know I want a love like my dad and stepmom. And that's not what I have with him," she says.

I frown, and she nods.

"Any idea what you'll do about him when you get home?" Dejah asks.

"None." She tosses her hands in the air. "What are you going to do when you see Josh?"

"Have lots of sex." I grab my wine and drain my glass.

Like a drug, I crave our safe intimacy. Breathing in the soothing sage smell of his skin. Intertwining our legs as we sleep with our chests pressed together. I just hope those moments are enough to offset the awkwardness I experience when our clothes are on.

"Stop bragging." Dejah rolls her eyes. "Where're you headed next, Lyndsay?"

"I leave for Poland in two days, and my last stop is Prague. I fly home from there on September thirteenth," she says.

"Really?" My eyes go wide. I had no idea we were going the same way. "I can't go back to Poland because I already used my single entry visa. But I'll be at the Twilight hostel in Prague and would love to hang out when you get there."

"I would love that too." Lyndsay nods. "I don't know how long I'll be in Poland, but I'll go straight to Twilight when I get to town."

Loitering in Prague sounds a lot more fun if I can hang out with Lyndsay.

A single candle flickers in Dejah's slice of Dobos Torta, a Hungarian favorite dessert with thin sponge layers, filled and frosted with rich chocolate buttercream. Lyndsay and I sing the first line of "Happy Birthday," and a nearby table of American businessmen join in.

Dejah's eyes shine with delight as she blows out the candle.

Vlad arrives as promised as we're finishing the last of our wine and cake.

We pile into a cab to Eli's plain white apartment building. Vlad jogs up three steps, leans on the buzzer, and the heavy front door clicks. We step inside, but we're still outside. The eight floors of apartments line the perimeter of an interior yard. There's a hip-height iron barrier at the edge of the breezeway safeguarding residents from tumbling into the courtyard below. We squish into the elevator and slam the gate closed, and the engine creaks as it lifts us to the fifth floor. Black iron ivy weaves through the railings overlooking the courtyard, but I have no idea if the fence is as functional as it is beautiful, so I walk close to the black apartment doors.

"Hey, man," Vlad says as a dark-haired, barely legal guy opens his apartment door. They complete a series of slaps and handshakes, then Vlad introduces us.

"Come on in." Eli grins, and two cute dimples sink into his cheeks.

Vlad charges down the honey-colored hardwood parquet, through the ten-feet-high French doors to a sitting room with high ceilings. Three velvet navy sofas edge a rich red Persian carpet. They face a floor-to-ceiling shelving unit holding a television, turntable, speakers, DVDs, and hundreds of records. And in the corner by the balcony door is a life-size cardboard cutout of Pamela Anderson posing in black lingerie. I smirk. Pammy worship—something these boys have in common.

"Nice place, right?" Vlad tosses his arms out and does a spin. "Eli's from Israel. He goes to university here, and his parents bought him this flat to live in while he goes to school."

Probably an overshare, but Eli doesn't flinch.

"I have drinks chilling in the fridge." Eli leads us to the kitchen.

The cabinet doors are open, and the shelves are bare. Dirty dishes teeter on the counter and overflow in the sink. There's an open bread bag beside a sticky knife and an open jam jar. I flatten my lips to hide a smile because this place looks like my college boyfriend's kitchen. He lived with three other guys from his hockey team, but Eli created this mess all on his own.

Eli scratches his cheek. "No clean glasses though."

"I'll wash, you get ready." Vlad rolls up his sleeves and fills the sink with soapy water. "You girls wait in the lounge while I take care of this."

Eli returns dressed in dark designer jeans and a button-down carrying a bottle of champagne. Vlad passes around clean glasses, and we toast Khadejah's birthday. The sound system is flicked on, and heavy rock pours from the speakers. We talk about music, school, and Pamela as we finish the champagne. For five people from five different countries and backgrounds, we get along just fine.

Once the drinks are done, we move the party to the bar Music Corner.

The shaky beat of "Strike It Up" by Black Box blares through the smoky room. Strobe lights flash over the crowd gyrating on the dance floor. My shoulders shimmy to the beat as we file through the crowd to the bar. I wave to the bartender in a tube top and her long blond hair bounces as she kicks up our drinks. Ken buys us five tequila shots, then we join the melee on the dance floor.

Shoulders bump, butts wiggle, and there are smiles all around.

"I'm going to buy a round," Lyndsay says. "Be right back."

Vlad throws his arm over Dejah's shoulder and pulls her to his side. His lips land on hers, and she throws her arms around him and kisses him back. I grin as they get lost in the bodies on the dance floor. Two dudes slap Eli on the back, and they shake hands and move to the side to catch up.

I push through the dancers to track down Lindsay at the bar. I yelp as beefy arms circle my waist before I reach her. My feet dangle as his one hairy arm bars me in place. His opposite hand snakes under the hem of my borrowed blue top. I launch my head back, hitting Beefy's hard chest as his rough fingers grip my stomach. I thrash, but his arm doesn't budge.

My heart stalls as his hand moves toward my chest. The music gets fuzzy. My head fogs, and air drains from my lungs as the compartment I locked after *the encounter* in Vilnius bursts wide open. Nausea boils in my throat as I'm thrust back to the moment at the bus station when *his* fingers invaded me and his sticky tongue lapped at my skin.

My body locks as Beefy's hand squeezes my breast.

Oh my God, it's happening again, and just like the last time, there's nothing I can do to stop it—

I'm ripped out of Beefy's arms.

Eli shoves me behind him and screams at Beefy in Hungarian until he stomps off.

"Are you okay?" Eli's dark eyes fill with concern as he checks me over.

"Thank you." I leap into his arms, and he wraps me in a hug. "Thank you, thank you, thank you," I whisper over and over as I cling to him.

He has no idea how much I appreciate that he stood up for me after no one helped me during *the encounter* at the bus station in Lithuania.

Lyndsay returns carrying five bottles of beer, and I peel myself from Eli's embrace.

"Everything okay?" she asks as she hands me a beer.

"Yeah, Eli's my hero." I force a smile. "He just saved me from an encounter."

But this wasn't an *encounter*. And neither was the one in Vilnius.

The bruises the ticket agent at the bus station left on my body have faded, but mentally they're still there. And I've done myself an injustice by calling it an *encounter*. Hiding behind that label like it would somehow diminish what really happened.

I down half the bottle of beer.

I was sexually assaulted in a bus station in broad daylight.

A deep ache pulses in my chest because now that I've called it out to myself, I can't put it back. And I don't know what to do with the loathing and anger lingering beneath my skin.

THAT'S A WRAP - BUDAPEST, HUNGARY

For the first time since we left London, Khadejah packs and I don't. Her flight leaves tonight, and my stomach churns as she rolls her clothes and stuffs them in Hulk.

I can't watch this.

"How about I get us breakfast and I'll meet you in the common room when you're done?" I ask as I pull on a sweater.

"Sure." Her face is somber.

"I'll come." Lyndsay grabs her wallet, and the two of us head out.

We traipse through the cool, cloudy morning to buy coffee

and croissants from a nearby bakery, then set up at a table in the common room. Khadejah joins us as I'm flipping through my tour book prioritizing what we'll visit.

Dejah, Lyndsay, and I spent the day after her birthday celebrations lounging under our cozy duvets, leaving only today to see the sights. A down day tucked in a warm bed with friends close by did wonders for my stricken heart. It was just what I needed to reflect on what happened on the dance floor and weeks ago in Lithuania.

I didn't disclose the details to the girls, but I'm ready to talk about it now.

Boxing things up to deal with later isn't sustainable and is a shitty way to live. I plan to tell Dejah before she leaves today because I know sharing what happened to me in Lithuania will help me move on.

"Why the long faces, girls?" Vlad pulls out a chair and kicks back after bringing in a group of French backpackers.

"It's our last day together," I say as I smother jam on my croissant.

"We should exchange information," Dejah says, gathering pens and paper.

Books are passed around. I write my dad's address and phone number under the 'C' tab in Lindsay's phone book and scribble my details on a paper for Vlad.

"It's time for Spice Girl names," Dejah says, then explains it as I pass out cigarettes.

Both are keen to get one.

"Lyndsay first since she's easy," Dejah says as Vlad lights everyone's cigarette. "Kindred Spice."

"Oh yeah, that's perfect." I felt that way as soon as we sang Billy Joel together.

"Guys, you're the best." Lyndsay jumps up and gives us each a hug. "I feel the same way."

"And I think Gentleman Spice is good for Vlad since he made sure we got everything we needed in Budapest," Dejah says.

"He sure did." I snort, and the four of us laugh.

Their lip-lock was a one-time amicable thing, with no pining on either side.

We arrange to meet back here before Dejah's shuttle leaves to say goodbye.

The four of us catch the same tram into town. Vlad gets off first for work—at his other job, which we know nothing about. Lyndsay disembarks in Pest—since she toured Buda on her first day here. Khadejah and I stay on till Buda Castle.

We enter the extensive castle grounds through the stone-arched Vienna Gate. We dodge elderly German tourists past baroque buildings and church towers. We speed-walk the scenic Tóth Árpád sétány promenade, but we can't see much because of the heavy cloud cover. I flirt with the doorman at the Matthias Church, he lets us in for free, and we breeze past intricate mosaics we could spend days admiring.

I take a drink from my water bottle as we lean against the fortress wall out of the wind to admire the many pointy cone towers on Fisherman's Bastion.

"This place is beautiful but hard to appreciate on a tight schedule," I say as I tuck my water away in my daypack.

"Yeah." Dejah gathers her hair and pulls it into a high ponytail. "But we've seen most of it—"

"Hello," a middle-aged Hungarian man greets us. "I would like to offer you both my tour guide services." His beady eyes are level with my boobs, and he's talking to them.

"I'm from Budapest and have done many tours …"

Dejah waves, but Boob Looker is laser-focused on my chest. "… and I can also tell you about …" he drones on.

Dejah winks and tips her chin to my boobs.

I nod. Show time. I stretch my arms out and flip my hair from side to side like I'm in an '80s hair shampoo commercial. Then I slowly peel off my sweater and stick out my T-shirt-covered chest.

"I can …" Boob Looker coughs and his eyes bulge. "Uh …"

"I think we're good on the tour, mate." Khadejah crosses her arms.

"Watch out for pickpockets. They're all over the area," he says before he scurries off.

"Dude, I had no idea my boobs were as entertaining as yours." We chuckle and reminisce about Burly's long conversation with Dejah's chest in Korčula.

"I'm hungry. I'd say we're done here." She swings her bag over her shoulder as I tug on my sweater.

I pale as we walk to the tram stop. Dealing with Boob Looker with Dejah is funny. But how will I manage this type of interaction on my own? It'll be cringy, uncomfortable, and impossible to laugh off.

Complex and tense Arabic music blares in the shawarma takeaway shop near the hostel as we order falafels. We commandeer the solitary table opposite the stacked lamb rotating on a vertical spit and tuck into our wraps.

"How are you feeling about Istanbul?" I ask as I dip my falafel in hummus.

"Great. The girls were already in town when I checked email on my birthday. I'm looking forward to seeing them and getting back to the heat," she says.

"I'm glad." I'm going to be on my own for a week waiting for Josh—which I'm not looking forward to—but that's my choice. She didn't choose to travel alone, so I'm relieved Gwen and Stella are there for her.

"We're heading straight to Lebanon when I get there. Four weeks should be heaps for us to travel overland and meet you in Amman on the twenty-ninth. If for some reason we're not at the airport, wait for us at the Inter Hostel. We'll join you within a few days."

"Inter Hostel in Amman. Got it." I crumple my falafel wrapper. "We need a pact. No Spice Girl name allocations without the other person present."

"Nah, mate, I can't promise that." Dejah's face blanks.

"What?" My mouth gapes. "How can you play without me?"

"Ha, you should see your face." She smacks the table. "Just kidding. Of course, I agree. We can pick it up again in a month."

"You had me there for a minute." I suck in a breath. "There's something I need to tell you."

"Sounds serious." She tips her fingers.

"It is." My throat ripples with revulsion, unease, and resignation. "I was assaulted in the bus station in Vilnius."

"What?" Her face goes sickly white.

I tell her everything, from the bruises to his mocking laughter that still haunts me.

I've learned that grief comes in many forms. The loss of your confidence. The loss of trust in people. The loss of ability to protect yourself from predators. And the loss of a loved one.

"I'm so sorry." She races to my side of the table and hugs me. "Why didn't you say anything?"

"There was nothing you, me, or Keith could've done." I twist my fingers as she retakes her seat. "I was humiliated. And I felt weak when we needed to be strong. It was easier just to pretend it never happened."

"Oh, mate." Her throat wobbles, and she swallows.

"I know." Pain grips my chest. "It all came rushing back to me when a guy groped me on the dance floor the other night. Eli came to my rescue, and when he did, he showed me there's some good out there. Now I just want to let it go. I mean, it was bad but not the worst thing that's ever happened to me."

No one died.

"I could have helped if you'd told me." Her eyes are misty.

"But you did help. You've helped me every day. And not just with this. I've been drowning in grief since my mom died. I figured I would find the space to heal along the way on this trip. But what I really needed was connection. I needed understanding, grace, and patience. And I needed to learn to laugh again." Tears sting my cheeks. "And you gave me all of that."

Grief needs to be shared. You can't do it on your own. I'll miss my mom for the rest of my life. But her death's no longer my first thought in the morning, and thinking about her doesn't cripple me. It was enough. All of it was enough. Each laugh, interaction, and crazy moment we spent muddling through this adventure gave me the courage to unbox the pain I've been swallowing for years. Khadejah helped me crawl out from the confinement of my grief so I could mourn and heal.

"Best time ever." She grabs my hand as a tear slips from the corner of her eye.

How am I going to get through the day without her friendship?

THE AFTER - BUDAPEST, HUNGARY

Lyndsay passes me a tissue as Dejah's airport shuttle pulls away from the sidewalk.

I can't believe this part is over.

"I'm off," Vlad says as he flaps his paycheck. "Today's the day I've been saving for, and I'm picking up my new car."

Lyndsay murmurs something to him before he leaves as I watch the taillights on the van fade out of sight.

"God, I hope he's worth it." I wrap my arms around my middle.

"Come on, you need a drink." Lyndsay nudges my shoulder.

"I knew I liked you." I swallow past the ache flaring in my throat.

We link arms and walk to an Italian restaurant Lyndsay scouted earlier. There are only two occupied tables in the small dining room, and the quiet atmosphere suits my mood. The willowy hostess guides us to a booth on the side of the room.

"Should we pool our money?" Lyndsay asks, emptying her pockets.

She leaves the country tonight and I leave in the morning, so we need to spend the rest of our forints. Metal coins clink on the dark tabletop, and crumpled blue and red notes with somber faces are added to the pile between us. I pick out coins to cover tomorrow's bus fare to the station before she counts our cash and shares the total.

"We have enough for two mushroom fettuccines and a pitcher of beer," I say after doing the calculation in my head.

"Done." She signals the dowdy server and orders our meals.

"I get why you're meeting Josh," she says as Dowdy leaves.

I blink. "You do?"

"Of course, Candace. He sparked a change. And you're living the life you want because of him. That's special."

"You're like the only one who gets it. He hasn't treated me well, but it's hard to let go of someone who set you free." And gives me the intimacy I long for.

She purses her lips. "Just remember to take care of yourself."

"I will. He hasn't made any promises for more than our time together. I'm going in with my eyes wide open." My stomach cramps. Even being mentally prepared, I can't guarantee this reunion won't smash my heart into a million pieces—*again*. But it's a risk I'm willing to take to spend time with him.

Dowdy plonks our pitcher on the table, and Lyndsay pours the beer.

"Cheers, to safe trips ahead." I clink my glass with hers.

"I'm nervous for tonight's train trip." Lyndsay picks at a thread on her shirt. "I traveled alone through Yugoslavia to get to Budapest. The Yugoslavian border police yelled at me then grabbed my boobs." Her eyes water. "I managed to get away from him, but I was petrified. There was hardly anyone on the train, so I ended up huddled behind the train conductor the whole night for protection."

I intake a breath as anger burns in my gut. "I'm so sorry that happened to you."

I love being a woman. I truly do, but fuck me, it sucks sometimes. I don't tell her what happened to me at the bus station. Not because I don't want to share, but she's about to board a night train alone, and now isn't the time for commiserating.

"Dejah and I have had our fair share of harassment, and it was awful. But tonight, you'll have nothing to worry about because I'm going to go with you to the train station, and we'll make sure you're in a compartment with other people. *Nice* people, who are going all the way to Kraków."

"Thanks, man." The worry lines in her forehead ease, and her shoulders loosen.

"I've got your back," I promise.

We devour our plates of creamy pasta and down our last drops of beer as Dowdy places the receipt on the table.

"Cool, we have enough for a small tip." Lyndsay smiles at the tally.

"Wait. Let's each keep a one forint coin for good luck." I pluck two coins from the cash pile, passing one to her and placing the other in my pocket.

"I'll take all the luck I can get." She clenches the silver coin in her fist.

We collect her pack from the hostel, and I escort her to the train station. We stalk through three train carriages until we find a compartment with other backpackers who speak English and are going to Kraków. I give her one last hug, then leap off the train as the whistle blows.

She pops her head out the compartment window.

"See you in Prague," I yell as the train screeches and groans.

"Thank you." She smiles. "I should be there in a few days."

I wave until the train is out of sight.

I'm alone. And I hate it already. Josh better be worth it.

BACK IN MY ROOM, I slide Pete's *The Crash* mixtape into my Walkman, pile my clean clothes on the bed, and start packing. I leave the frisbee by the window because I can't use it by myself. Then I toss our salad containers from Split in the trash because they're a pain to carry, and I'll never use them without Dejah's influence. I plan to exist on my favorites—cheese, bread, and chocolate—for the next four weeks.

Between songs, I hear a knock at the door, and on the other side is a grinning Vlad bouncing on his toes.

"I have my new car downstairs. Want to take a spin? You'll be my first passenger."

My brow furrows. It's sweet and also sad he's at my door. Does he not have any friends or family to share this moment with? He's been around the hostel most days, but I don't know his situation. I've been so wrapped up in my decision and parting ways from Dejah that I haven't asked him anything about himself.

But this I can do.

"I would be honored. One sec." I grab my sweater off the bed and follow him outside.

He leads me around the corner with a cocky swing in his step to a three-door red hatchback.

"This is it, my 1986 Fiat Uno." He unlocks the door with the key.

I slide in the passenger seat as he hops behind the wheel.

I click my seat belt in place, and Vlad hits the gas.

My head rears back as he zooms into the streets of Budapest at breakneck speed. I reach for the 'holy fuck' handles above my head by the door frame, but there are none. I cling to the door handle and pump my invisible passenger brake as he leans over the steering wheel, racing to a red light. I brace my hand on the dash as he slams on the brakes at the last second, screeching to a stop just inches from the bumper ahead.

Note to self: add being a passenger with a new driver *and* riding on the back of scooters with strangers to the *don't* column beside not talking about Russia.

He races past the Buda Castle, crosses the Chain Bridge over the Danube River to Pest on the east side, then loops

338

around again with no concept of street signs, merge, yield … they mean nothing. It's like every sign screams *more gas* or *go faster*.

He must 'know a guy' because there's no way he passed his driver's test.

I don't know much about Vlad, but I do know I won't be asking him for a lift to the train station in the morning because I'll be safer taking the bus.

IT'S NOT THE SAME - TRAIN STATION, BUDAPEST, HUNGARY

Barney on my back, I pause before I exit the glass hostel door at the crack of dawn the next morning. It's only hours into Saturday, and there are packs of drunks stumbling down the sidewalks coming off a large Friday night. Maybe I should've asked Vlad for a lift.

"Hey, Candace." The weak-chinned strawberry-blond American veterinarian I played darts with a few nights before sashays to the door wearing his backpack. "I'm headed to the train station. Do you want to share a cab?"

"Uh." I cringe because I'm out of cash. "I can't contribute because I only have enough local currency for the bus."

"It's no problem, I was going to pay anyway." He shrugs.

"Thanks." I sigh. "I wasn't looking forward to a solo bus trip. Who knows what or who I would run into right now."

His head twists, and his forehead wrinkles.

We're ten steps into our one-block walk to the taxi stand when three broad drunk guys yell at us in Hungarian from the opposite side of the road.

"You'd think they'd have something better to do." I drop my gaze and double-time it.

The drunks cross the street and trail us, their shouts getting more aggressive as they close in. I hurry to the waiting taxi on the corner. We hoist our packs in the trunk, and the men scatter as we jump into the backseat of the car.

I sigh as the driver takes off, but the veterinarian's vibrating with anger.

"I've never"—he shakes his head—"not once in my month-long trip had people yell or chase me."

"It happens all the time," I say. "At least they didn't flash us."

"Pardon?" His jaw ticks.

"Oh yeah, I've seen all kinds of penises, oh, and masturbation." I fiddle with my seatbelt.

"You're not serious." He blinks.

"Oh, I am." Dudes have zero idea what it's like out here for women.

"I … I …" His mouth opens and closes.

"It's okay. I'm used to it." My shoulders slump. I hate that I've normalized it.

"What a terrible thing to be used to." He frowns.

"It is." His acknowledgement doesn't change how we've been treated. But maybe now that he recognizes what women deal with, he'll be mindful and be an advocate when help is needed, like when Eli was there for me.

The taxi pulls up to the station, and we say goodbye because he's off to Warsaw.

From Budapest, I transfer trains in Vienna for Prague.

I roll open the compartment door as the train chugs out of Vienna. I say hello to the solitary woman inside and her shoulders snap back. But then she slouches when I tell her I'm Canadian and not American like herself. But my nationality doesn't deter her from complaining about the food, the trains, and why no one speaks English. In *Austria*, where they speak *German*. My fingernails dig into my thighs as she rants. I can't sit here for another five hours. I make my excuses and drag Barney down the hall to a different seat.

In this cabin, there's just me and a couple. They're all over each other and are a pair of shorts and a tiny skirt away from having sex on the opposite bench. This scenario isn't great, but it's still better than listening to Train Girl from the first compartment.

I turn to the side and write in my journal, leaving the couple to their business.

I hope I meet some decent people in Prague until Lyndsay or Josh arrive. I shudder at the thought of being stuck with someone like Train Girl. That's totally *not* who I want to spend my time with.

ADJUSTMENT - PRAGUE, CZECH REPUBLIC

A sense of familiarity wraps around me as I enter the Twilight hostel in the late afternoon. Frowning Crosby is behind the bar, rock music blares over the speakers, and backpackers fill the tables. But this time my boots don't stick to the floor, the tang of stale beer and puke no longer lingers in the air, and the tables and chairs match.

"You're back. Where's your tiny friend?" Crosby asks as I approach the bar.

"Istanbul." I sigh. We truly overstayed last time if he recognizes me and that Dejah's not here after all the faces that pass through in a summer. "What happened in here?"

"Overdue revamp of the bar." He thumbs through the papers in front of him. "Green Room?"

"Sure." I hand him some cash.

My stomach twists as I walk down the same dull tile floors to the Green Room. The same six wooden bunks line the wall, and the warning note I taped above the window a month ago is still in place. But there are two new faces in the room. A smiley guy with pale cheeks is sitting on Dejah's bunk wearing the backpacker uniform of jeans and a T-shirt over his chubby body. And a broody guy with blond hair wearing a silk jacket, balloon pants, and a billowy scarf around his neck is sitting on the bunk near the window.

"Hi, I'm Richard," Smiley on Dejah's bunk says. "I'm from California."

"Candace, from Canada." I linger in the doorway because although I spent a week in this room, it feels off because I'm not with Dejah.

"I'm Lincoln from Australia." Artsy guy near the window tips his chin to the bunk below Richard—the bunk I slept in last time. "That one's free."

"Thanks." I drop Barney on the floor by the bed. "Are you two traveling together?"

"No." Richard giggles, and Artsy Lincoln purses his lips.

I didn't think so because they're complete opposites.

My chest ripples with loneliness as the good memories Dejah and I had here roll through my mind: the stolen jacket, the guys who knew my brother Pete, and the frat boy Chads. My throat dries. I should have asked to stay in a different room.

"Everything okay?" Smiley Richard asks. "We can swap beds if you'd like."

"No, I'm good, thanks." I straighten my spine.

No wallowing. I need to make new memories and get into the groove of traveling on my own. Which means making friends. These two seem decent and are a good place to start.

"Want to grab a beer downstairs?" I ask, and they both agree.

I kick Barney under my bunk and make sure the window's locked before leaving.

Lincoln and I get a beer, Smiley Richard a Coke, then we sit at one end of a long table. Lincoln's hands fly around his face as he recounts his day touring the churches, towers, and gardens inside Prague Castle. His fresh flamboyance makes me smile, and his excitement distracts me from the sadness in my chest from missing Dejah.

A guy drinking a pint by himself at the end of our table scans the bar through his thick glasses. His scrawny shoulders are slouched but filled with tension, and his shaggy sandy blond hair falls over his forehead. My heart catches as it recognizes the loneliness and longing on his face. I hate to see someone alone, and the more friends, the merrier … as long as they're not like Train Girl.

"Hey," I shout.

He turns his head and stills.

"Want to join us?" I wave.

He blinks.

"Yes, thank you." He collects his beer and moves to join us. "I'm Ben, from Chicago."

He thrusts out his hand, offering a strong handshake as we introduce ourselves.

"How long have you been here?" I ask.

"Two days." Ben adjusts his glasses and fidgets with his shirt.

"I just got here." He doesn't need to know I spent a week here last month.

"Do you like card tricks?" Ben pulls a deck of cards from his pocket and flips the top open and closed with his thumb.

"Who doesn't?" I've never seen a card trick in my life, but I'm throwing this guy a bone because he looks like he could use one.

"Hi gang," a girl with short blond hair and average build says as she sits beside Lincoln with two other girls in tow.

"Candace is in our dorm room," Lincoln says. "The girls are in the other beds."

"I'm Leah," the average blond says in an Aussie accent. "Mila." She points to the sultry brunette with golden skin who's sitting beside Smiley Richard. "And Mary." She flicks her wrist to the sour-faced third girl next to her.

Ew. I'll be giving Mary a wide berth; she has Train Girl annoying written all over her miserable scowly face.

"What's up?" Sultry Mila asks in a Latina accent.

"Ben was just about to show us a card trick," I say.

Ben's Adam's apple bobs as he shuffles the deck. His social awkwardness falls away as the cards swoosh and dance between his fingers. All conversation stops as he entertains us with fancy hand moves and countless well-executed card tricks.

"Mate, that was sweet. Where did you learn those?" Lincoln blinks.

"I went to Magic Camp for six summers." Ben's cheeks go pink, and his jaw tenses.

"I was entertained," Sultry Mila says, and Ben exhales.

"I'm starved. Any interest in going for dinner? I saw a cool place by the castle," Lincoln asks our motley crew, and everyone is keen.

We zip up our coats and wander in the light rain to the tram two streets away. Two dudes and a dog are waiting in the transparent shelter at the tram stop. I rush inside, hoping I can pet the dog and get some puppy love. The motley crew huddles outside because there's no more space in here.

"Yo, what's up," the brawny dude not holding the leash says in an Australian accent.

"Hi." I smile at Brawny, then gasp as I turn to the other guy.

He has long dark curly hair in a low ponytail, dark sunglasses covering his eyes, and the yellow Lab dutifully sitting at his side has a harness that reads: Property of The Seeing Eye Dog.

"Mate, she's gawking. And she's hot." Brawny snickers.

"Sorry." My cheeks heat as I glare at Brawny for outing me.

"Hello." The second guy turns toward the direction of my voice. "I'm Angelo, and this is Ernest." He motions to his dog.

"I'm Candace. Are you here on vacation?"

"Ernest and I are backpacking around the world; we've been on the road for two years." Angelo smiles and strokes Ernest's head.

My lips part. *How?* I find it difficult getting around, and I can see.

"That's so cool." My mind spins with questions. Like how does he deal with all the different currencies? Manage the languages? Buy dog food? "How … I … How do you get around?"

Angelo shrugs.

"I stay at hostels and hook up with other travelers whenever I can, like Dex." He tips his head to Brawny.

"I … You …" My thoughts get tangled on my tongue.

"This is us," Brawny Dex says as their tram approaches.

"Bye, Candace." Angelo raises his hand in my direction.

I slump against the wall of the shelter as Angelo, Dex, and Ernest board the tram going in the opposite direction. The challenges Dejah and I have faced pale in comparison to Angelo's journey. Talk about putting my solo situation in perspective. I need to pull up my big girl panties and make the most of my time.

I WALTZ into the Internet café the next morning, buy a large cappuccino, and settle at a desk. I've treated myself to two hours. I intend to savor every email and compose long-winded replies.

I lick the foam off my lips as my email loads. My inbox lights up with unread messages. I scan the names. None are from Josh. I huff. I was hoping to have something saying he would get here sooner, but I can check back tomorrow.

I click on Khadejah's note first and breathe out a sigh of relief. She arrived safely in Istanbul, and Gwen and Stella were at the airport to meet her. The last of my guilt washes away knowing she's safe and has company.

I move on to Vasilii's email. He's still sorting things out in Russia after his mother's death and won't be able to join me in South Africa as we planned. But he wants to meet me at some point when things settle down. My heart throbs knowing what he's going through. I'm sad I'll miss him after my safari, but we can meet up in Australia or Asia.

Who's next … oh, there's one from my brother Pete.

I could write for three hours and still not be able to tell you everything I have to say.

I miss you.

Love Pete

I fold forward as pain pierces my chest. I haven't spoken to Pete in two and a half months. That's the longest we've gone without talking. I minimize my calls home because by calling collect, my dad's phone bill is exorbitant. But I've left calling Pete way too long. I check my watch. I'm all messed up with time zones, but I think it's a six-hour time difference between here and where he goes to university. It should be nine in the morning there.

The rest of my notes will have to wait; I need to talk to him. I shut down my email, abandon my coffee, and race out to the pay phone beside the Old Town Hall and Astronomical Clock. I pull out my phone book and jab the buttons to reach the Bishop's Gaiters' football house where he lives during the school year.

"Hello," some dude answers.

"Hey, can I talk to Pete?" I ask as I tap the plexiglass sheltering the phone.

The dude huffs, and the phone clinks.

"Hello?" Pete's voice rumbles over the line.

"You're home." My eyes water.

"*Candace*," he whispers.

We talk for ages, maybe not for three hours but a long time. He tells me about his football training camp, the upcoming season, and the empty beer cases stacked in their living room after last night's party. I share the funny parts of our trip, like Curler Commando in Zakopane, the Meditator Yoga Guru who works directly for Jesus from Croatia, and the pineapple upside-down cake I had on my birthday in Korčula.

"I'm glad you're having fun. But I don't understand why you need to travel for so long," Pete says.

My eyes burn as I will the lump in my throat to disperse. Mom got cancer when he was nine and I was fourteen. She died eight years later but was sick most of those years. I didn't want him to feel abandoned, so I stepped in as much as I could when my mom was too sick to be there. I showed up to watch him play sports, took him back-to-school clothes shopping, drove him to a buddy's house, played cards—anything and everything I could do I would.

"I know me being away is hard. But it's easier for me out here. I don't ache from missing her quite as much being away from home. And I need this time to get to know myself." Time I never had growing up. I was a teenager, and being a carer not only for my mom but for my family was all-consuming. Taking time for me and putting myself first has been one of the hardest things I've ever done. And I've had to leave him to do it.

Tears burn my eyes as my knees threaten to give out from my betrayal at leaving my family. But I couldn't give *or* get the support any of us needed because we were all burnt out from caring for my mom.

"I miss you." His voice cracks, and so does my heart at the sound of it.

"I miss you too." My chin wobbles.

"I think it's great that you're doing what you need. But traveling's something I have no desire to do, so it's hard for me to get it." He clears his throat. "Are you happy?"

I clench my hand around the phone receiver.

"If you asked me that two months ago, my answer would have been no. But I've come a long way since I left London. Some days out here are hard, but yeah, I'm happy." It doesn't make my abandoning him any easier to swallow, but I haven't been able to say that *honestly* in many, many years.

"How about you?" I ask.

"It depends on the day," he mutters.

"Ah, Pete. I wish I could be more help." I squeeze my eyes shut and will myself not to cry. "Traveling works for me. I don't know what your answer is. But I do know you'll figure it out. It takes time." And work. Lots of work. Reflection, a willingness to make what you need a priority, and help. "Do you have people you talk to?"

Slow steady breaths echo over the line.

"Sometimes," he says, and my heart cracks that little bit more. "Do you still see yellow butterflies?"

"Yes." Letting him change the subject is probably a mistake, but there's only so much I can do from a phone booth in Prague. But I can share happy stories. "She's here with me in a lot of places, like Lithuania, Poland, and Croatia. I also light a candle in every church I visit. Which is a lot."

"I'm glad."

"Me too." Like Dejah, my family doesn't think I'm crazy because I believe my mom's spirit lives in a yellow butterfly.

"Did you know Dad was gifted a fancy phone with call display from the phone company? He got it for being in the top one percent of their long-distance users in Canada." Pete chuckles.

"Oh my God." I cringe, so glad I'll be half a world away when the phone bill for this call arrives in the mail. "Good luck with your football season. I love you, little bro. I'll try to call more often."

"Bye, Can."

My heart wanes as the dial tone drones in my ear. I drag myself to a bench just off the main square and stare into space. The cold air numbs my skin as guilt slithers through my chest while I replay every word of our conversation. Then I question and over-analyze every decision I've made that's led me to sitting right here. Am I being selfish by traveling and leaving my family? And what about my future?

I dig my fingertips into my skull and groan. Ugh, I hate feeling like this. This is why being alone sucks. There's no one to commiserate with when I drag myself down the mental garbage path—

"Hey, Candace."

I yelp as Smiley Richard pops down on the bench.

"Richard, you scared the crap out of me." I press my palm to my chest.

His chubby face falls, looking like a scolded puppy.

"Sorry, I was just in my head. It's nice to see you," I say, and his smile returns. "Want to grab dinner? There's a place around the corner called Hogo Fogo. They do amazing deep-fried camembert."

"Sounds nice." He jumps up and holds out his hand to help me off the bench.

"Thanks." My heart warms as I accept his help. "You really did come along at the perfect time." Because he completely snapped me out of my over-analyzing death spiral.

We sit at a different cherry wood table than *my usual* in the front of the basement restaurant. The bright modern art on the walls is a familiar comfort. I order a beer, him a Coke, and of course, two plates of fried camembert. Being with Smiley Richard is easy; he's a gentle, young soul you want to take under your wing.

"Are you not a fan of beer?" I ask after I take a long drink of my amber ale.

"I've never had alcohol before." Smiley Richard fiddles with the straw in his Coke.

I bite back a grin and lean forward. "Do you want to try a beer now?"

Watching Smiley Richard get drunk for the first time would be hilarious. I'm sure he'll be even more bubbly than he is now. Maybe I could even convince him to go to a club.

"I do." His neck pulls taut. "But not so far from the hostel."

Well, that's not a no … seems I have a new mission.

SOUR MARY - KUTNÁ HORA, CZECH REPUBLIC

Average Leah, Smiley Richard, Sour Mary, and I board the early train to Kutná Hora to visit the church made of bones.

My gut turned when Sour Mary from Minnesota invited herself along while Average Leah, Smiley Richard, and I were getting ready in the Green Room this morning. But before I could say no to Sour Mary, Smiley Richard agreed. I strive to be inclusive, but like Train Girl, she rubbed me the wrong way when I met her. There were lots of people around that night, so I could avoid her, but I doubt I'll be so lucky today.

As the train rolls down the track, Sour Mary talks about herself and when she's not talking about how great she is, she makes cruel, ignorant digs about the locals. My jaw hurts from clenching as I refrain from challenging her to keep the peace in our group. Average Leah is staring out the window scrunching her fists, and Smiley Richard has clammed up.

I race off the train and rush ahead to the church to avoid Sour Mary.

The Sedlec Ossuary—Church of Bones—is *decorated* with the bones of over 40,000 people. A missing twinge flares in my chest as I admire the creativity and symmetry of the skulls and bone placement in the bone chandelier dangling over the church entrance. Khadejah would love this place; it's a Morbid Spice Girl dream. I buy her the most gruesome postcard I can find with a close-up of a long wall of skulls from the gift shop.

Sour Mary mouths off the entire return trip to Prague.

Smiley Richard's cheery chat about the skulls and the booklet he bought to show his parents when he gets home isn't enough of a distraction from Sour Mary's negativity now coating my skin.

She ruined our day trip.

I stare out the window and block her out. This is the last time I get sucked into hanging out with someone who sets off my Spidey senses. God, I miss Khadejah and our easy friendship.

I hope Josh arrives early or Lyndsay shows up soon because I don't fancy my chances of rooming with Sour Mary for another four days without strangling her in her sleep. I like Smiley Richard and Average Leah, but I'm ditching these people as soon as this train rolls into Prague.

OVER WAITING - PRAGUE, CZECH REPUBLIC

I lie and tell the bone church day trip gang I need alone time, then hustle to the Internet café when the train arrives in Prague.

I buy two hours, an extra-large coffee, and slurp back the bitter brew as my email loads. There's a new addition in my inbox. A note from Josh received this morning. Before I open it, I send out good vibes hoping it says he'll be here sooner than we originally planned.

Baby, I can't get there before the 12th. I'm leaving Tallinn today for Vilnius. Then I'm going skydiving in Warsaw. I look forward to seeing you in a few days.

Josh xo

Skydiving? A rush of anger heats my throat. Is he freaking kidding me? Skydiving isn't for me, but I hate that he's happily ticking activities off his list while I'm burning time doing crappy day trips with the likes of Sour Mary.

I shake my head. I'm an idiot. I forgot the best part about traveling alone. I'm beholden to no one. I set my schedule. And I choose who I spend time with.

So screw it. I'm leaving for Český Krumlov first thing tomorrow morning. My guidebook raves about its beauty, museums, and castle. Dejah and I skipped visiting there to save time for Croatia. And I didn't head there as soon as I arrived in Prague because I was hoping to go with Lyndsay. But I'm done waiting around. I'll leave Lyndsay a note at the hostel, and hopefully she can meet me there. I send an email to Josh, then Lyndsay—as a backup—letting them know my plan and that I'll be back in Prague by the 12th.

I cross my legs, light a cigarette, and spend the rest of my time getting lost in news from home. Happiness and not jealousy weaves in my chest as I read baby, job, boyfriend, and family news. As much as Pete doesn't covet the life I'm leading, I don't yearn for his or any of my settled friends at home.

I might be considered too old to be living out of a backpack.

I could be messing up future job prospects.

And at times I'm consumed by guilt about being away.

But I need the variety each day brings, and right now that's what's important for me.

From: Candace

To: My friends

Date: September 6, 1998

Subject: It's cold HERE

We took a ferry from Dubrovnik to the island of Korčula. This little piece of paradise proclaims to be the birthplace of the great explorer Marco Polo, but Venice also claims him as its own. I've been to both places and if I had a choice, I'd rather grow up on the exquisite island of Korčula.

From there we traveled four hours north by ferry to Hvar, another island. Khadejah and I met an Australian guy who speaks Croatian and made communicating way easier. I celebrated my birthday there. We ate seafood and washed it down with a strong local wine.

We met loads of Italians; with Croatia being just across the Adriatic Sea, it's a popular vacation spot for them. But the Croatian people were distant and hardly spoke to us the whole time we were there.

The train from Croatia to Budapest traveled alongside Hungary's largest lake, Lake Balaton. Cottages were squished between the train tracks and the shore of the lake. I thought it was odd that in a landlocked country, train tracks occupied prime waterfront real estate. The tracks were probably built ages ago, but I thought they would have moved them to expand lake living. Anyway. We spent five days in Budapest, sightseeing, organizing for the next leg of our trips, and celebrating Khadejah's birthday.

Khadejah flew from Budapest to Istanbul on Friday and I left for Prague early Saturday morning. It's just as beautiful the second time around but the weather is a bit cooler than last month. I could spend a year in this city and not see everything; it's a special place.

I'm going to stay in Czech for another two weeks then head over to Oktoberfest in Munich with Josh. After that, I'll travel to the Netherlands to visit Irma (my old roommate from Toronto). And at the end of the month, I'll fly to Jordan to meet up with the girls again.

Candace xoxo

BACK IN THE HOSTEL, I check with Crosby, but Lyndsay hasn't checked in. I buy a beer and set up at a table away from the crowds, crack open my book, and read up on Český Krumlov to prepare for my trip in the morning.

Smiley Richard joins me and places a pint of beer on the table.

"Today's the day then?" I ask, tipping my chin to his frothy glass.

He nods, takes a long drink of his beer, and his baby face pinches.

"Okay, I'm here. But I need about thirty minutes to do some research."

I flip pages and write notes in the margins next to where I'd like to stay and spots I'd like to visit.

"I'm going to get another one," he says.

I blink at his empty pint glass.

"Fine, but slow down on the next one." I tut.

He returns.

"Done." I fold the corners on a few pages and close my book. "I'm going to the bathroom. I'll be right back. Okay?"

He nods.

On my way back from the toilet beside the bar, I buy another beer for myself and one for Smiley Richard. I place his new beer next to his empty glass. He snatches it and gulps it down like I just offered him a cool beverage after he mowed the lawn on a hot day.

"What the heck, Richard? Did you drink all three pints like that?" I cross my arms.

"I might have had shots as well," he giggles.

"How much did you drink?" I was across the table from him. How did this happen?

"Three beers …" He hiccups. "And two shots of tequila at the bar while I was buying them."

My eyes go wide. He drank all that in under an hour.

He blanches then slaps his hands over his mouth and speeds for the door. I take off after him, hoping he doesn't spew all over the revamped bar because Crosby will lose it.

I follow the sounds of heaves and splashing water to the last stall in the unisex toilet. Smiley Richard's not so smiley when his head's over the bowl. And here I thought he was going to be a fun drunk.

I lean against the door and light a cigarette as he projectile vomits. There's no dance club in our future. My night will be spent babysitting Not So Smiley Richard in the hostel toilet. But I don't have to hold his hair back or drag him home like I did for Dejah in Hvar. Man, I'm looking forward to getting out of here. Český Krumlov better be as magical as my book says because I need it.

CHAPTER 8
KEEP PADDLING

WEDNESDAY, September 9, 1998

WHITE DRAGON ROOM - PRAGUE TO ČESKÝ KRUMLOV, CZECH REPUBLIC

I enter the common room at nine the following morning to check out. Smiley Richard was snoring away with drool leaking down his chin, so I didn't say goodbye. But I left him my dad's address and pain tablets on his backpack.

"You gone for good this time?" Crosby asks as I pass him my key to the Green Room.

"Yup." I pull my note for Lyndsay out of my pocket. "Can you put this on the—"

My lips part. Tacked on the message board behind the bar is a paper with *my* name scrawled on it.

"That's for me." I wave at the note. "Can I have it?"

He yanks it off and slaps it on the bar.

Candace,
I hope you're still here.
I'm in the White Dragon room.
Come find me,
Love Kindred.

My heart expands like The Grinch when he learns the meaning of Christmas. Lyndsay and I have only known each other for a handful of days, but we have a rare friendship connection that I value even more after spending one miserable day with Sour Mary.

With Barney on my back, I bound up two flights of stairs to the White Dragon room.

I rap on the door. No answer. I huff and keep knocking.

A shirtless white guy opens the door, and his jaw ticks as he crosses his arms.

"Hey," I say. "I need to see Lyndsay." I try to peer past him, but it's pitch black inside, and I can't see anything.

"Never heard of her," he says in a South African accent.

He moves to shut the door, but I wedge my hiking boot in the doorway.

"Please, I know she's here." I cling to the door frame.

"Mal meisie." He flicks his hand and stumbles back to his bunk in the far corner, leaving the door open.

"Thanks." I drop Barney in the hallway and steal into the dark room.

"Lyndsay," I whisper as I feel my way to a bed in front of the window.

My fingertips press against a hard snoring body that smells like stale beer and farts.

I wrinkle my nose. Not her.

I turn and stub my toe against a double bunk. Damn, this place is like a maze.

"Lyndsay." I tiptoe to the other side of the room and there's … a sink, hot plate, and kettle? I groan. Man, I missed out by not trying a different room. This one's cool if you discount the farty guy.

"I'm over here," a groggy female voice calls from the corner I haven't investigated.

Lyndsay pops her head up, and I dash over and hug-tackle her in her bed.

"Oh my God, it's good to see you," I whisper. "I'm so freaking glad you're here. Get up and come with me to Český Krumlov."

"I just got here late last night." She rubs her eyes.

"You can sleep later. Come on. It'll be fun." I bounce on the edge of her bed.

"Okay." She swipes her hair out of her face. "But I need a shower."

"Yes, you do," I joke, poking her in the ribs. "I'll wait for you in reception."

Lyndsay's hair is wet and slicked back when she strides into the common room wearing her backpack. She stops at the bar and has a chat with Crosby. Then she stomps over to my spot at a table by the door.

"Sorry, man." She wrinkles her nose. "I submitted my laundry last night, and it won't be ready for a few hours."

"If anyone gets the importance of laundry it's me." I flip my hand in the air. "I have no problem waiting. The train leaves on the hour for Český Krumlov, and the last one's at three. We have loads of time. Let's put our big packs in the storage locker, and we can grab some food."

My smile's so bright it lights me from the inside out as we saunter across Charles Bridge in the sunshine to Joe's Garage, the restaurant Josh introduced me to last month. We slide into a booth overlooking the Vltava River and order coffees and nachos. My stomach growls as the server drops a mountain of chips drowning in gooey cheese on the table. We dive in, scooping heaped portions on our side plates.

"I arrived safe and sound in Kraków. I loved it there, but it wasn't the same as being with you and Dejah." She drags her chip through the sour cream.

"I get it. Some of the people I've met here have been the worst." I shove nachos in my gob. "I've been in Prague, for crying out loud. One of the most beautiful cities ever, and I've been bored out of my mind."

We devour the platter and blissfully while away the hours ordering coffee after coffee. I sigh because my last few days waiting for Josh won't be about burning time; they'll be about having an adventure in Český Krumlov with Lyndsay. And I can't wait.

SOMETHING ABOUT ... - ČESKÝ KRUMLOV, CZECH REPUBLIC

We step out of the station in Český Krumlov well after dark and follow the map in my book to the place I earmarked to stay at while Smiley Richard was chugging pints.

Pristine brown and white houses with bright, orange-tipped roofs line the cobblestone streets. The cloudless night sky is lit up with glittering stars. There are no cars, no crowds; it's still—like the whole town's asleep. The air is cool and crisp and smells of campfire. A pleasant tug of nostalgia swirls in my chest. The smell reminds me of nights spent by the firepit laughing over a glass of wine with my family at my aunt's cottage in Northern Ontario.

This town is like strolling through a fairytale, but it's more than that; it has a *feeling*. A pulse that wraps around you, lightening your steps, like there's a little less gravity here to weigh you down.

"Do you feel it too?" I ask as I rub the raised hairs on my arms.

"Yeah. Wow." She shivers. "This place is magical."

"Even the hostel is beautiful," I say as we arrive at the gray stone cottage.

Windows with white shutters flank a heavy oak door with a dragon spewing fire carved straight into the wood. We remove our shoes as directed by the sign above the door and pad socked feet across the carpet into the main room. Artistic wood carvings of birds and fairies hang on the walls above two slouchy denim sofas. In the far corner is an acoustic guitar leaning against a shelf crammed with paperbacks and board games. The adjoining large communal kitchen has a rustic wooden table with a dozen mismatched chairs and a cozy cushioned nook in the corner where you can eat, read, write, or hang out.

Our dorm has three rustic bunks made from yellowish-white tree trunks. No one is here, but packs are lining the walls, and there are rumpled sheets on all but two bottom beds.

"I can't wait for tomorrow," Lyndsay says as she drops her pack next to a clean bunk.

"Same." I grin.

Because after walking through the enchanted streets, I know all the things on my list like visiting the castle and the Egon Schiele Art Centrum are going to be way better than I ever anticipated.

THE PERFECT DAY - ČESKÝ KRUMLOV, CZECH REPUBLIC

Warm morning air and a cloudless sunny sky greet us as we leave the hostel carrying a photocopy of their quirky hand-drawn map. Lyndsay traces her finger along the exaggerated points of interest, the tipped turrets in the castle, the castle gardens, and the four bridges over the river snaking through the city to our first destination—a stack of pancakes.

Tables line either side of the door of the narrow café leading to a counter with a cash register and a tall man with a mustache flipping pancakes at the grill. I freeze in the doorway because the song playing over the din of the milk steamer and clattering forks on crockery is the pop-rock tune "Fall from Grace" by Amanda Marshall. My skin tingles at hearing an up-and-coming Canadian artist in a tiny town in the south of the Czech Republic.

"I have this CD." I grip Lyndsay's forearm. "I saw her live in Toronto before I left home. This music is a sign that today's going to be awesome."

"Never heard of her," she says. "But I trust you. Let's grab a seat. I'm starving."

We snag a two-top and order two cappuccinos and two orders of deluxe pancakes.

"This is how I know it's going to be a great day," Lyndsay says as the petite blond server places two yellow mugs on the table with real chocolate pieces melting on a swirly tower of frothy milk.

"Totally." I nod and grab my mug.

My eyes widen as a stack of five fluffy pancakes dotted with fresh strawberries and topped with a scoop of ice cream, whipped cream, *and* chocolate sauce are placed in front of me. I snag my fork and knife off the table, then sigh as the indulgent sweet mix melts on my tongue. I power through until my plate is clean, so glad my shorts are loose to allow room for pancake bulge. The food was so good that whatever comes next today is a bonus.

I pat my tummy as we exit the café and wander the winding cobblestone streets to the 13th century Český Krumlov Castle. We skip the costly guided interior tour, opting to visit the grounds with the help of our guidebooks.

We stroll through the lush grass and manicured bushes in the three-tiered castle gardens to the Cascade Fountain, where marble statues of water deities lounge between the water spray.

Next, we lean between the statues of apostles on the ledge of the Cloak Bridge. The five layers of stone arches on the bridge are similar to a Roman aqueduct, holding up the cobblestone footbridge we're on and the Baroque corridors above. It fills the chasm between the castle and cliffs and has sweeping views of the city. I click through half a roll of film snapping shots of the forest green Vltava River snaking through the dreamy town to the green rolling hills beyond.

"Every building is beautiful. Every road and bridge are immaculate," I say as we wander past stone buildings that arch and flow with the winding street.

"I ... It's ... I've no words." Her head cranks from side to side, taking it all in.

We pause in front of the willowy gold human shapes on the smooth white façade of the Egon Schiele Art Centrum.

"Want to do this tomorrow?" Lyndsay eyes the entrance. "It seems too nice to go inside."

"Yes." I nod. "I want to see it, but I don't want to waste this beautiful day."

"I can't believe I'm saying this after the stack of pancakes we polished off, but are you ready for lunch?" She pulls the quirky map from the pocket of her jean shorts and taps the cartoon pizza. "It's on the next block."

"Lead the way," I say.

Most days I exist on one meal, snacks, caffeine, and cigarettes.

But it takes energy to have a great day, so I'm all in.

Reggae music is playing, a mural of Bob Marley's head is painted on the brick wall opposite the window, and a wooden oven is firing up thin-crust pizza in the back. We sit beside Bob's chin, and our large pizza is served by a man with dark skin wearing a red and green Rastacap over his chunky dreadlocks. I salivate as I pull a slice off the tray, dragging the cheese from the slice next to it, and we don't speak again until the pie's gone.

"How about we try canoeing down the Vltava?" I say as we pay the bill.

"Canoeing?" Lyndsay wrinkles her nose.

"Why not?" I point to the hand-drawn canoes next to the 'i' for information office in the center of town on the quirky map. "The map hasn't led us astray yet."

We enter the 'i' office beside the river and ask about renting a canoe—a very Canadian pastime I've only done a few times, but it's not like it's hard.

"You can rent one for three hours," the 'i' office lady with fiery red hair and loads of freckles says. "Then you'll be collected at a campground along the river."

She indicates the spot on her topographic map taped to the counter with actual streets, a blue river, and green space.

"A one-way trip. We can do that." I look to Lyndsay.

"Uh, *totally*. How do we know where to stop?" she asks.

"You'll need to carry the canoe around the rapids in town. Then paddle until you reach the spillway. There's a bypass to the right of the spillway. Canoe down the bypass channel to the campsite just past it, and our truck will pick you up there at five-thirty," Fiery says.

My forehead furrows. She lost me at spillway. I have no idea what that is, but I'm sure we'll figure it out.

"Sounds great," I say as we pay.

Fiery passes us each a wooden paddle and a life jacket. We follow her outside to a brown barn the size of a single-car garage behind the tourist office. She slides a key in the padlock and the black door scrapes against the ground as it opens. She lifts her chin to the solitary red plastic canoe inside.

I blink. A whole barn for one canoe? So weird.

We drop our stuff by the door and enter the dank barn. Lyndsay and I wrap our fingers around the front rim of the canoe, and Fiery shoves from the back. We heave it across the splintery wooden floor slats in short bursts till it's out of the barn.

I stretch my back as Fiery locks the barn door and strides away.

Here in the center of town, the river is narrow and waist-deep in the middle. And according to Fiery's map, we pass under one pedestrian bridge before we reach the rapids. But first, we need to get the red beast to the water ten meters away. I grimace because I twinged a muscle in my side just getting it out of the barn.

"Well … do you want to push or pull?" Lyndsay asks.

"I'll push," I say as we drop our daypacks and gear in the canoe.

I dig my feet in the grass and shove from the back as she pulls it backward from the front. I groan as we inch the canoe along, taking four breaks before we reach the riverbank.

"I've only ever used wooden canoes. I had no idea anything plastic could be so heavy," I say as we shove it into the water just as a couple stroll past holding hands. "Ever canoed before?"

"This is my first time." She wipes her brow and arches her back.

"We got this." I roll my shoulders. "Front or back of the canoe?"

"Uh … back?" She shrugs.

We click our life jackets closed and settle on the seats. We dig our paddles into the rocky river bottom, guiding The Red Beast to the middle of the river. We catch the current flow and fishtail. My knuckles go white on the paddle handle as we spin and hurl backward under the pedestrian bridge.

"Dude, you're in charge of keeping us straight," I say as people stop on the bridge to watch us.

"I'm supposed to steer back here?" she screams.

The current picks up speed as we approach the bubbling rapids.

"Forget about that for now. Paddle to shore," I shout.

We side-paddle and manage to reach the shore—still backward—just before the river gradient drops to the white water. I hop out, and my sandaled feet sink ankle-deep into the cool water, then we haul The Red Beast onto the riverbank.

The angry rapids continue around the bend and the portage

route to the calm river past the rapids is a downward slope with grassy patches and big rocks.

"The lady said to walk around them like it would be easy." Her cheeks puff as we contemplate the steep pitch.

"There's no path." I huff.

How are we supposed to get this over downward terrain when we can barely drag it on a flat surface?

"Maybe we should chance the rapids." She leans her forearm on her paddle wedged in the pebbles on the bank.

"We can barely make it through regular water. A bubbling fast ride is not going to end well for us." I tilt my head to the rocky slope. "We can drag the canoe down."

I think.

We toss the paddles in the canoe. I grab the front, and we manage to lift it an inch off the ground. But the plastic around the edge cuts into my hands, and my pelvic floor screams with each step.

"Dragging a dead body would be easier than this." I grunt as sweat soaks my brow.

The canoe gets lighter.

What the ...?

I look back, and a man in a ballcap and corduroys has joined our portage. His beefy bicep flexes as he carries most of the weight from the center of the canoe. The three of us easily navigate the slope and dump The Red Beast back into the river.

"Thanks." I wave to Ballcap Man as he silently ambles away.

"We couldn't have managed without his help," Lyndsay says in between heaves.

We settle in new positions, this time with me in the back to steer. I drag the paddle against the side to keep us straight, like I learned from my cousin at my aunt's cottage.

"We're off now," I call out as we pass under a different bridge.

"We are," Lyndsay says. "This reminds me of the time I was with my brother and I went white water rafting—"

My body jolts like I've been in a car collision. I wince and knead my neck.

We're grounded. The Red Beast is sticking out of the water, half on top of the *only* big rock in the middle of the river. The tilt of the canoe makes it sit low in the water. One wrong move and the water will come in over the side. I push one way with my paddle, Lyndsay the other, trying to get us off the rock. I'm getting splashed as the river rushes past. A crowd is gathering on the bridge, waiting to see if we'll flip. I don't think the odds are good of getting out of this the right way up.

"This feels like having a massive spill on the black diamond under the chairlift while skiing. Why are the most difficult runs under the chairlift, anyway?" I ask as water gathers at my feet.

"Focus, man." Lyndsay tuts. "Forget this." She leaps out into the rushing river—which comes up to her waist—and shoves the canoe off the rock.

"We're free," I shout and toss my arms in the air as she throws her top half into the canoe and shimmies her legs in.

The fast-moving water spins us around. I'm laughing so hard a bit of pee slips out as we're dragged backward down a set of mini rapids.

Once we're well outside of town, we're on our own. Just us, the river, and the tall thick trees lining the shore. The late afternoon sun reflects off the water and heats the air, so we whip off our life jackets and T-shirts and canoe in our lacy black bras and shorts.

"Want to take a break?" Lyndsay points to a craggy Russian Olive tree on the bank leaning over the river.

We park in the still water under the shade of the tree, light cigarettes, and dangle our feet over the edge of the canoe as the sun dances through the thin silvery-green leaves.

"I'm so glad you asked me to come here. It's awesome." She glides her hand through the clear water.

"It wouldn't have been the same without you," I say as the

soft breeze coaxes the delicate fall leaves off the branches, sending them fluttering into the river like confetti.

The best places are even better with the right person.

"Hey, do you know what a spillway is?" she asks as we get ready to move on.

"No." I dip my paddle in the water as I push us away from our shady oasis. "But we'll figure it out."

"Yeah, we will," she says.

I smile. At long last, I have my perfect day. And it's everything I dreamed it would be.

"We've got company." She thrusts her paddle toward the canoe speeding our way.

We haven't seen anything but trees and water since we left town.

"Shit, where's my top?" I'm still in my bra. I scramble for my T-shirt, but the solo shirtless guy is level with our canoe before either of us has time to dress.

My brain stalls at his rippling muscles flexing with each deep stroke.

"He must paddle this river a lot to look like that." Lyndsay gapes as he powers past.

"Totally." I sigh as he races around the river bend. "They should add him to the hostel map."

"I don't think there's enough room on the page for all those muscles." She giggles.

As we continue our trip, she tells me about her best friend Cindy, who loves hiking and works with her at the hospital. I tell her about Stephanie's green wooden canoe she inherited from her uncle, which hasn't been in the water in years because it lives in her backyard. Then we commiserate about missing *Saturday Night Live* and share our favorite skits.

"I hear rushing water. We must be getting close to this spillway," I say.

"Whatever it is." She scoffs.

"True that. Let's pull over before we reach it and survey the situation."

We yank on our T-shirts and heave the front of The Red Beast on shore then edge down the narrow bank toward the sound of rushing water. There's a one meter artificial concrete drop on the left side of the river. The water falls evenly over the level slope like an infinity pool edge.

"So that's a spillway." I swipe my hand across my mouth.

On the right is the bypass channel. It's two meters wide with manmade stone barriers on either side. The water rushes between the channel, picking up speed as it shoots down the ramp churning at the bottom, where the river levels out.

"It looks like a canoe water slide." Lyndsay's brow furrows.

"Or a log ride at an amusement park."

My stomach contracts. How are we going to get down the drop and remain upright in the washout at the bottom in The Red Beast? But we have no option but forward because we just walked the entirety of the riverbank. We're surrounded by thick forest and marshland with no path to portage The Red Beast.

With my butt parked on the bench seat at the back of The Red Beast, my heart pounds as we paddle toward the bypass.

"You scared?" I ask as the sound of rushing water increases.

"Yeah, you?"

"Oh yeah." I grip the paddle tighter.

"I'm afraid we'll bash into the sides as we go down the canoe water slide." Her voice is strained.

"I'm worried about the whirlpool at the bottom."

"I didn't even think of that," she cries.

A man dressed in a yellow banana hammock screams at us in Czech from shore as we approach the chute.

"What does he want?" Lyndsay asks as Banana Hammock's arms wave and his round gut jiggles.

"Keep paddling. Maybe he watches rookies like us do the water run for fun." I try to sound cheery, but this is going to be a shit show.

"Get down on your knees!" a woman from shore screeches from beside Banana Hammock.

We drop off the seats to the floor, grip both sides, and scream as The Red Beast tips over the edge. I fling from left to right as we bash into the walls of the stone barrier. My body jolts as the heavy canoe plunges into the whirlpool like a rocket, soaking my hair and clothes. I dig my fingernails in the plastic as the back end of The Red Beast lifts off the water and the front end floods. My stomach drops as the whirlpool spins us in a pirouette. Then spits us out. The canoe crashes—right side up—with a mighty bang on the water, soaking us with one last wave.

"Are you okay?" I ask as river water drips down my face.

"I think so." She swipes her soaked hair away from her eyes.

My hands are still shaking when we reach the campsite beach and drag The Red Beast out of the river. My clothes are soaked through to my underpants, and water streams off the bottom of my daypack. I pull out my camera, turn it on, and slump with relief when it whirs to life. But my new castle postcards are a congealed mess at the bottom of my bag.

"I'm gonna need new cards," I say as I lay my bag to dry next to The Red Beast.

"Worth it," Lyndsay says, wringing her T-shirt.

"Yeah." I grin. "I would love to do that again."

"Me too." She chuckles as we collapse on the rough pebbly shore.

I close my eyes, lean back, and let the late-day sun warm my chilled skin.

I *would* have done this trip alone if Dejah hadn't offered to join me.

I would have ridden every filthy train and bus alone. Bemoaned every wrong turn, lamented every bad experience, and marveled at every sight—alone.

I could have done it. But I would rather eat *the sandwich* and tag team Austin and Keith on the boat to Hel than have done this trip by myself. Because it wouldn't have been the same. None of it would have been without Keith, Owen, Lyndsay, and of course Dejah.

"Best day ever." I swallow past the rise of emotion in my throat.

A *perfect* day.

"Totally agree." She sighs.

I reach out and squeeze her hand, and she squeezes back.

This trip has been an uphill battle of harassment, food woes, language barriers, and cultural differences.

And grief, so much grief.

Before my mom died, I faced things head-on. But after, I didn't have it in me. So I buried it. Swallowed it. Expecting it to go away.

Boy was I wrong.

Because to come out the other side I can't hide when life strikes back.

But I couldn't do it alone. I needed help. And I got it through hugs, hours upon hours of talking about everything and nothing, and a team to share the burden. Hands down, though, my best medicine has been nicknames, inside jokes, and having amazing friends I can laugh about it all with.

A LOT OF VAGINAS - ČESKÝ KRUMLOV, CZECH REPUBLIC

Lyndsay and I pause as we enter the airy Egon Schiele Art Centrum the morning after our perfect day because Egon had a thing for the woman's nude form and vaginas.

Lots of vaginas.

Hairy ones. Bald ones. Detailed. Sketched. Front on. From behind.

All just right here. On the walls. And they're exquisite. We spend ages admiring the pen strokes hugging the curves of the women's hips, thighs, breasts, and of course vaginas.

In the next room are *The Seasons* by Alphonse Mucha. Each panel has a woman in a floral setting representing the seasons of the year. Innocent *Spring* is dressed in translucent white, sultry *Summer* is adorned with red poppies, fruitful *Autumn* is wearing a crown of chrysanthemums, and frosty *Winter* is standing next to a snow-capped bush.

We stare at them for an hour. I'm so glad we left the museum for today when we had the time to appreciate it, because this place, like everything in this town, is perfect.

In the gift shop, I choose a stack of postcards to replace the ones I had to toss yesterday, of the city, *The Seasons*, and my favorite—more conservative—vagina poses. I also buy a poster print of *Summer* and a standing female nude by Egon Schiele along with a big cylinder to mail them home in. Because one day —who knows when— I'll hang these two unique pieces in my house. And each time I look at them I'll remember this most epic place *and* my perfect day.

My steps are soft, but my heart is heavy as we traipse to the station for our return journey to Prague. It's my last night with Lyndsay because tomorrow is Josh day. I'm excited to see him but sad to say goodbye to her. Josh has some big shoes to fill, and doubt swirls in my chest if he can.

QUEENS AND STAIRS - PRAGUE, CZECH REPUBLIC

I wriggle on the hard plastic seat as the tram rolls down the rails in Prague to The Dock hostel. I twist my icy fingers on my lap as Lyndsay counts the stops on the map until ours. I press my forehead to the window but can't see anything through the black night and lashing rain. I fear we left the last of the warm summer days behind in Český Krumlov a few hours ago for fall weather.

Lyndsay said I should branch out from the Twilight Hostel— *she's right*—so we're trying a new place. But frustration steeps in my gut with each passing minute because Twilight is a five-minute walk from the train station, and this ride to The Dock is taking *forever*.

I shiver as we step off the tram into the downpour. The freezing rain soaks through my yellow jacket as we march in circles looking for the hostel.

"The Dock." Lyndsay points to a tiny sign about the size of a letter envelope—tucked in the bushes—that we missed on our first five loops of the area.

My back aches as we climb the steep and slippery worn concrete steps to a long building with an oversized wooden door. It creaks as we enter the vast vestibule. This is the type of place the *Scooby Gang* would assemble to solve a spooky mystery. With the dark wood wainscotting wrapping around the space and twelve-foot-wide sweeping staircase on the left, it's begging for a *Scooby Gang* grand entrance moment.

But there's no one here. The deserted check-in desk opposite the staircase makes my heart long for Crosby's grumpy face. I stomp to the counter and drip on the blue paisley carpet, hoping someone shows up at the desk soon. But if I see Shaggy or Fred, I'm out of here.

"It's dinner time. You'll have to wait to be checked in," a woman with a dour face and gray hair says as she trudges past and enters a room down the hall.

I ball my fists. I would already be out of the shower if we'd stayed at the Twilight hostel.

Two cigarettes later, the door behind the check-in desk swings open.

"There's dinner leftovers if you're interested. I can check you in after." Dour Face flips her hand to the door she disappeared through ages ago. "Feel free to leave your bags here."

"Thanks," Lyndsay says as we abandon our packs.

Shivering from the cold and boots squishing with each step, we burst through the mystery door. And like a record scratching in a dance club, the buzz in the large cafeteria ceases. Sixty sets of eyes swing to us dripping in the doorway.

"What's with this place?" My brow wrinkles as people whisper and point.

"I feel like the new girls who arrived halfway through the school year," Lyndsay whispers.

"Well, screw them." I square my shoulders and sashay through the long tables to the buffet on the left side.

We load our trays with bowls of oily red soup and plates of clumpy tomato penne, then face the room. Lyndsay tips her chin to the table with empty seats next to two girls with ponytails wearing fleeces. As soon as our trays hit the table, the girls stand and leave.

"Was it something we said?" I ask their retreating backs.

"Did we miss the secret handshake?" Lyndsay asks, and I shrug.

We make short work of our bland but warm meal and return to the front desk.

I pass Dour Face my passport, and she flicks through the pages and pauses as she reads my name.

"You had a phone call today." She wrinkles her nose. "From a … Josh?"

"*What?*" I still. Is he already in town? "What did he say?"

"I told him I'd never heard of you," she says.

The blood drains from my face as she jots my name in the ledger on the desk. Josh and I only made plans to meet in Prague. We never said specifically *where*. And she blew him off. Did Dour Face just mess up my Josh reunion?

"He might call back tomorrow," Dour Face says as she slaps my passport on the counter and grabs Lyndsay's.

"We'll find him. Don't worry, man." Lyndsay pats my hand.

"Okay." I nod as I shove my passport in my money belt under my pants.

I'll email him tomorrow; it might take time, but we *will* find each other.

"Here are your keys to your lockers." Dour Face passes us each a small silver key with a number on a yellow tag. I've never had a locker before, although we could've used it in the Green Room with all the thefts. "It's best to lock your things up. I'll show you to your beds." They must have the same sticky finger problem here, too.

We climb the sweeping grand entrance staircase. Dour Face stops on the half landing, pulls back a thick red velvet curtain, and points to the two beds behind it against the wall. The cots are covered in scratchy brown blankets and sag in the middle.

I press my lips together to bite back a giggle.

"Is this a joke?" Lyndsay asks no one because Dour Face has disappeared.

My shoulders slump. I could use the *Scooby Gang* right now. Because Daphne would be equally horrified, and Velma would have clever words of advice. But it's too late. We already paid, and I'm not getting back on the tram with Barney in a downpour. We're stuck here tonight, but hopefully, I find Josh tomorrow so we can stay somewhere else.

"This must be where they put the outcasts," I say as I yank the curtain aside and enter our zone.

"Yup, we gotta learn that secret handshake." Lyndsay drops her bag on the floor and sinks onto a cot.

"Totally." I unlace my boots and rub my cold feet.

"So how are you feeling about Josh day tomorrow?" she asks, crossing her legs.

"Excited. It's a different experience being with him, more intense. We tend to stick to ourselves and stay in private rooms." I wave my arms around our dark space. "Not this type of luxury on the stairs." I sigh and smooth my hands across my damp pants. "I'm also nervous."

"Why?" She tips her head.

"I'm taking a huge gamble on a guy who doesn't have a good track record."

In my dreams, our time together will be sunshine, laughing, and getting lost in each other. But what if we have a terrible time? Or a great one and he leaves me broken all over again?

She frowns and leans forward.

"Candace, you listen to me." We lock eyes. "Our time together has been some of the best days of my trip. No way would I have had that much fun canoeing with anyone else. Or even gone canoeing in the first place. You're an awesome person. No matter how much Josh changed your life, if he doesn't appreciate how wonderful you are, then he doesn't deserve you."

I swallow back my tears as she leaps off her bunk and wraps her arms around me. My heart lightens as I sink into her warm embrace. Once again, a friend has made everything better with kind words and a hug.

I'm going to miss her.

"I need a drink or ten," I mumble into her shoulder.

"I've got that covered." She stands and rubs her hands together. "There's a cabaret, which is highly recommended by *Let's Go!* for Saturday night fun."

"Cool, I haven't done that. You shower first, and I'll watch the bags."

She exits in search of the bathroom. I poke my head out the curtain and yell, "Peek-a-boo!" when she's halfway down the steps.

She snorts and stumbles but rights herself with the handrail.

"We should put on a stage performance later, or at least scare a few people going to their beds," she shouts.

"Oh, that's so on!" I holler.

I sit crisscrossed on my itchy blanket and run my fingers through my hair.

"*Meow.*" A black cat waltzes through the small gap at the bottom of the curtains with his tail up and leaps onto my lap.

"Hello, beautiful." I stroke his silky fur, and a loud purr rumbles from his chest. "You're the shining light of this place. Yes, you are." He leans into my strokes as heavy footsteps march past on the stairs, sending vibrations through my bed. "That's going to suck," I say to the cat. "I've stayed at a lot of bizarre places, but this one's the strangest. It's even worse than the place above the strip bar in Tallinn."

Lyndsay bursts through the drapes.

"Where did that come from?" She points to my cat.

"No idea, but I'm naming him Scooby," I say as I gently place him on the bottom of my bed. "It's noisy in here."

"No problem. We'll stay out late, come back drunk, and sleep through the stair traffic," she says as she rummages through her bag for clean clothes.

"Sounds like a plan."

We get ready in record time, leave our pajamas on our beds—mine beside Scooby—then shove our large packs in our lockers. We catch the tram into town in the drizzling rain, dash across Charles Bridge, then zigzag back streets to a three-story red brick building behind a seven-foot wrought iron fence.

"This is the place." Lyndsay snaps her guidebook closed.

"Really?" I wrinkle my nose at the three security cameras pointed at the sturdy black gate with no signs anywhere.

"How do you think we get in?" Lyndsay pops on her tiptoes and peeps through the iron bars.

A guy with shoulders double the size of mine and a stumpy neck lumbers down the paved path from the building. Keys jingle as he unlocks the gate and jabs his meaty finger at the descending stairs on the side of the building.

"Uh, you sure you want to do this?" I tense at the top of the dark stairwell.

"It'll be fun. *Let's Go!* said it's the place to be." She links her arm with mine.

The bad outings I've experienced like the mud bath, the trip to Hel, and the Zakopane boat trip have come from personal recommendations. And aside from The Dock and the hostel in Zakopane where I got cellulitis, my blind faith in guidebook recommendations have mostly panned out.

"What's one more leap?" I say.

My tummy flutters as we creep down the concrete steps to

the basement level. The black door leads to a dimly lit hallway with a dude behind a glass window on the left and dance music leaking through the closed door at the opposite end of the corridor. We each pay a five-dollar cover charge and step through our second mystery door of the night, hoping for a better result than earlier at The Dock cafeteria.

Dance music thumps in my chest. An enormous disco ball spins above the stage at the back of the long room, lighting up the crowd in twinkly rainbows. The lush red walls are covered with framed glossy photos of nude dudes, and the wall-mounted lighting has red heart-shaped shades. On the left near the stage are three long tables of people wearing party hats and one tall person dressed in a sparkly pink onesie with a birthday sash. And the right side of the room is packed with men so pretty my eyes hurt to look at them.

I grin. Door number two for the win tonight.

But I have no idea where all these people came from.

"We're in the right place," I scream in Lyndsay's ear over the music.

"Oh yeah." She directs us to the bar near the door.

Beer bottles in hand, we choose neutral ground beside a pillar in the center of the room between the birthday gang and the pretty people.

"Welcome!" The bar goes wild when a Cher lookalike in a low cut red dress glides on stage and introduces the show with a rousing rendition of "Believe."

Back-up dancers join the performance. Their makeup is flawless, and they ooze confidence as they spin and shimmy in their vibrant clothes and sky-high heels under the disco ball.

"I feel ugly." I sigh at my hiking boots, boring black pants, and T-shirt. It's especially hard to feel normal in this room filled with shiny, beautiful people.

"Me too, but we got ready in ten minutes, in a stairwell." She points to her mirror outfit and flat hair from the rain.

"I know, but it sucks feeling like less." I hide my short, naked fingernails as the dancers raise their sparkly manicured hands in unison on stage.

"You're not less. You're just living differently." Her eyes brighten. "And you wouldn't have it any other way, not even for an updo and sequined dress."

"You're right." I nod as my insecurities ebb and fade. "I couldn't pull off that dress anyway."

"Me neither." She shrugs. "But it's okay because we're together, so we're fine."

My chest squeezes. I'm so freaking lucky to have met these people.

A Celine lookalike in a gold miniskirt takes over for Cher and starts the soft opening lines to "My Heart Will Go On."

"No matter what I'm wearing, I don't have legs like Celine," I say, admiring the definition in her thighs and calves.

"You don't." She nudges my shoulder. "But you have a great smile."

I chuckle and hook my arm around her waist. We sway and shout the words along with Celine about not fearing and how our hearts will be okay.

My throat tightens. This stupid song kills me every time. And don't get me started on *the door*. Rose and Jack could have both gotten on. I scoff. If my mom and I could surf an air mattress together at my aunt's cottage, surely Jack and Rose could have—

I blink. A memory that would have torn me up months ago isn't.

I was so wrong when I thought raw pain and grief were all I had left of her. I have joyful childhood memories. Everything she taught me about friendship and caring for others. And I never lost her love; it was just misplaced for a while by my sadness.

The room explodes into song with Celine as she belts out the last line.

A heartwarming tingle glides down my back, ending at my toasty toes in my hiking boots. I'll never be the person I was before her death. I'm the person who's survived grief, assault, good days, and sad ones. And I like this new me.

The bar erupts with applause. Lyndsay curls her thumb and index finger between her lips and whistles. I throw my arms in the air and clap as Celine takes a bow. Eagerly awaiting whatever glittery act comes next.

THE END

The adventures continue in Book Three: Hello, I Am Here
Prague, Czech Republic to Cairo, Egypt

OTHER BOOKS IN THE BACK IN A YEAR SERIES

ACKNOWLEDGMENTS

This one was hard to write. The travel adventures came easy; it was spinning them into a story that dealt with grief and assault that took work. There was much introspection, and it was difficult and healing at the same time. As I was wrestling out the story, I kept thinking of the movie *The Empire Strikes Back* and how dark yet funny it was. I cried like a baby when Han Solo was frozen in carbonite. And I remember thinking he was never going to come back from it. But he did. And that's what this book is to me. Dark but light at the same time. And that's why it's called *Life Strikes Back*. Because it did.

I've done countless versions and rewrites, and I'm fortunate to have a great support group around me. My dad, Les MacPhie, was the first to read these books and has been cheering me on ever since. My brother, Kevin MacPhie, gave me encouragement and support to continue when I thought this might be a terrible idea. And is very good at finding the funniest way to describe things.

Chantal Plowman is the most supportive book coach anyone could ever ask for. She read every word of the first very rough and rocky draft. Her thoughtful and kind feedback gave me the courage to keep writing.

Suzy Vadori, my developmental editor, can noodle out any parts of a book that need work. She has a fantastic learning feedback style that I was desperate for and has taught me to do better and be better. Thanks Suzy.

To Kasi Simmering who diligently went through line by line looking for inconsistencies and grammatical errors. Mostly correcting my liberal use of commas, misplaced apostrophes, and hyphens.

My sister-in-law Caroline Gordon is excellent with a red pen on all my grammatical errors and the final line in the sand when it comes to editing.

Farrukh Bala, for his perfect cover design, and Melanie McNicholl, who designed the beautiful map and chapter icons.

To Plin Gonzalez in Miami, thank you for ensuring Juanma said all the right things.

To Stuart Brisgal, also in Miami, for being my sensitivity reader for the Holocaust site visit. Your kind feedback warmed my heart.

To my niece Cristina, who has a keen eye for cover design review. To my daughter Sloane, who listens and shouts out alternative words when I'm stuck on a part. To my son Slater, who manages to always know the perfect moment to pop his head into my office and give me words of encouragement. To my daughter Anneek, who provides countless hugs and builds puzzles with me when I need a brain break.

And to my husband, who comes up with not-so-creative excuses to peer over my shoulder to catch a few lines of the book on my computer monitor. And then insists on getting credit for any word he suggests whether I use them or not. You annoy me, but I love you more than I can put into words. And that's saying something since I 'do' words. Thank you for supporting me in my writing journey.

For anyone who has suffered from any type of abuse, I encourage you to reach out for support, from friends, family, church, or organizations like The National Sexual Assault Hotline at 1-800-656-HOPE, www.endingviolencecanada.org, or www.respect.gov.au/services.

What I learned writing this is that if it makes you

uncomfortable or hurts to think about, then it's important not to keep it locked inside.

You matter.

Candace xoxo

ABOUT THE AUTHOR

Born in Montreal, Quebec, I spent years backpacking and working around the world. I've a Bachelor of Commerce degree, an MBA, worked for twenty years on four different continents, and now call Calgary, Alberta home.

I got married, had kids, and things got busy. Time was moving by quickly, and my kids were growing up fast. I shifted gears and quit my job to spend time at home. During the COVID lockdown, I had time on my hands, decided to try writing, and wrote the Back in a Year series.

When I'm not at my computer yelling, "Just a few more pages then I'll make dinner," I love hiking in the Rocky Mountains, swimming, reading romance novels, and making up new cake recipes. I especially like to laugh and spend time with my husband the silver fox and my three awesome kids.

Feel free to follow me on:

Instagram & TikTok: @candacemacphie

www.candacemacphie.com (has loads of information including trip photos)

EXERPT FROM BOOK THREE: HELLO, I AM HERE

SATURDAY, September 12, 1998

FOUND - THE STAIR LANDING, PRAGUE, CZECH REPUBLIC

Dour Face from the front desk flings open the thick red velvet curtain on the hostel stair landing. I groan as light streams into my and Lyndsay's enclosed sleeping space.

"Candace, telephone." Dour Face thrusts a cordless phone the size of a shoebox with a foot-long antenna in my face and marches away.

I narrowly miss poking out my eyeball as I pull the clunky thing to my ear.

"Hello?"

"Candace."

I bolt upright in my cot.

"Josh." My hand trembles around the bulky receiver.

"I'm in Prague," he says.

"You found me." My voice cracks.

He chuckles, and my skin sizzles.

"Wake up baby, then meet me at Joe's Garage beside Charles Bridge at noon."

"Yes." I press my fingertips to my lips.

"I can't wait to see you. Bye baby."

The line clicks, and I clutch the phone to my chest.

Holy shit.

He's here.

And I'm going to see him in three hours.

MAGIC BEN'S RIDDLE – PRAGUE, CZECH REPUBLIC

There's one flashlight and four people.

All four people must get across a bridge in pairs using the flashlight for each trip.

Each person takes a different time to cross:

10-minutes

5-minutes

2-minutes

1-minute.

What's the fastest cumulative time to get everyone across the bridge?

ANSWER

1-minute and 2-minutes go first with the flashlight. 1-minute returns with the flashlight.

That's 3 minutes.

10-minutes and 5-minutes take the flashlight and cross together. Then 2-minutes goes back over the bridge with the flashlight.

That's 12 minutes.

Lastly, 1-minute and 2-minutes cross together with the flashlight.

That's another 2 minutes.

The fastest time is 17 minutes.

BOOK CLUB QUESTIONS

1. What response do you think the author is trying to elicit from the reader?

2. What parts of the book you could relate to? What parts were difficult to relate to?

3. Discuss the book's structure, language and writing style. How well did the author draw you in and keep you engaged?

4. What were the most admirable qualities of the main characters? Would you have wanted to know them or are they similar to people in your personal life?

5. There are a lot of relationships in this book. Which did you think were the most important? Which were the biggest detriment?

6. Compare *Life Strikes Back* to book one *Finding Color*. Is it similar? How would you compare or contrast the books?

7. What is your lasting impression of the book?

8. What advice would you give the main character?

9. What question(s) were left unanswered in the book?

10. What question(s) would you ask the author?

Manufactured by Amazon.ca
Bolton, ON

38998285R00236